SPECIAL TIME

Super Mario

The All-Star Video Game Changer

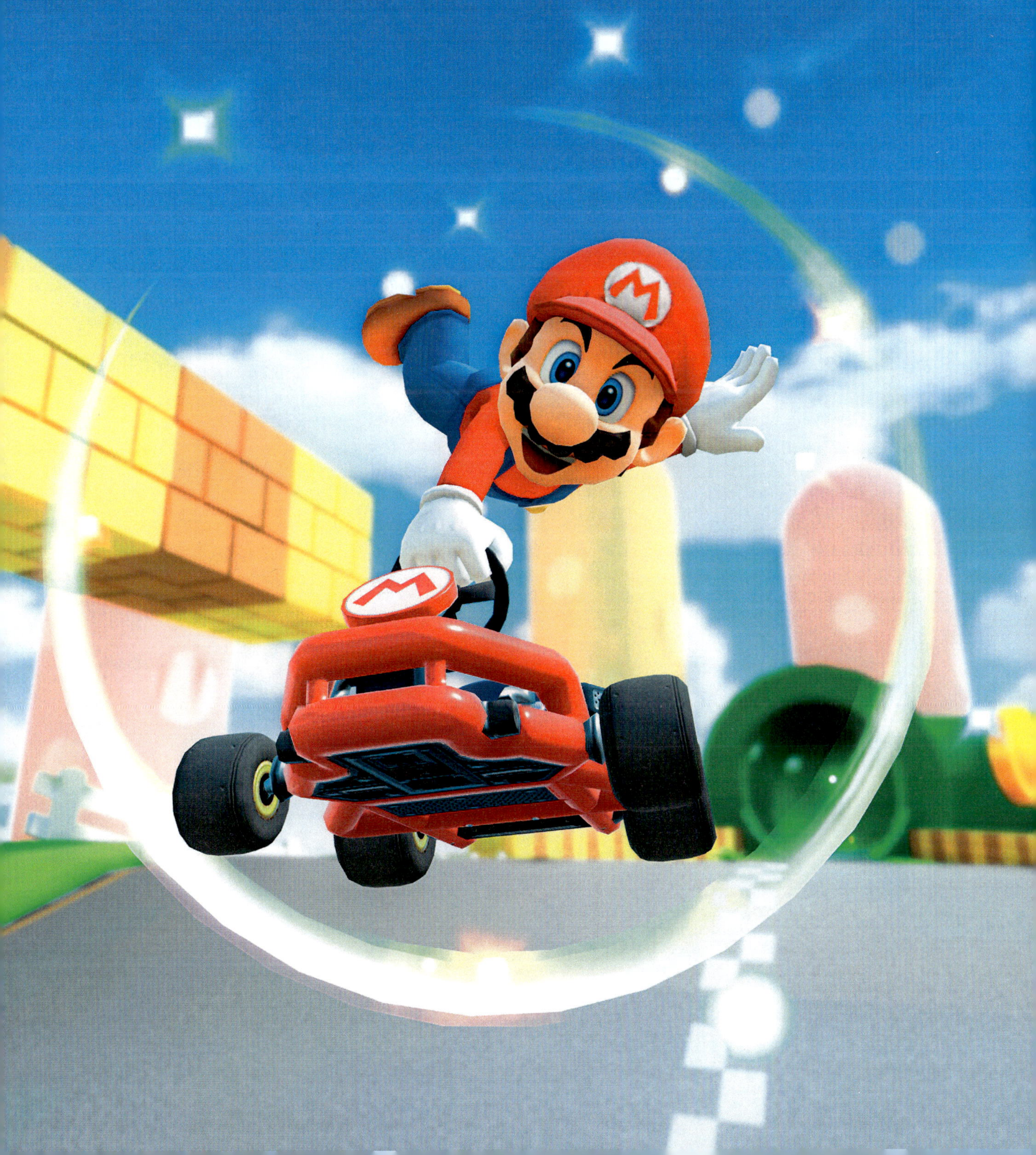

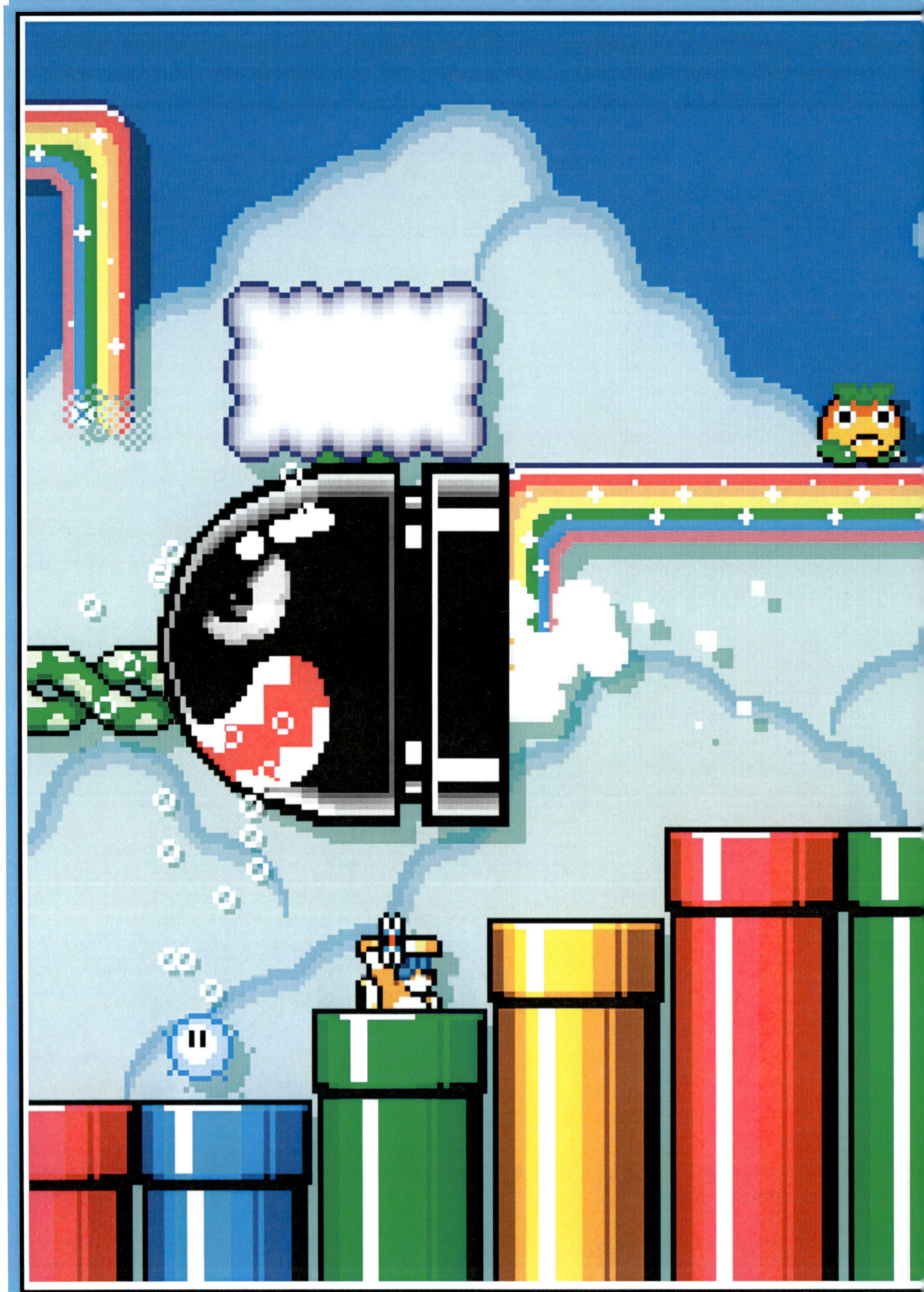

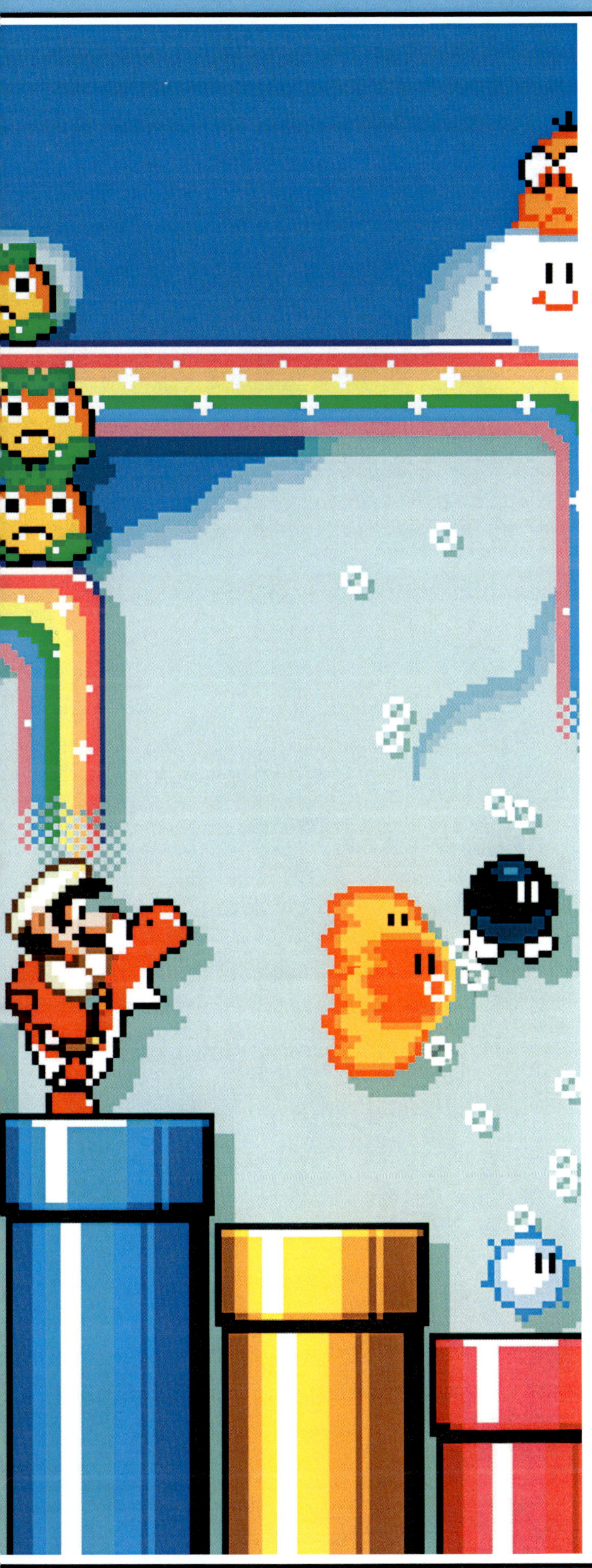

CONTENTS

There are more than 60 sample courses in 2015's Super Mario Maker.

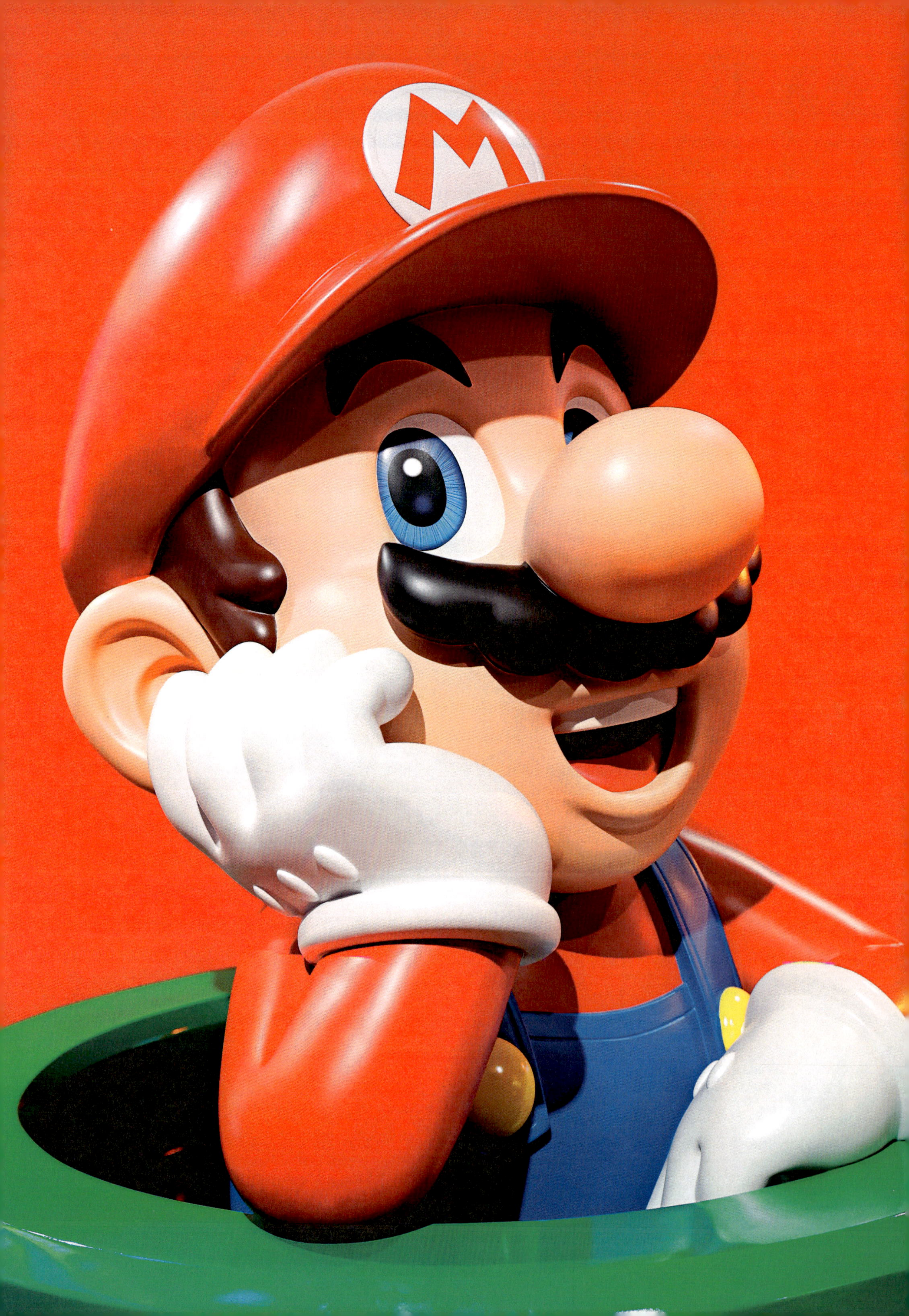

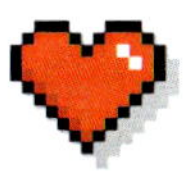

STILL SUPER AFTER ALL THESE YEARS

What began as an 8-bit platformer game has spawned a global multimedia franchise.

BY COURTNEY MIFSUD INTREGLIA

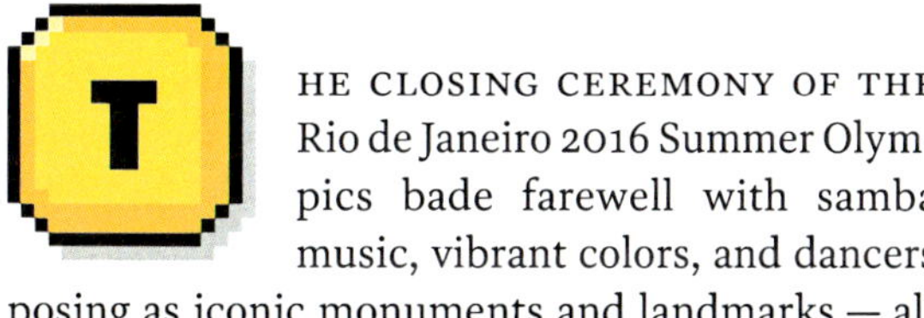

THE CLOSING CEREMONY OF THE Rio de Janeiro 2016 Summer Olympics bade farewell with samba music, vibrant colors, and dancers posing as iconic monuments and landmarks — all befitting the carnival traditions of the host city. Beyond bringing the Games to an end, an Olympics closing has one other agenda item — to introduce the nation hosting the following Summer Olympics. On August 21, 2016, shortly after a choir of Rio children sang the Olympic anthem, a film titled *Warming Up Tokyo 2020* was broadcast to the audience. The glossy promotional video showcased various sporting icons throughout the next host city, along with well-known Japanese pop culture mainstays, such as Hello Kitty and Doraemon.

But in a surprise cut, the video showed late prime minister Shinzo Abe, in a Toyota Century, worried that he wouldn't make it to Rio on time. Fret not—Abe morphed into an animated Mario, dove into a green pipe in Tokyo, and emerged as a human figure from a green pipe on the field in Rio de Janeiro holding a red ball and waving a red Mario-style cap.

"To be honest, when [Tokyo Olympic Organizing Committee head Yoshiro] Mori first came to me with the idea [of appearing at the ceremony dressed as Mario], I didn't like it," Abe explained to *Nikkan Sports* in a 2020 interview, laughing. "'Is it really OK for a prime minister to dress up like Mario?' I asked. As much as possible, I wanted to avoid any politicizing of the Olympics, and it's a 20-hour flight to Rio. But during Mori's term as prime minister, I was his deputy chief cabinet secretary, so he was something of a mentor to me. 'You're the only one who can do this, since you've been serving as prime minister so long and are recognized internationally,' he said, so I ended up doing it." The promotional escapade inspired immense enthusiasm online, with "Abe Mario" the top trending topic on Twitter.

Mario is a mustachioed Italian American plumber and the mainstay of Nintendo's fortunes. Considering game sales alone, the Mario video game franchise has sold more than 900 million units worldwide across more than 200 games, making it the best-selling video game franchise of all time. The primary Super Mario series has sold more than 495 million copies worldwide. In terms of gross revenue, including merchandise, events and film, Mario is a financial juggernaut.

The Mario franchise has earned more than $55 billion worldwide and is the second-highest-grossing video game franchise after Pokémon (which has grossed more than $90 billion). Scores of video games have taken inspiration from the original *Super Mario Brothers* video game of 1985, which first appeared 40 years ago, on Nintendo's earliest home console, the 8-bit Nintendo Entertainment System (NES). Mario has lent his likeness to toys, mugs, beauty products, and a highly successful feature film (and one not-so-successful flick). As Prime Minister Abe's warp in 2016 shows, Super Mario is also a tool of geopolitical influence, with Mario as a global ambassador.

A CHILDHOOD MAINSTAY

Mario's first visit to the Olympics was not his 2016 appearance. Almost a decade before, the iconic Italian plumber faced off against a blue-haired hedgehog named Sonic in a series of video games tied to Olympic events. The Mario & Sonic at the Olympics series kicked off in 2007 for the Wii with the Beijing 2008 edition, called *Mario & Sonic at the Olympic Games*. Games tied to the 2012 London Olympics, the 2016 Rio Olympics, and the 2020 Tokyo Olympics followed, as did several entries tied to Winter Olympics.

When Mario & Sonic failed to pay a visit to the Paris Olympics in 2024, the world noticed. And Lee Cocker, an executive producer on the series for 17 years who worked on every game, had to issue a statement confirming that the series was over. "My Twitter blew up, my social media blew up, my emails blew up," Lee told the BBC. "Loads of people messaging me, saying, 'We love that game. We grew up on that game.'"

Connecting with children is part of Super Mario's ethos, ingrained since the franchise's earliest iterations. Super Mario's primary creator, designer Shigeru Miyamoto, has said that the content of his games is based substantially on the experiences of his own childhood. "I can still recall the kind of sensation I had when I was in a small river, and I was searching with my hands beneath a rock, and something hit my finger, and I noticed it was a fish," Miyamoto told *The New Yorker*. "That's something I can't express in words. It's such an unusual situation. I wish that children nowadays could have similar experiences, but it's not very easy."

The player in a Super Mario game behaves similarly to a young Miyamoto. The players rolls down hills, jumps around, encounters fish in rivers, and explores caves, woods, and old ruins. While the basic-level architecture of Mario games features clouds, hills, flowers, and aesthetics familiar to small children

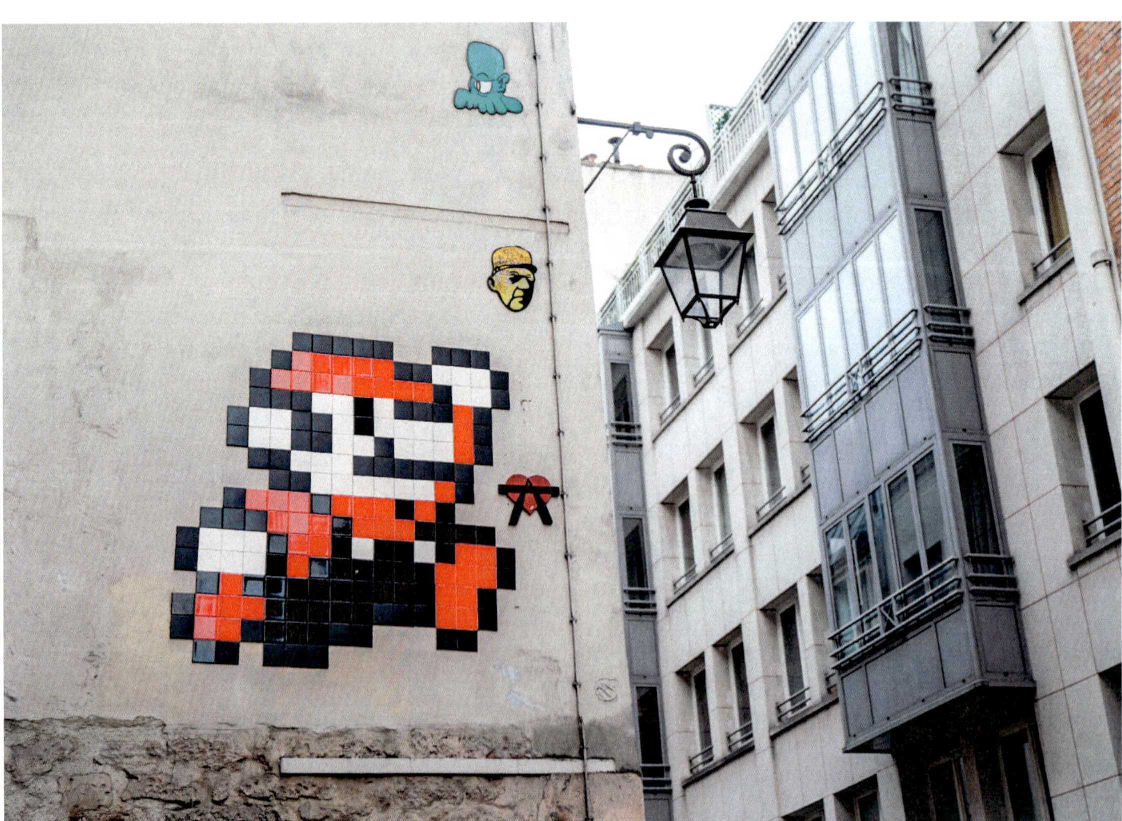

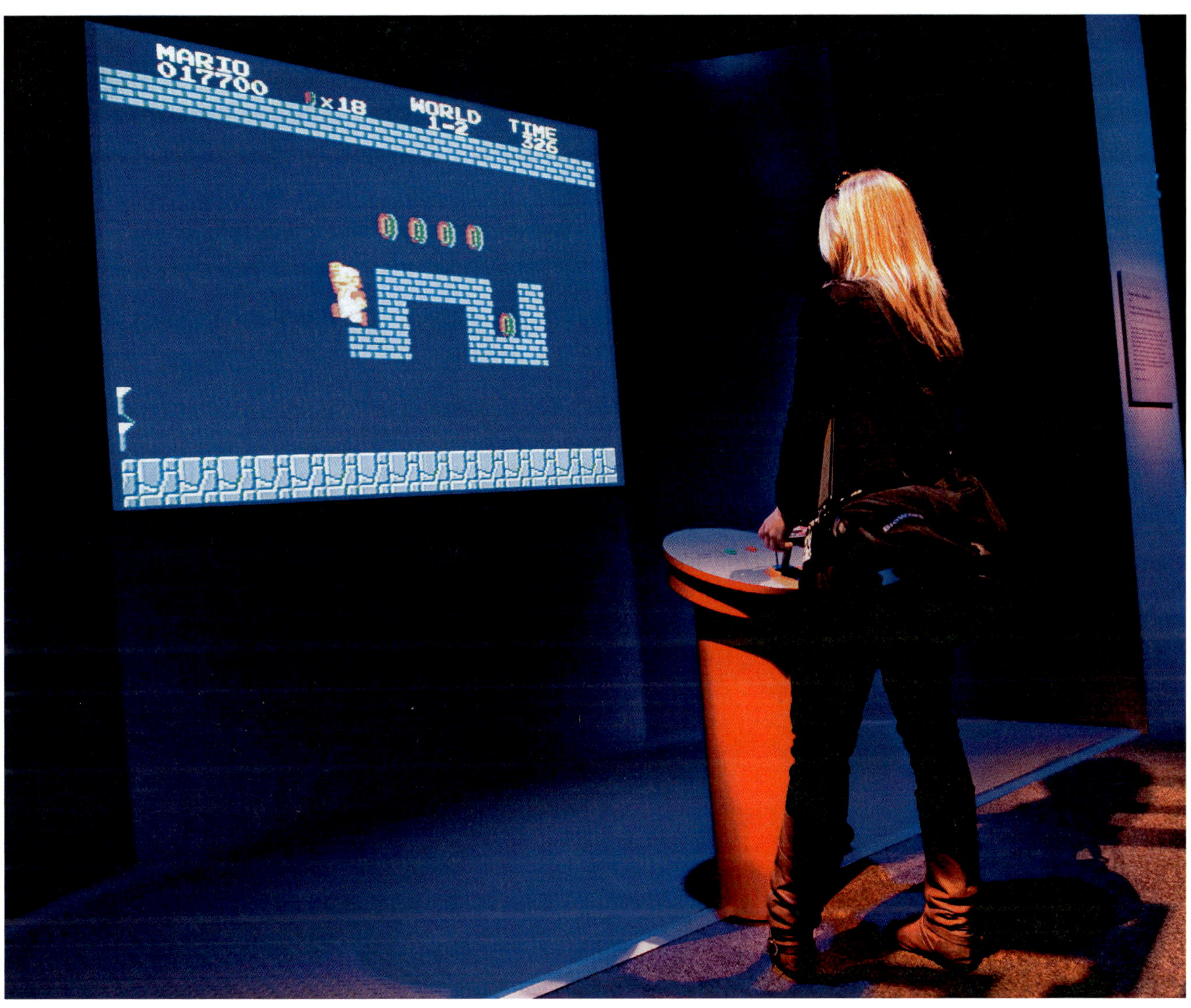

Above, Super Mario Bros.*, during a media preview of the exhibition "The Art of Video Games," at the Smithsonian American Art Museum, in Washington, D.C. Opposite, street art by Invader in Paris.*

across the world, some key elements are firmly rooted in experiences sourced from a Japanese childhood. Those clouds and flowers are often adorned with eyes, a reflection of the native Shinto tradition of animism, in which each element of the natural world includes nature-spirits named *kami*. Many enemies throughout the games are based on *yokai*, monsters and ghosts of native Japanese folklore.

Games with moderate difficulty levels tend to be the most enjoyable for players. When a game is too easy, players may quickly lose interest, as there are no significant challenges to overcome. If a game is too difficult, players — especially children — may become frustrated and give up, leading to decreased engagement.

Mario games strike a balance between repeated successes and the thrill of new challenges. "A lot of the so-called action games are not made that way," Miyamoto said. "All the time, players are forced to do their utmost. If they are challenged to the limit, is it really fun for them?" But when it comes to Mario games, as well as others he's created, like the Legend of Zelda series, Miyamoto said, "You are constantly providing the players with a new challenge, but at the same time providing them with some stages or some occasions where they can simply, repeatedly, do something again and again. And that itself can be a joy."

MUSICAL LEGACY

Mario's main musical theme, the "Ground Theme," as it's officially known, is one of the most recognizable video game themes of all time. The jaunty rhythm and snappy melody occurs in 1985's *Super Mario Bros.* David Gibson is the digital project coordinator for the recorded sound section at the Library of Congress National Audio-Visual Conservation Center. For nearly two decades, he has worked to oversee collection and preservation activities for video games at the Library of Congress. In 2023 he penned a tribute essay to the Ground Theme and its composer Koji Kondo. "From their initial inception, video games incorporated sound effects and music to enhance the gameplay experience. From the audible blips heard when a player makes contact with the ball in *Pong* to *Pac-Man*'s famous *wakka-wakka* sound, early game developers recognized that sound was an integral component of engaging the player, by creating a multisensory experience," explained Gibson. "As sound chips for arcade and home consoles became more sophisticated, game developers continued to broaden the sonic palette for games released throughout the early 1980s. Inspired by these developments, Koji Kondo built upon the existing framework of video game sound design in an effort to create something altogether more 'musical.'"

Upon seeing the overworld levels in an early version of *Super Mario Bros.*, Kondo initially wrote a "laid-back, relaxing" piece that would invoke the feeling of a "carefree walk," he explained to *Nintendo Minute* in 2014. But he thought that tone did not fit the game.

Kondo decided instead to create a new piece with a tempo that would match the game's speed and the rhythm of Mario's movements. "Perhaps the most impressive fact to consider when evaluating the Ground Theme from a musical standpoint is its relative complexity, particularly given the limited palette of sounds available via the early sound chip that shipped with Nintendo's Famicom and Nintendo Entertainment System platforms," explained Gibson. "Kondo was essentially working only with four channels to create this work: two pulse-wave channels, a triangle-wave channel, and a noise channel. Kondo worked out the melody in advance and then programmed the notes for each channel into the computer. By combining his musical theory background with the technical skills that he quickly acquired as a Nintendo employee, Kondo was able to communicate his musical ideas in captivating ways, alternating melodies between the three 'melodic' channels and employing the noise channel to create driving rhythmic variation."

In 2023 the Ground Theme, often just referred to as the Super Mario Bros. theme, was recognized as a key contribution to U.S. history. It was one of the 25 songs added to the Library of Congress's National Recording Registry that year, along with Mariah Carey's Christmas classic "All I Want for Christmas is You," Daddy Yankee's "Gasolina," and Madonna's "Like a Virgin."

This was the first time a video game theme was ever added to the registry. "For many children of the 1980s, the opening notes of the *Super Mario Bros.* Ground Theme served as an introduction to the musical world of Nintendo, given that the game was included with a purchase of the Nintendo Entertainment System by 1988," wrote Gibson. "The first six notes that greet the player upon starting the game immediately set the mood for this thrilling home-gaming experience. As Mario and Luigi's universe has continued to expand, the Ground Theme stands as an early testament to the power of video game music to inspire, captivate and excite."

ENDLESSLY FOR THE FANS

Perhaps no such indication of Mario's reach is more obvious than the success of the 2023 film. Released on April 5, *The Super Mario Bros. Movie* was a major box office success. It earned more than $377 million worldwide in its opening weekend, making it the biggest global release ever for an animated film, beating out the previous title holder, *Frozen II*.

While movies adapted from video games have a history of falling flat, a number of factors helped *Super Mario Bros.* succeed where others have failed. There was an all-star cast, a hefty budget (more than $100 million), and swaths of beloved characters to bring to the big screen. But it was the fans and their memes, illustrations, and hashtags that drew triumphant support. On Twitter and TikTok,

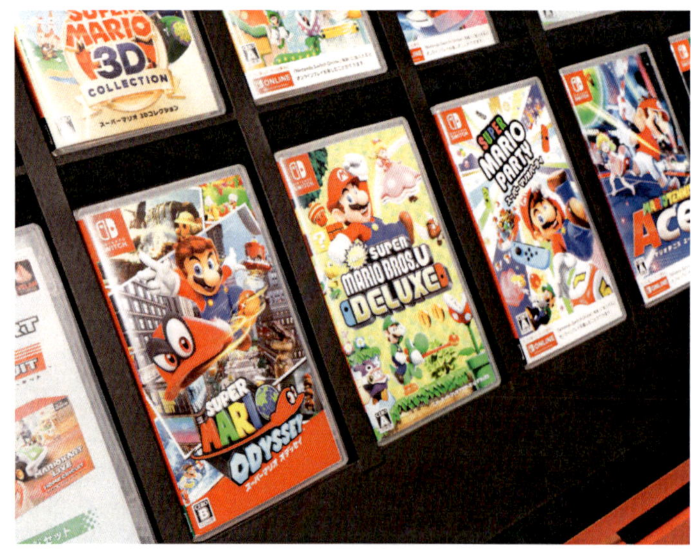

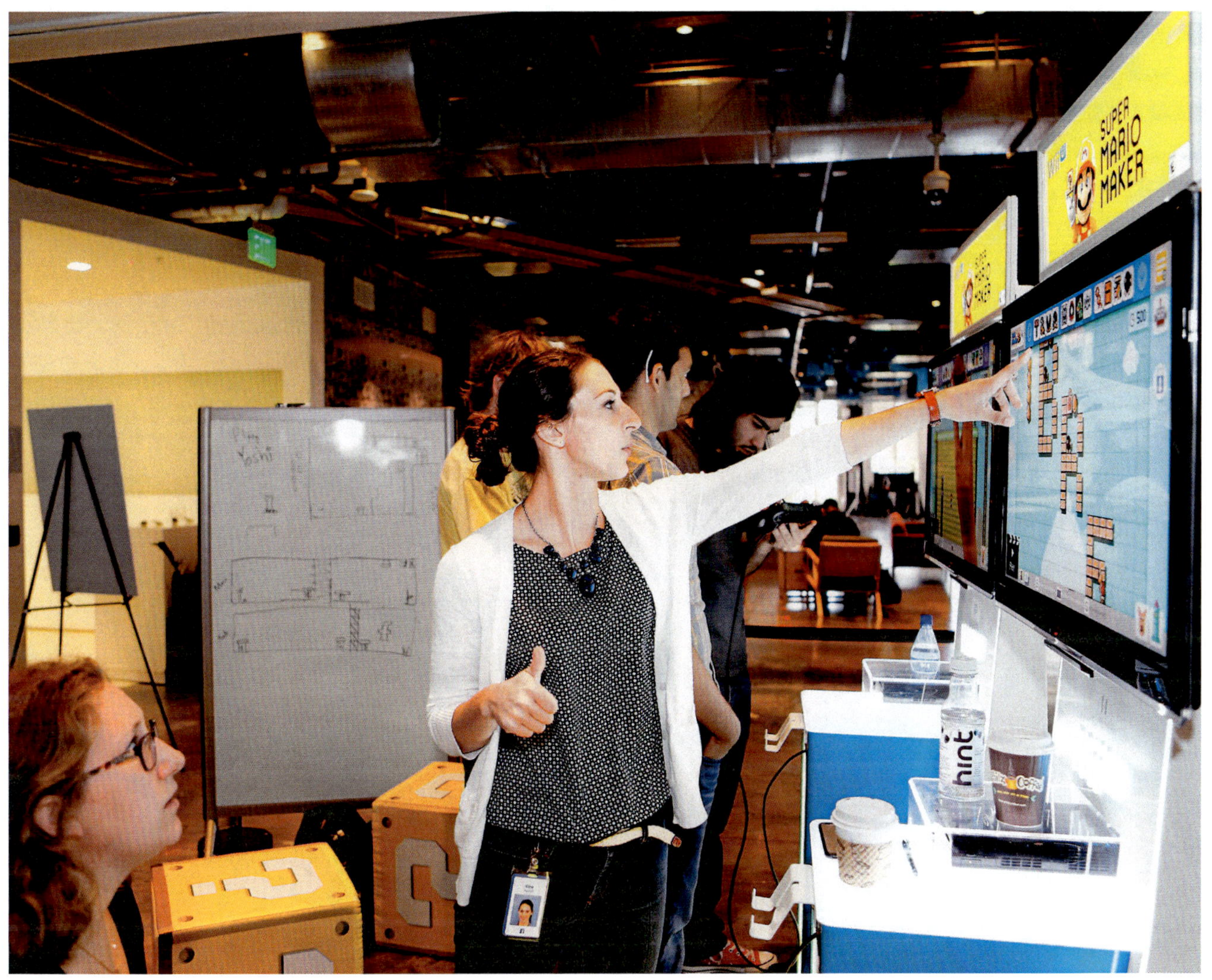

Above, Nintendo hosted a "hackathon" event using Super Mario Maker *at Facebook HQ in Menlo Park, Calif., in 2015. Opposite, more than 20 Mario games have been released on Nintendo Switch since its 2017 launch.*

hashtags like "Super Mario Movie" and "Super Mario Bros" have accumulated roughly 4 billion views. The latter was one of TikTok's highest-trending tags during the release month, according to data from TikTok's Creative Center. Viewers have also gathered on Reddit, with Mario's subreddit fostering a community of over 130,000 and Nintendo's subreddit logging in at over 2 million, as fans shared comedic fan art and movie spoilers within the threads.

While Nintendo might have unintentionally turned fans into marketers, the company was a bit more intentional when they turned players into game developers with 2015's *Super Mario Maker*. The platformer and game creation system, released for the Wii U, allowed players to create, play and share courses online based on the style of previous Super Mario games.

"*Super Mario Maker* is a bit of an answered prayer for every kid who grew up with graphing paper and a dream, and I've been able to spend a few days, and one intense night, with the game," Polygon's Ben Kuchera exclaimed in 2015, in an article previewing the game ahead of its release. "I played one level where someone used Bowser's flying craft, a fire flower and a scrolling level to create a bullet hell shoot 'em up. That's just the beginning. The community, which is tiny in these prerelease days, is already coming up with great stuff. When more people are involved it's going to get very strange, very quickly. And many of those strange experiments are going to be delightful."

Forty years after he entered homes around the world on 8-bit NES, Mario is still a figure that inspires joy, nostalgia, and, most of all, an urge to stomp on mushrooms over and over again. With a parent company putting out new and exciting games every year, and a reach that extends to global leaders and musical denizens, Mario's going to stay super for a very long time.

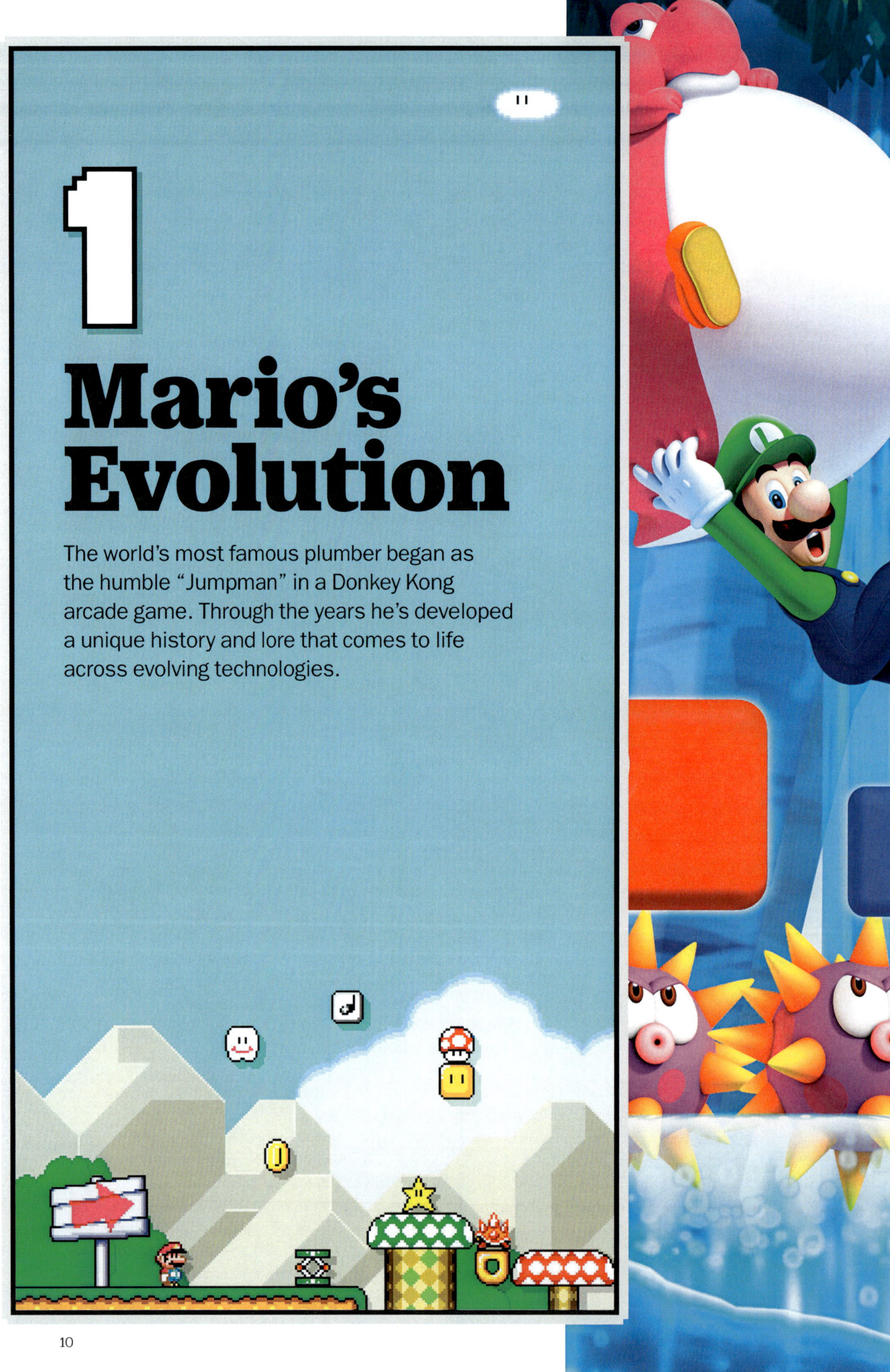

1

Mario's Evolution

The world's most famous plumber began as the humble "Jumpman" in a Donkey Kong arcade game. Through the years he's developed a unique history and lore that comes to life across evolving technologies.

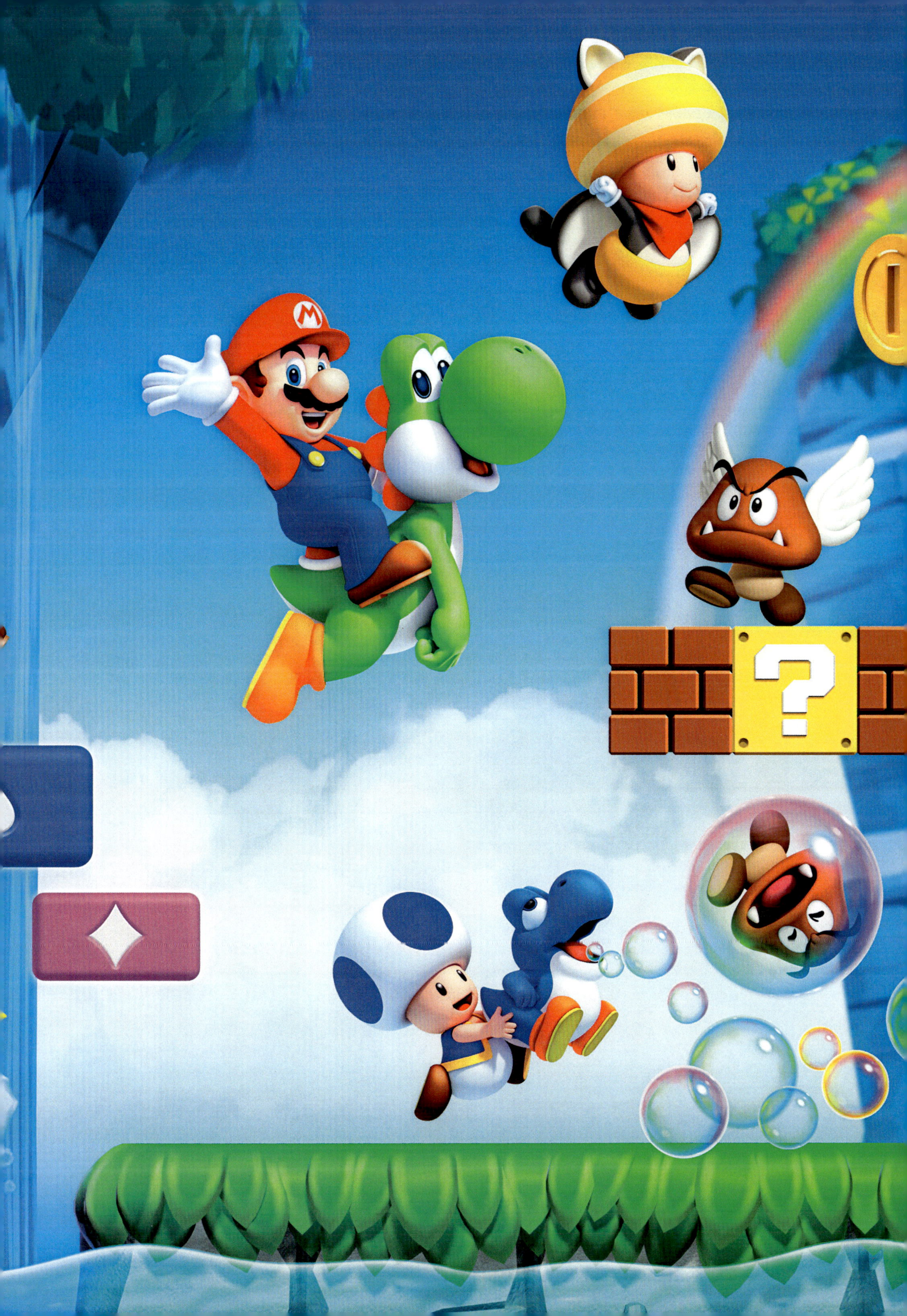

IT'S ON LIKE DONKEY KONG: THE GAME'S ORIGINS

Mario began as a side character in an earlier Nintendo game. The company's storied history sheds light on his full journey.

BY ASHLEY ABRAMSON

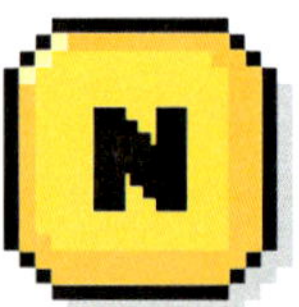

INTENDO HAD A PROBLEM. TWO thousand unsold *Radar Scope* game cabinets, part of the Japanese company's first foray into U.S. arcades, were collecting dust in a Tukwila, Wash., warehouse. Whatever Nintendo did with these 2,000 cabinets would be the difference between profit and loss — and either cement or diminish its place in the American market.

First released in 1979, the shoot 'em up arcade game saw major success in Japan. The next year, eyeing a new market, Nintendo of America's then president, Minoru Arakawa, sent a large shipment of *Radar Scopes* to the States. But games like *Pac-Man* and *Space Invaders* proved to be steep competition, and *Radar Scope* never took off.

The unlikely solution — the story-driven, graphically playful *Donkey Kong* — stood in contrast to the austere shooting games and the dark, dingy arcades that defined the early 1980s. Here was a game that was bright, colorful, even cute, complete with an original soundtrack. It was a breakout success: At just the right time, before the arcade crash of 1983, *Donkey Kong* solidified Nintendo as a contender in the arcade battle and positioned the company for success in the home market.

But perhaps the most significant part of Nintendo's U.S. comeback? The origin of Nintendo's mascot, a mustachioed Italian plumber named Mario. Now arguably as recognizable as Mickey Mouse, Mario is a testament to the value of risk-taking and perseverance — lessons that can also be learned in his eponymous games.

NINTENDO'S STORIED HISTORY

Long before it infiltrated arcades and living rooms, Nintendo was Nintendo Koppai, or Nintendo cards. Founded by artist and craftsman Fusajiro Yamauchi in 1889, the company created and sold popular illustrated playing cards called *hanafuda*. The name Nintendo, it's said, roughly translates to "leave luck to heaven," a nod to the players who gambled with the cards.

Throughout the 20th century, Nintendo stayed in the Yamauchi family. Fusajiro's son-in-law, Sekiryo Yamauchi, took over as the second president, leading the com-

Donkey Kong 3 *debuted in 1983, two years after we first met Mario (then known as Jumpman) and the titular giant ape in the original* Donkey Kong.

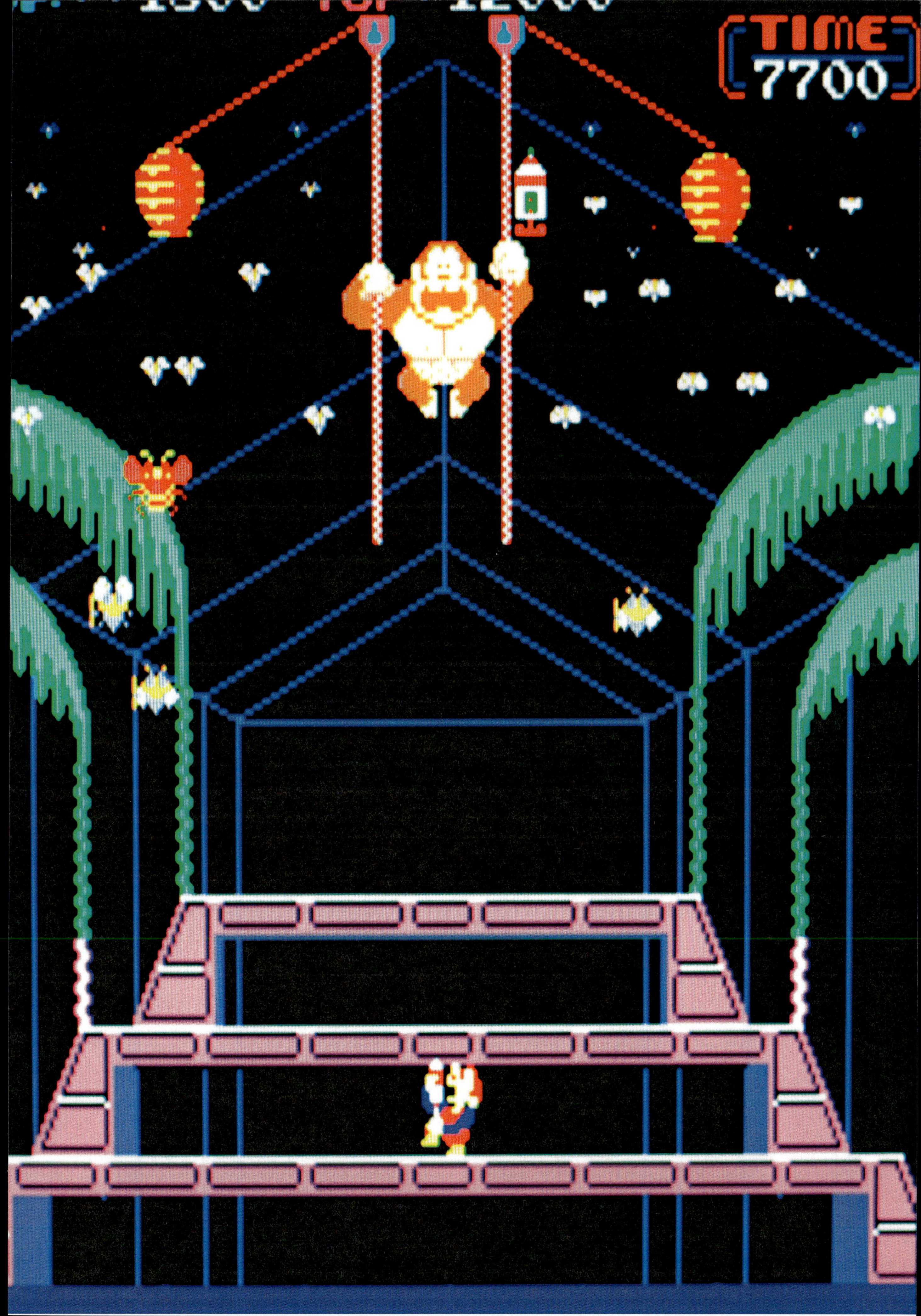
TIME
7700

pany from 1929 to 1949. Disgrace struck the family when Sekiryo's son-in-law, Shikanojo Yamauchi, abandoned his family. Sekiryo's daughter, Kimi, filed for divorce and moved in with her sister, leaving their young son Hiroshi with his grandparents. When Sekiryo suffered a stroke in 1949, he asked his grandson, Hiroshi Yamauchi, to take his place at Nintendo.

Hiroshi, who had eliminated all of Nintendo's existing managers, had a different vision for his great-grandfather's company, experimenting with revenue streams from instant rice to taxis and love hotels that couples could rent by the hour. None of Hiroshi's eccentric ventures stuck, so he decided to refocus on Nintendo's original niche: entertainment.

A toy called the Ultra Hand, first created by a Nintendo maintenance worker at home on the weekend, steered the company in a new direction. The Nintendo Games Department was established in 1969, overseen by Hiroshi Imanishi, a Nintendo executive inspired to expand into the toy market. Integral to Nintendo's success in toys and games was Gunpei Yokoi, hired by Nintendo in 1965 to maintain the assembly line that produced the company's playing cards. But Yokoi was clearly far more than a maintenance worker: He was an inventor. In 1970, Nintendo released Yokoi's gadget, which went on to sell more than a million units.

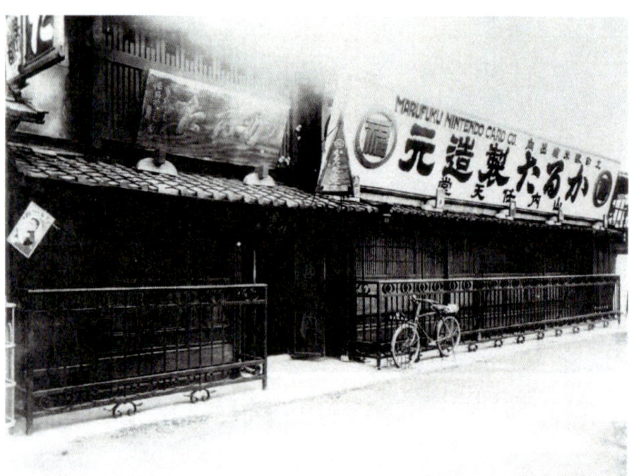

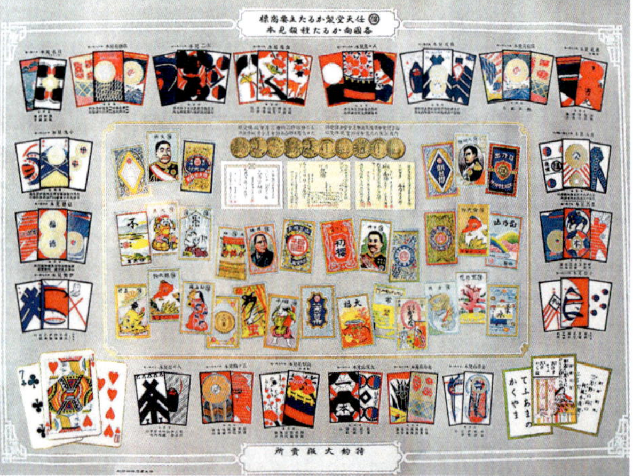

The Ultra Hand was only the start of Nintendo's new market. Yokoi also helped create a pitching machine, a periscope-like device, and even a love tester, a meter that would read the "love" between two people. Notably, Yokoi's creations generally created new experiences with existing technology, making products more accessible and affordable.

"The Nintendo way of adapting technology is not to look for the state of the art but to utilize mature technology that can be mass-produced cheaply," Yokoi once said, according to David Sheff's 1993 book, *Game Over: How Nintendo Zapped an American Industry, Captured Your Dollars, and Enslaved Your Children.*

One of Yokoi's most important creations was the Nintendo Beam Gun, a toy gun that used solar cell technology to "hit" physical targets yards away. The toy gun, a collaboration with Yokoi's colleague Masayuki Uemura, had a light sensor on the end. The game included physical targets, such as a plastic beer bottle constructed of pieces, with display lights — so if a player aimed the gun at the sensor, the gun would "fire," causing the bottle to "explode." The gun grew so popular in Japan that Nintendo created clay ranges inside old bowling alleys; this, some critics argue, was Nintendo's first real arcade game (though it used 16 mm film instead of computer-generated images).

In late-1970s Japan, popular games like Taito's *Space Invaders* made video game arcades a distinctive part of Japanese culture. (To this day, these "game centers" are a popular leisure activity in Japan.) Recognizing the importance of entering the arcade niche, the company eventually created computer generated imagery (CGI) arcade games. Throughout 1978 and '79, Nintendo released its own original CGI games, including *Computer Othello*, *Block Fever*, and *Space Fever*. Nintendo's successful 1980 release, *Game & Watch* — a video game the size of a calculator with a digital clock in the top corner, a Game Boy prototype — was inspired by Yokoi's observation of a fellow train commuter fiddling with a calculator.

The progression from cards to toys to games seems natural, but Nintendo's new niche represented a shift toward "serious" game play. "Working in the gambling-type space, Nintendo had always understood people crave entertainment and distraction,"

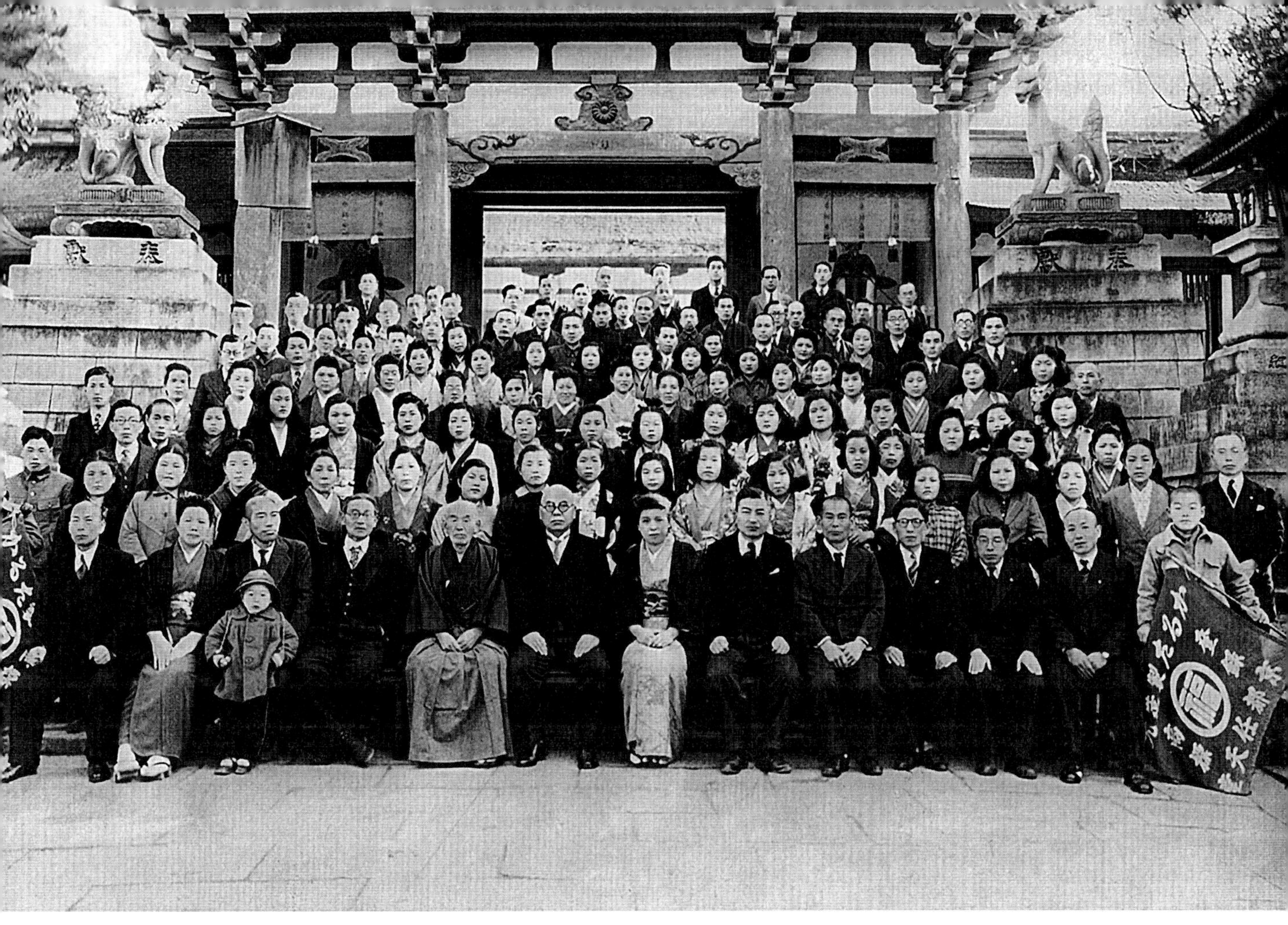

In 1889, Fusajiro Yamauchi founded Nintendo in Kyoto, Japan (opposite, top), as a small business that produced and sold Japanese playing cards (opposite, bottom). Above, the Nintendo Card Company staff in front of the Fushimi Inari shrine, in Kyoto, 1949.

says Jennifer deWinter, dean at the Illinois Institute of Technology and author of *Shigeru Miyamoto: Super Mario Bros., Donkey Kong, The Legend of Zelda.* Rather than simply indulging players' dopamine systems, the next generation of games would connect with players on a far more meaningful level.

GOING WEST

From the mid–20th century on, Nintendo was stable, but its leaders recognized the company wasn't on par with global entertainment leaders like Disney. "In the mid '60s, Yamauchi got a licensing deal to put Disney characters on the back of trading cards, and that's when he realized Japan was one small market in the global economy," says Jeff Ryan, author of *Super Mario: How Nintendo Conquered America.* "Becoming a big success in Japan wasn't the end all, be all. It was becoming a world power."

The U.S. arcade boom of the late 1970s and early '80s was the perfect opportunity for the Japanese company to enter the American market. Hiroshi asked his son-in-law, Minoru Arakawa, to take Nintendo to North America. Nintendo of America was born in 1980, ultimately headquartered in Redmond, Wash. *Radar Scope* would be its first arcade release.

When *Radar Scope* — Nintendo's failed arcade game — fell through, Yokoi started a competition within the company to design a conversion kit for the existing game. A young industrial designer, Shigeru Miyamoto, had joined Nintendo in 1977 as a staff artist. Inspired by manga, a Japanese genre of comic books, Miyamoto initially wanted to be a cartoonist. His dad set him up with an interview at Nintendo, and Yamauchi was impressed by Miyamoto's designs on children's clothes hangers. In the late '80s, the author of the Japanese book *Denshi Yuugi Taizen: TV Games* asked Miyamoto if he saw himself as an artist or engineer. "I think I'm somewhere in between the two. What I aspire to be, personally, is an entertainer with a lot of good ideas," Miyamoto replied.

Given his earlier career aspirations, it makes sense that Miyamoto's design submission was based on another famous cartoon. Miyamoto wanted Popeye to be the protagonist of his game, but the company couldn't get the rights. Instead, Miyamoto created his own Popeye-themed game, where a good guy would fight a villain to save a girl. Donkey Kong — "donkey" for stubborn and "Kong" for gorilla — replaced Bluto, and a princess named Pauline stood in for Olive Oyl. Standing in for Popeye: a protagonist named Jumpman, a carpenter with a blue shirt, red hat, overalls and a trademark mustache. Ryan calls Jumpman a "digital Adam," the first video game character that looked and acted like a real human being.

As revolutionary as Jumpman was back then, his design was primitive, driven by the technical constraints of the time. The game had a three-color quota, resulting in Jumpman's outfit choice. Given the low pixelation, Miyamoto used the mustache to bring attention to Jumpman's face. "In order to show his nose better I gave him a mustache, and to make his running animation easier to understand, I gave him those overalls," he said in a 1986 interview with the Japanese magazine *Famimaga*. Some pop culture experts theorize Miyamoto found inspiration in an issue of an early 1980s magazine called *Popeye*, which featured a cover model dressed like Jumpman. "It's meant to represent western working-man fashion," says Frank Cifaldi, executive director of the Video Game History Foundation.

Jumpman's outfit, it turns out, also suited his job (or perhaps it was in part inspired by it). *Donkey Kong* takes place in a construction site, where Jumpman runs across the screen fighting Donkey Kong. Whenever Jumpman dies, he rises again (up to three times, the standard in gaming). Because Miyamoto was more of a designer than a programmer at the time, a team of programmers brought the game to life. Nintendo replaced the guts of the *Radar Scope* game cabinets with the new game, repainted the exteriors, and hoped for the best.

At first, *Donkey Kong* was a hard sell: It was definitely a thematic and graphic risk, compared to other popular games of the day. "Arcade vendors and sales crews were as comfortable with shooting games as the kids dropping quarters into them were," Ryan writes in *Super Mario*. "How do you sell a title about a carpenter fighting a monkey who throws barrels at him? With a name that makes no sense in English? . . . It didn't fit into any recognizable category — not a sports game, not a shooter, not even a driving game." But once it hit its first arcade, the game earned more than *Radar Scope* ever had.

Raking in $200 million for Nintendo, *Donkey Kong* blew up, fundamentally changing Nintendo's course — and that of U.S. video games. "All of a sud-

Nintendo produced a series of toys, such as the Ultra Machine (below left, top) and the Ultra Hand (left, bottom), before creating the handheld Game & Watch console (right). Opposite, future business magnate Richard Branson playing Space Invaders *in London, 1979.*

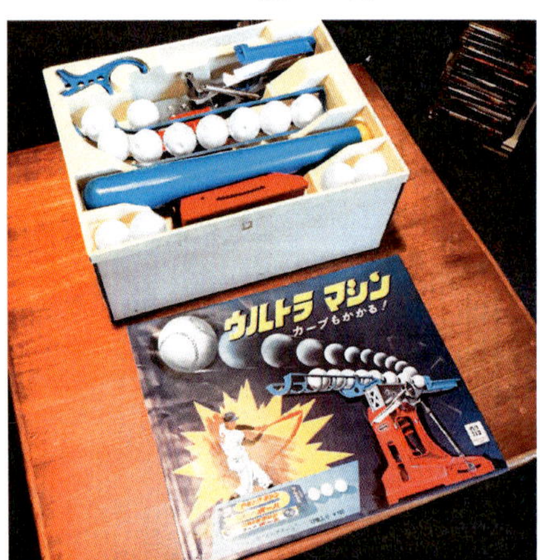

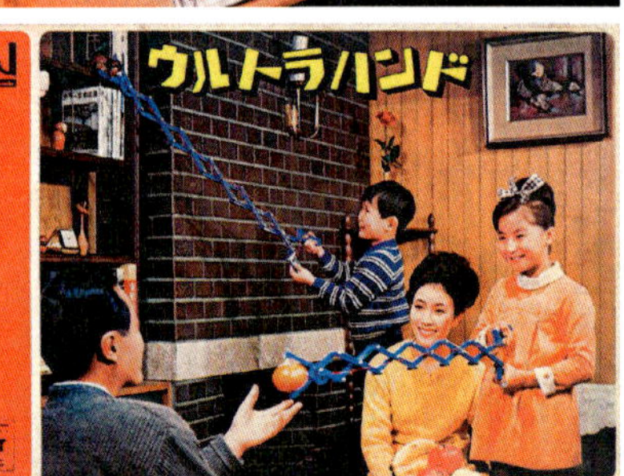

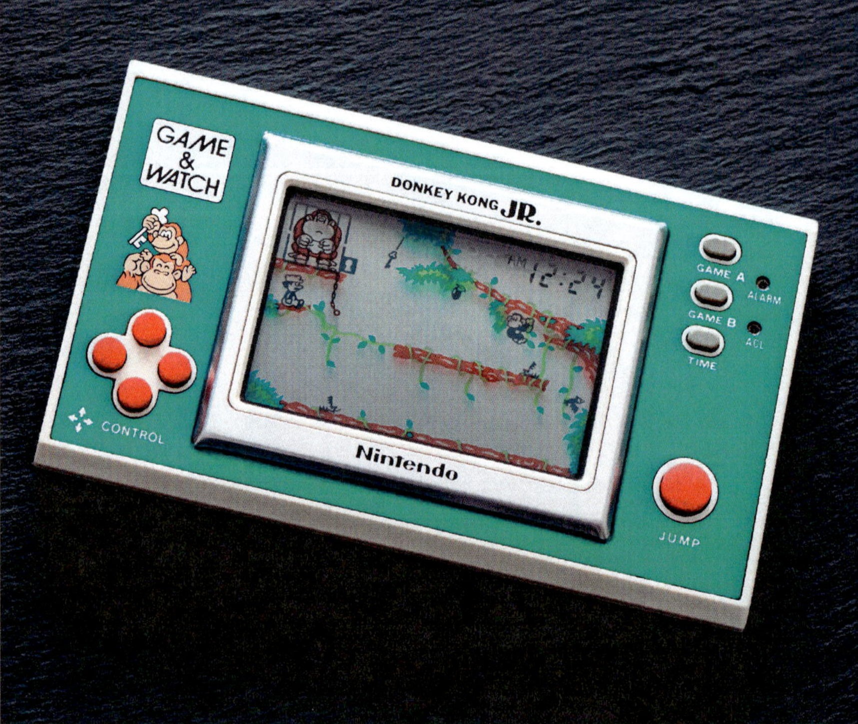

den we see a bright and colorful game with a *kawaii* cuteness, which changes what the arcade environment feels like," says Matthew Payne, PhD, associate professor of film, television, and theatre at the University of Notre Dame, who studies the cultural history of video games. Thanks to this new, squeaky clean image, Nintendo could work its way into homes, too.

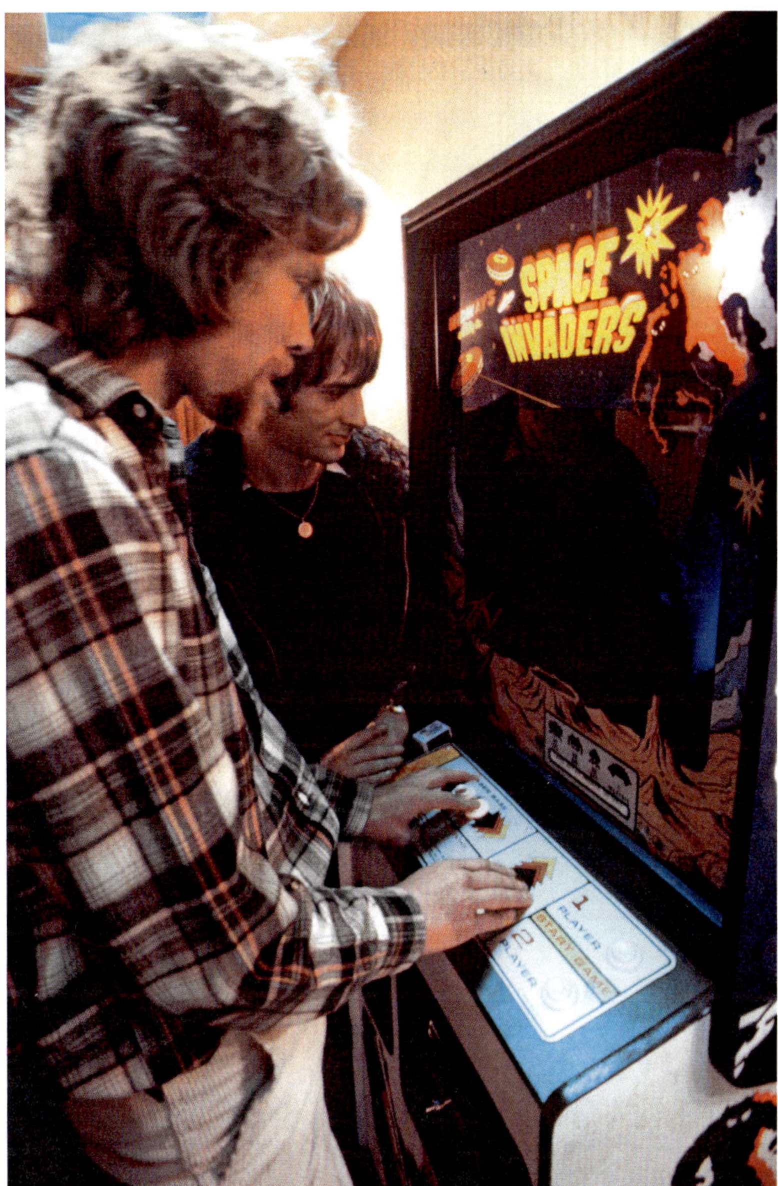

JUMPMAN BECOMES MARIO

In 1983, Jumpman emerged from *Donkey Kong*'s construction site into his own world — and with a new name. As legend has it, Mario was named after Nintendo's mustachioed landlord, Mario Segale, who came storming into the Tukwila warehouse one day, angry that the rent was late. It's said that Segale was nearly jumping up and down in frustration, an inspiration for the character.

Mario Bros., released as an arcade game in 1983, is set in a sewer full of pipes. Instead of a carpenter, Mario is a plumber, accompanied on adventures by his taller brother, Luigi — allowing for two-player games. This new two-player mode wasn't just a money grab but a reflection of Miyamoto's belief that games should forge social connection. "When they test games, even single player games on a handheld device, Nintendo tests with groups to see if it's interesting enough for people to watch," says deWinter. "The introduction of a two-player game emphasizes that social aspect."

Along with expanding gaming opportunities, the presence of Luigi strengthens Mario as a character. Cifaldi describes Mario as a "blank slate character" without a distinct personality. Compared to Mario, Luigi is typically more cautious. While both characters share capabilities — there are no games where Luigi can't do all the same things as Mario — Luigi tends to be more easily frightened and might even hide behind Mario. As the more reluctant protagonist, the taller green player highlights Mario's bravery and boldness, helping create a persona players can relate to or be inspired by.

Mario's heroism takes place in a world inspired by Miyamoto's childhood experiences, which have historically served as inspiration for Nintendo games. In *Mario Bros.*, Miyamoto expressed his love for jumping, sliding, crawling, and collecting on childhood playgrounds. For adults, playing feels nostalgic. For kids, it just feels like being a kid. "There's something so joyful in everything Mario shows up in," says deWinter. "It's bright, fast, slippery, and loud. It's the absolute weightlessness of being that comes with unfettered childhood."

The playful, joy-filled nature of Mario's world turned out to be an asset. *Mario Bros.* exploded in popularity just before the arcade crash of 1983 to 1985, marked by emptying arcades and dwindling sales. Nintendo earned a family-friendly reputation just as the company released its first at-home game console in Japan, the Famicom (Family Computer). The console was released in the States as Nintendo

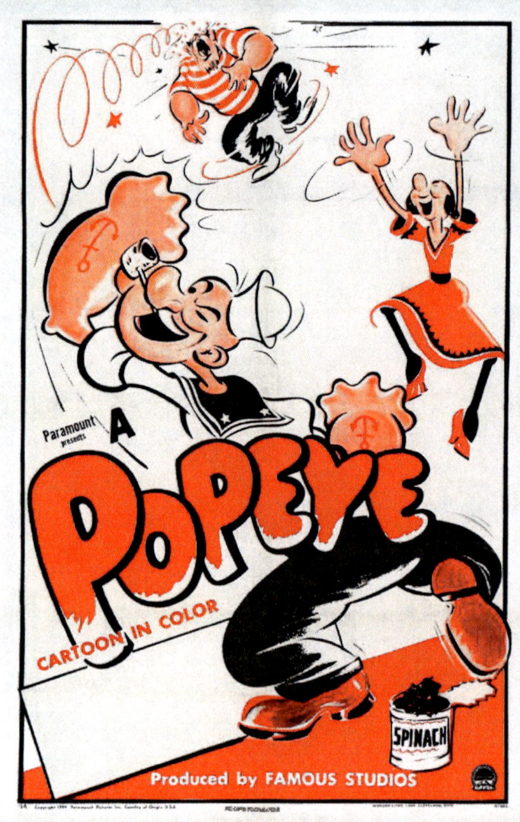

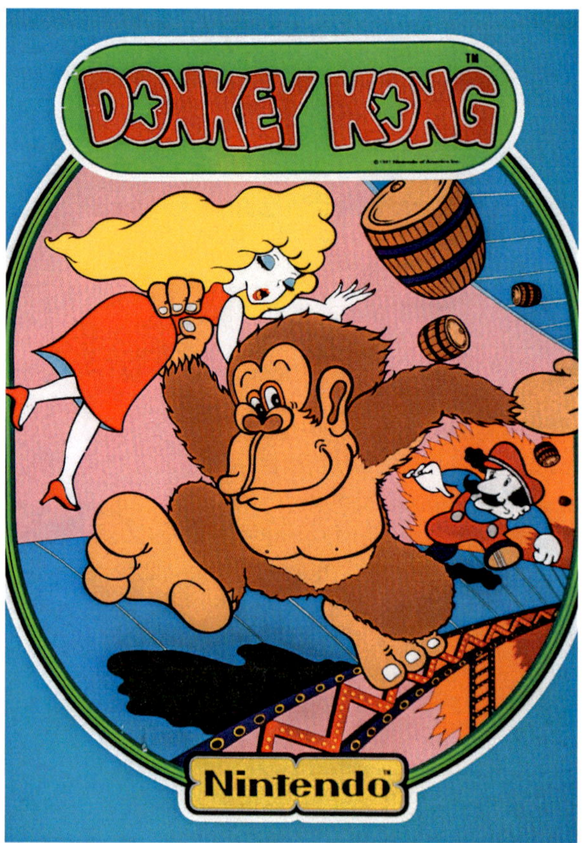

Nintendo originally intended to make a video game based on the Popeye characters, but was denied a license, so the characters of Mario, Donkey Kong, and Pauline were developed for Donkey Kong *(1981). Opposite,* Super Mario Bros. *was originally released in September 1985 in Japan for the Family Computer, before a U.S. release for the NES.*

Entertainment System (NES) in 1985, with the games *Super Mario Bros.* and *Duck Hunt* included. In 1988, Nintendo introduced *Super Mario Bros. 2*, to critical acclaim.

Now, Mario wasn't only a household name. His games were a household staple, too. *Super Mario Bros. 2*, Sheff writes in *Game Over*, "gave kids the sort of power they couldn't get anywhere else. It was safe for them to make mistakes while playing, because there was always another chance. The things that ordinarily made kids popular at school were not important when they were playing. Also, they had found an arena in which they could beat the pants off their parents, not to mention confound them with an incomprehensible vernacular ('I'm in the second world of the Sub-Con, but I can't get past the miniboss')."

Along with courageously battling Koopas and Bowser to rescue Peach, Mario led Nintendo's successful pivot to the home game market. Suddenly, parents didn't have to be afraid of bringing shooting video games into their homes, now that they had a lovable character on an adventure to save a princess. "Mario as a character allowed for product differentiation, but this squeaky clean image very clearly started to skew games as a toy or leisure pursuit for children," says Payne.

THE NINTENDO CRAZE

Nintendo kept growing, up against giants like Sega and PlayStation. Rather than emulating what these brands did to gain popularity, Nintendo stayed on its own path, focusing on original characters and concepts. "Mr. Yamauchi back in the day would tell us that we are not good at fighting: 'We are weak — so don't go picking fights with other companies,'" Miyamoto told the *New York Times* in 2024.

The approach worked. Nintendo, which boasted $3.4 billion in U.S. sales by 1990, kept finding ways to fit into peoples' lives with new games and consoles (many of them featuring Mario). Released in 1989, the Game Boy became the biggest portable game on the market, but not necessarily because it was the

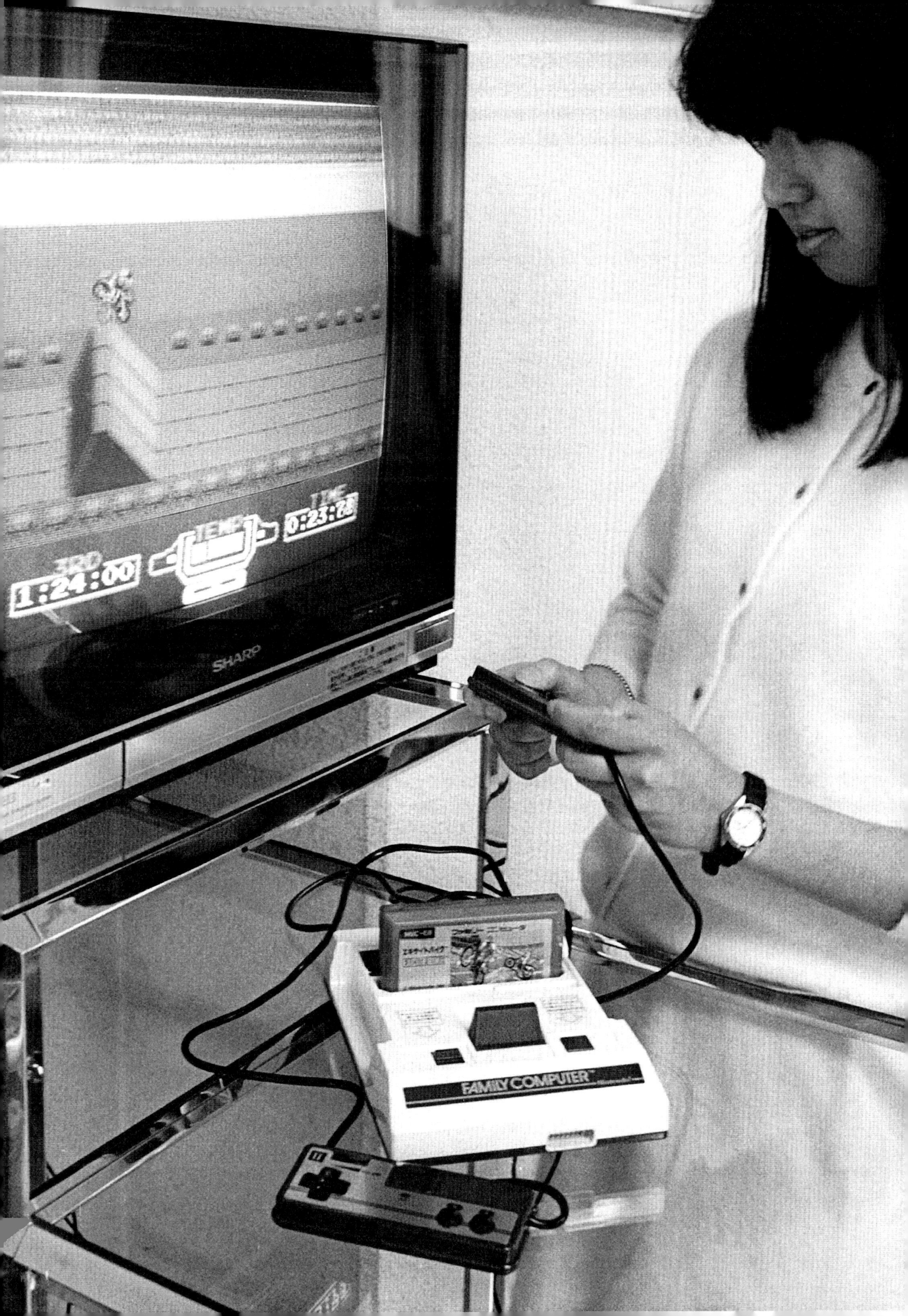
3RD
1:24:00
TEMP
TIME
SHARP
FAMILY COMPUTER

best. Nintendo had long prioritized new experiences with existing technology rather than creating fancy new technology, in order to stay accessible to consumers. "Sega had a larger colored screen, but Nintendo made Game Boy smaller to keep the battery life longer and the price point lower," says deWinter.

The Super Nintendo Entertainment System, or SNES, followed in 1991 and was the first home console with a memory card, allowing players to log their progress when they stopped playing the game. With it came *Super Mario World*, which took place in a new land with a new story (and a new character: Mario and Luigi's dinosaur companion, Yoshi). Nintendo 64 arrived in 1996, and in *Super Mario 64* consumers had a new way to explore Mario's world: in 3D. Game Boy Color came out in 1998, followed by 2001's Game Boy Advance and GameCube and the Nintendo DS, in 2004. The most recent console, the Switch, released in 2017, has since introduced plenty of Mario games (including a return to side-scrolling, in *Super Mario Wonder*).

Since *Donkey Kong*, Mario's has had dozens of games named after him across all of Nintendo's gaming systems. In addition to popular games like *Mario Kart* and *Mario Party*, he's been part of plenty of spin-offs, from teaching kids typing on PCs to refereeing sports on Wii games. Miyamoto also used him as a fill-in character when he was designing other games, such as *The Legend of Zelda*. "It started out as Mario running around a dungeon, because Miyamoto was thinking more about the gameplay itself than a story or character," Cifaldi says. In that way, Mario is like an actor placed in roles by Nintendo, a right-hand man during the creative process.

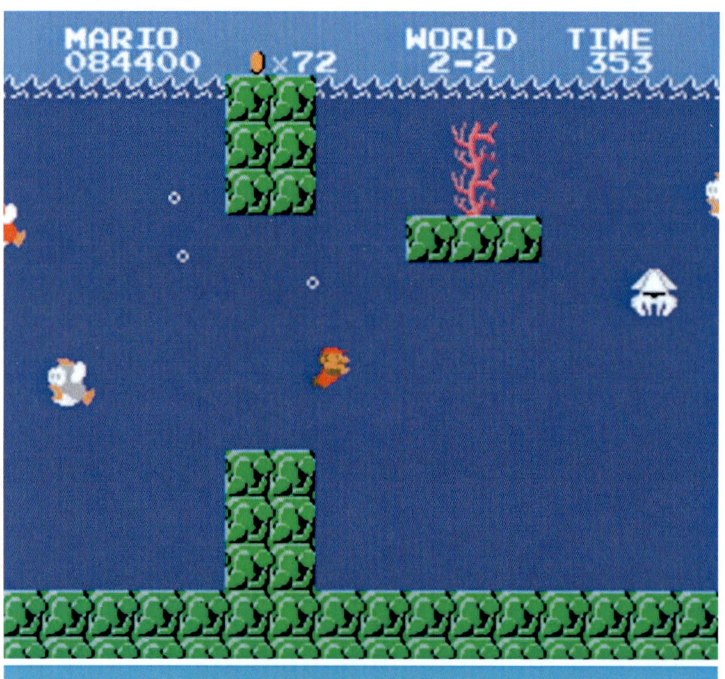

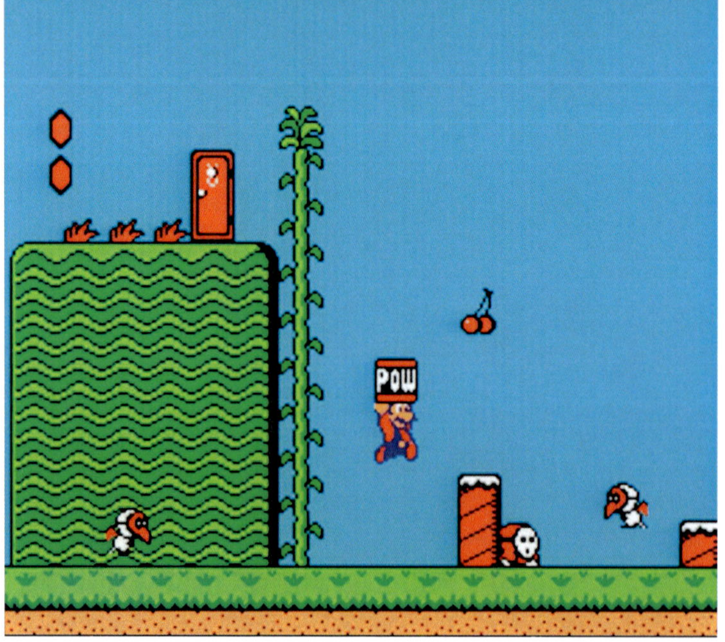

A 2020 article published in *The Ringer* calls Mario "the video-game-character equivalent of type-O blood." Like other big-name characters, he doesn't have a lot of discernible character traits other than being a good guy who wants to do what's right. That adaptability is part of what makes Mario universally appealing: "We all want to be the hero, and being such an easy character to put ourselves into, Mario helps us live out that fantasy," says Cifaldi.

MARIO'S MARK ON CULTURE

Since the Nintendo craze of the 1980s and '90s, Mario's celebrity has only grown: Along with Mario games, there are now Mario clothes, bedsheets, board games, backpacks, and Mario-inspired movies and theme parks. According to Q Scores, an online database that scores public figures and fictional characters based on their popularity and likability, Mario's level of familiarity among Americans ages 6 and older has increased

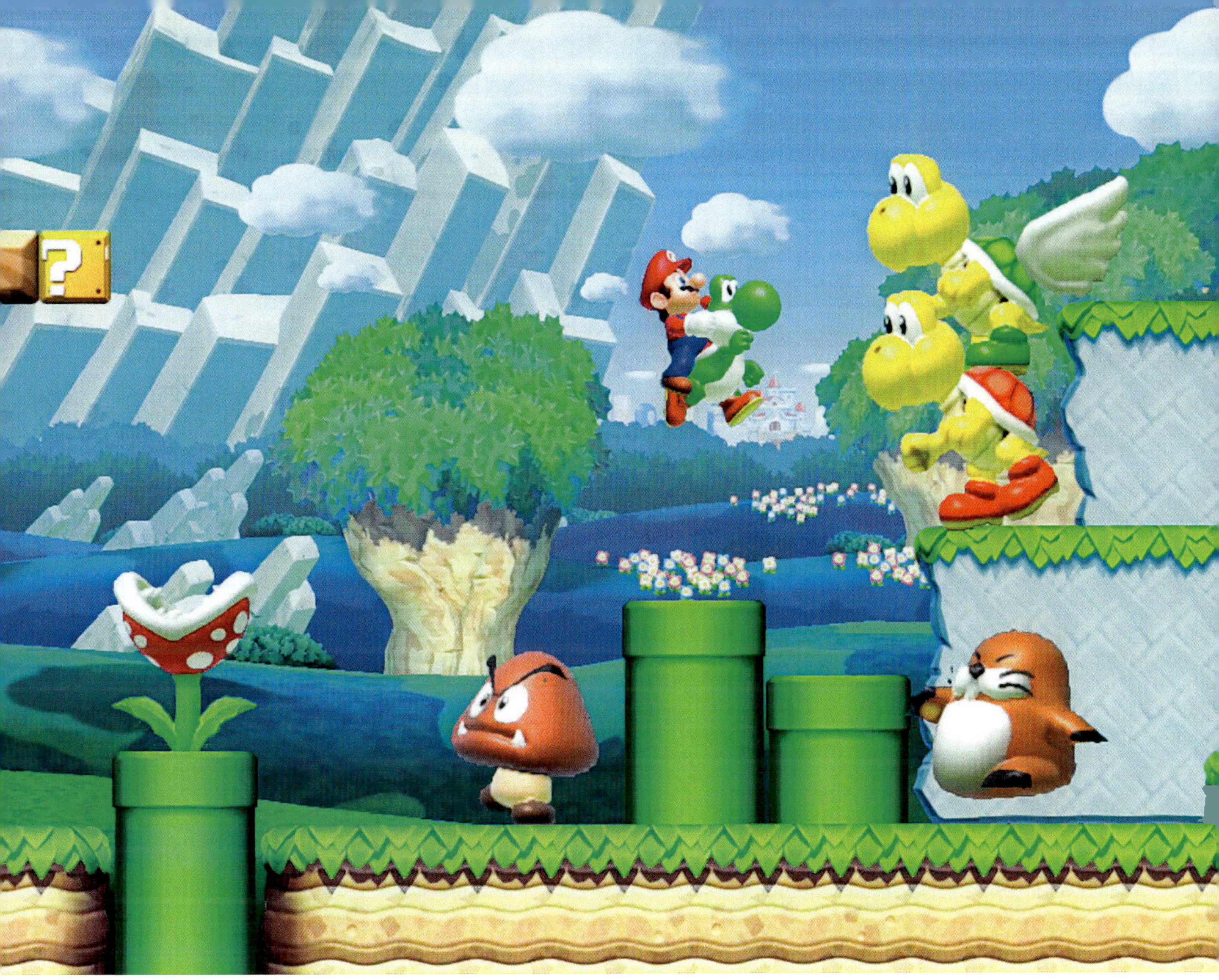

Super Mario games have progressed immensely since the 8-bit NES versions of the '80s and '90s (opposite). Super Mario Maker *(above) allows players to create their own levels for others to explore.*

from 60 percent in 1996 (when Q Scores began) to 72 percent as of 2020. Mario's Q Score—his measure of likability — sits at roughly 30 percent, meaning that 30 percent of people familiar with Mario say he's one of their top characters.

It could be said that Nintendo, in large part, has Mario to thank for its legacy. "I do believe that the quality of something hinges on whether or not it's sought several decades after its creation," Miyamoto said in a 2020 interview with *The New Yorker*. "Walt Disney didn't create everything that Disney put out, but the idea that a company could make these long-lasting symbols—that's something I've admired. We're finally at a point where people who played with Nintendo's characters as children are playing with those same characters with their children. That longevity is special."

All this fame hasn't changed Mario too much over the years, aside from some minor cosmetic changes necessitated by advancing technology (more colors and a more detailed face, for starters). But is there really anything to evolve in a character like Mario? To do so would be to alter what makes him so appealing, so enduring in the first place. "He's just a timeless hero. His only opinion is that good is right and princesses shouldn't be held against their will," says Cifaldi.

Experts have their own theories about why Mario has stood the test of time. But in the end, Miyamoto would probably suggest that Mario's looks and personality, or lack thereof, don't matter as much as what we experience when we play with him. Like Nintendo did during the *Radar Scope* challenge of the 1980s, Mario gets back up and tries again when he faces obstacles, which makes for a lesson in resilience — and a pretty fun game. "No one in history has lost more than Mario, but he always springs back up," says Ryan. "So long as you want to keep going, Mario will keep going with you."

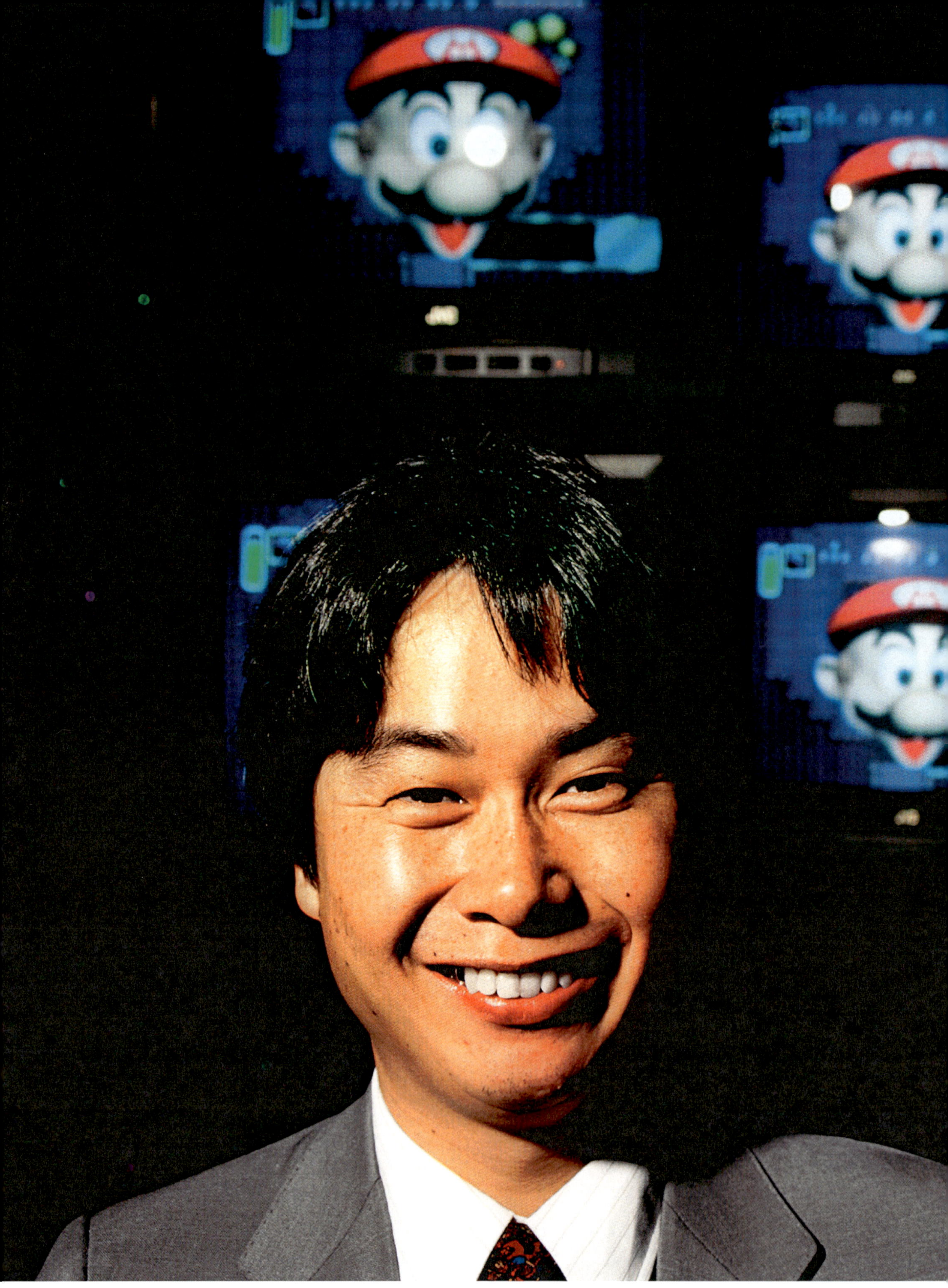

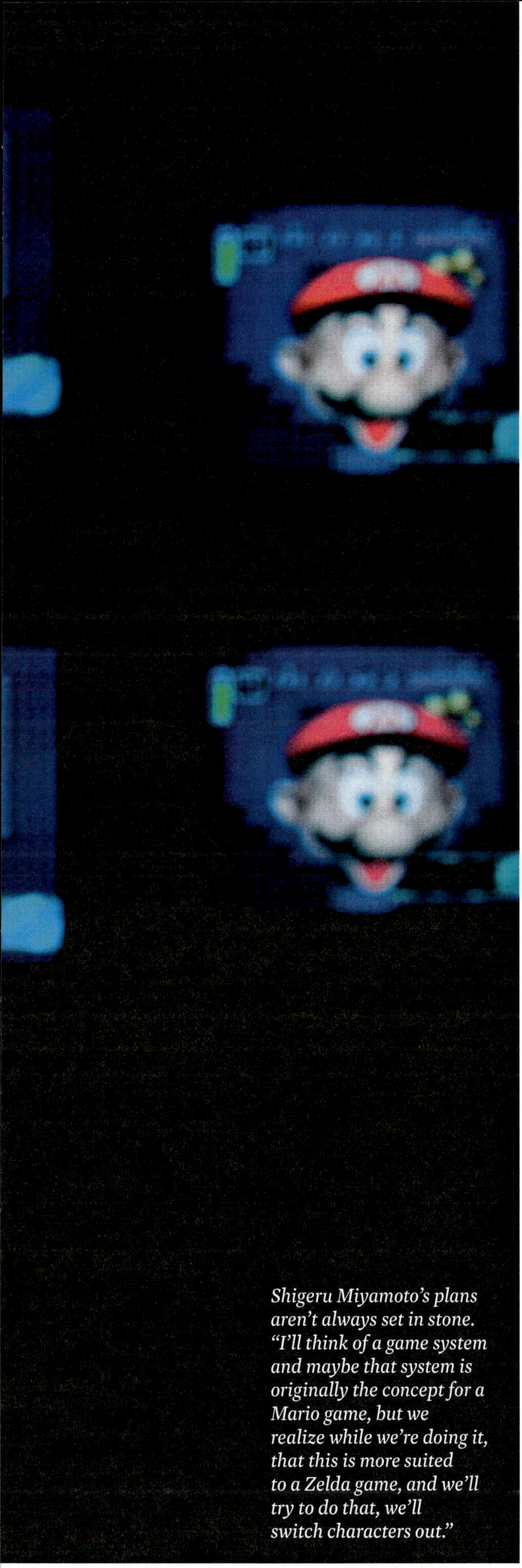

MARIO'S MAKER

In 2010, for the *Super Mario* 25th anniversary, TIME spoke with the game's creator, Shigeru Miyamoto.

BY EVAN NARCISSE

Shigeru Miyamoto's plans aren't always set in stone. "I'll think of a game system and maybe that system is originally the concept for a Mario game, but we realize while we're doing it, that this is more suited to a Zelda game, and we'll try to do that, we'll switch characters out."

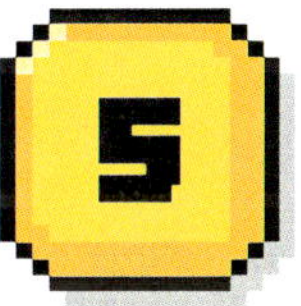

UNDAY, NOVEMBER 7, 2010, WAS the day of the 40th New York City Marathon, and thousands of runners journeyed through the city as fast as their feet could take them. One very special visitor to the city didn't lace up a pair of New Balance kicks but has nevertheless been running his own personal race for more than two decades.

The year 2010 would mark the 25th anniversary of *Super Mario Bros.*, a game that ushered in a new wave of financial success and creative ferment for the home video game console business. Shigeru Miyamoto is that game's lead creator and has worked at Nintendo since 1977. Miyamoto, initially hired as a staff artist, now holds the title of senior managing director and general manager, entertainment analysis & development division.

Miyamoto came to the United States to celebrate the 25th anniversary and wowed fans with a surprise appearance at the Nintendo World store in Manhattan's Rockefeller Center. Gamers young and old hooped and hollered when Miyamoto took the stage, and it's easy to understand why. In person, Miyamoto evinces the same impish liveliness of his best work, and a conversation with him also makes plain the thoughtfulness that sharpens the games he works on. I spoke with him two days before his Nintendo World appearance, and he held forth on the importance of simplicity in game design.

Nintendo is a company that's been around for a long, long time now, and many view you as an integral part of its longevity. Do you think of your own legacy and things you've done before when you are creating new games? Do you use them to inspire you?
I don't really think of things in terms of legacy or where I stand in the history of Nintendo or anything like that. The important thing for us is to make sure that we're having fun in our job.

So I really try to focus on, again, not only myself enjoying what I'm doing, but looking at my staff, and making sure that they're having fun in their jobs as well. Especially when you're working on a series, there are times when you're doing some repetitions, some work that maybe you've done before. You really want to make sure that the people working on it are approaching the project in a way that they're not getting bored or frustrated, and that they're thinking of new things and new twists and new appeals. That's something we look at as well.

Your career with Nintendo actually started a little bit before, with *Donkey Kong*, and we all know it became a big hit. But when *Donkey Kong* became popular, why shift the focus to Mario? Why make him the focus of a new series of games? Why not a new character?
Well, the first reason is that Donkey Kong is just too darn big. And because he's so big, we actually created Donkey Kong Junior to try to come up with the same sort of character but in a smaller, more manageable size. And as we were looking at an 8-bit size, Mario became a much easier character to use.

So that's the first reason. My original goal was that I really wanted to use Mario in a lot of different games. So, for example, in the original *Punch-Out!* you'll see Mario and Donkey Kong in the audience.

"I think there are a lot of people who think that 'Wow, simple is pretty cool!' They look at the older games and think of them as amazing," says Miyamoto.

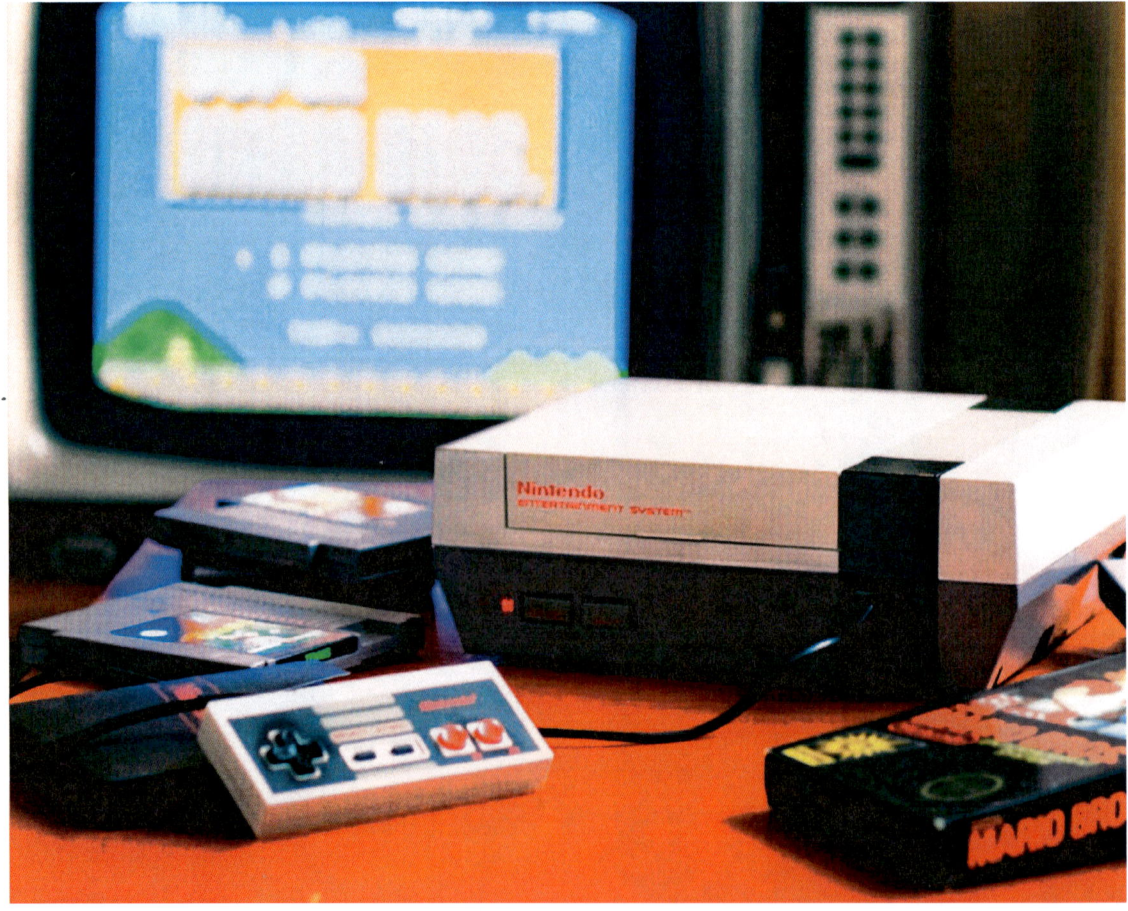

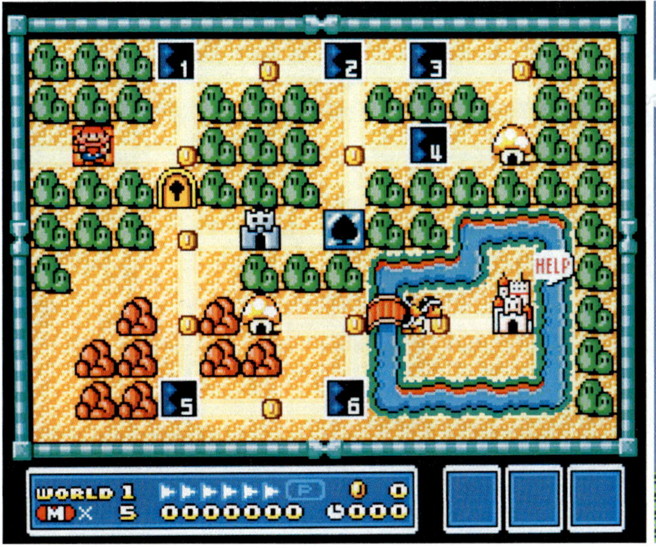

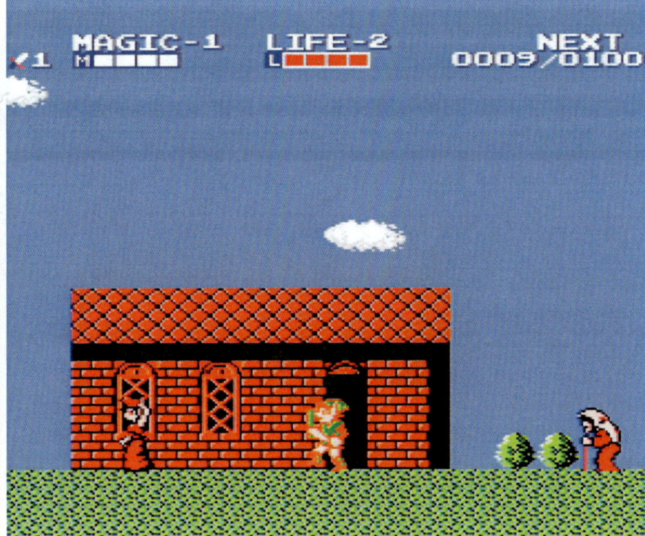

You'll see Mario is the referee in *Tennis* [a 1984 Nintendo Entertainment System game].

And then it became taking Mario and Luigi both and putting them in different situations in various games, and that was the direction I decided to take.

So, even from the beginning, you envisioned Mario as a character you would put in different settings, in different genres?
Exactly right. And it's sort of common among the popular culture in Japan that a creator will take that same character and have him appear in different manga. It's also sort of like, maybe, Hitchcock appearing in all his movies. It's sort of cool to have that character appearing here and there, whether or not they have a large role or not.

But, Hitchcock appeared as Hitchcock. Do you see yourself as Mario?
[*Laughs*] Yeah, I'm a little embarrassed, but Mario is sort of my doppelgänger.

You started your career as an artist, not in programming, but in drawing and designing. Do you think that's informed your game design sensibilities in a particular way?
Yeah, I think part of it has been very influential, in that my industrial design background has allowed me to be able to take these concepts that I have in my head and be able to put them down on paper.

I have people on my teams do their own drawings and bring out the creation of their own ideas just to make sure that they're true to what they have in their heads. So in terms of thinking of design as building a structure into which we put in everything else, that's the core for what we flow everything into. It hasn't changed all that much.

That's where you start, with a structure in mind, and then you fill it in with all these different concepts?
You're right. And then you take that and look at how people will respond to this. And you try to make that structure into something that people will enjoy playing and being a part of.

Mario has become a universal character like Superman or Mickey Mouse. What does he symbolize for you? Is it a spirit of adventure? Or adaptation?
Well, as I said earlier, I start with the game system [the rules and ideas that will go into the experience]. So I'll think of a system and maybe that is originally the concept for a Mario game, but we realize while we're doing it that this is more suited to a Zelda game, and we'll try to do that, we'll switch characters out. But how I think of Mario is sort of as my go-to actor. So when I'm creating that new system, I start by plugging Mario in to see how he will react or what we can do with him in this design. He's like the trusted guy you throw in to see how the system is working.

That's funny, because a lot of the times Mario always seems very harried, or the character himself is like, "I don't understand what is going on? I guess I just have to figure out the stuff that's in the world." So it's funny that you say you just drop him in a situation for the player to control.
The player is the one who is playing the game and Mario is sort of their surrogate vehicle for enjoying that game. And because we know it's Mario, there's a sense of reassurance and familiarity. The player can think, "Even though I don't know what's going on, at least I'm Mario."

You're talking about fitting Mario inside new game designs. What's been the most difficult part of sustaining creativity over the last 25 years? Were there

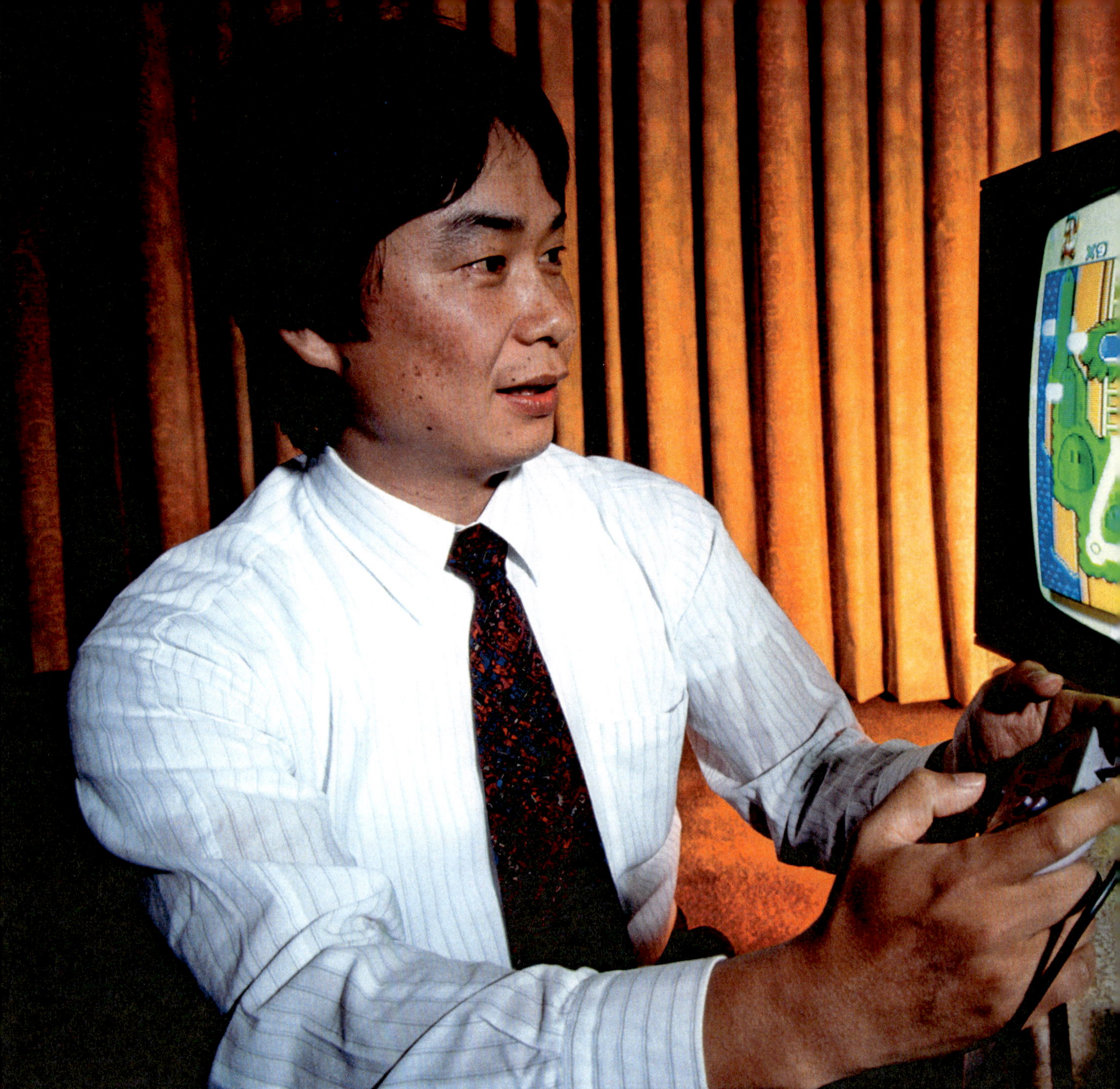

Miyamoto playing Super Mario World *on an SNES console. The game, known as* Super Mario Bros. 4 *in Japan, released in 1990.*

moments of doubt in which you thought you might not be able to fulfill a concept or create a mechanic in a game?
I look at Mario as being equal to digital technology of the time. When we first started, we were looking at, let's say, 8-bit limited technology. There are always limitations to what you can do.

But the fun in that, and the job for us, is to take that and see what could happen, rather than complaining and wondering about what we can't do and wondering, "Oh, if only we could do this?"

We create by looking at what we can do and using our energies to utilize that technology to the fullest, to maximize its potential. And of course, as technology grows and advances, that refreshes our ability to look at Mario in new ways, and to be able to do new things with him. And it's really been for me a very natural process in that, as technology advances, so does Mario.

Do you have favorite aspects of the remastered editions of the older games?
Well, I look back and play some of these games and there are a lot of places where, to be honest, I'm a little embarrassed. I look at *Super Mario 3*, and I'm like,

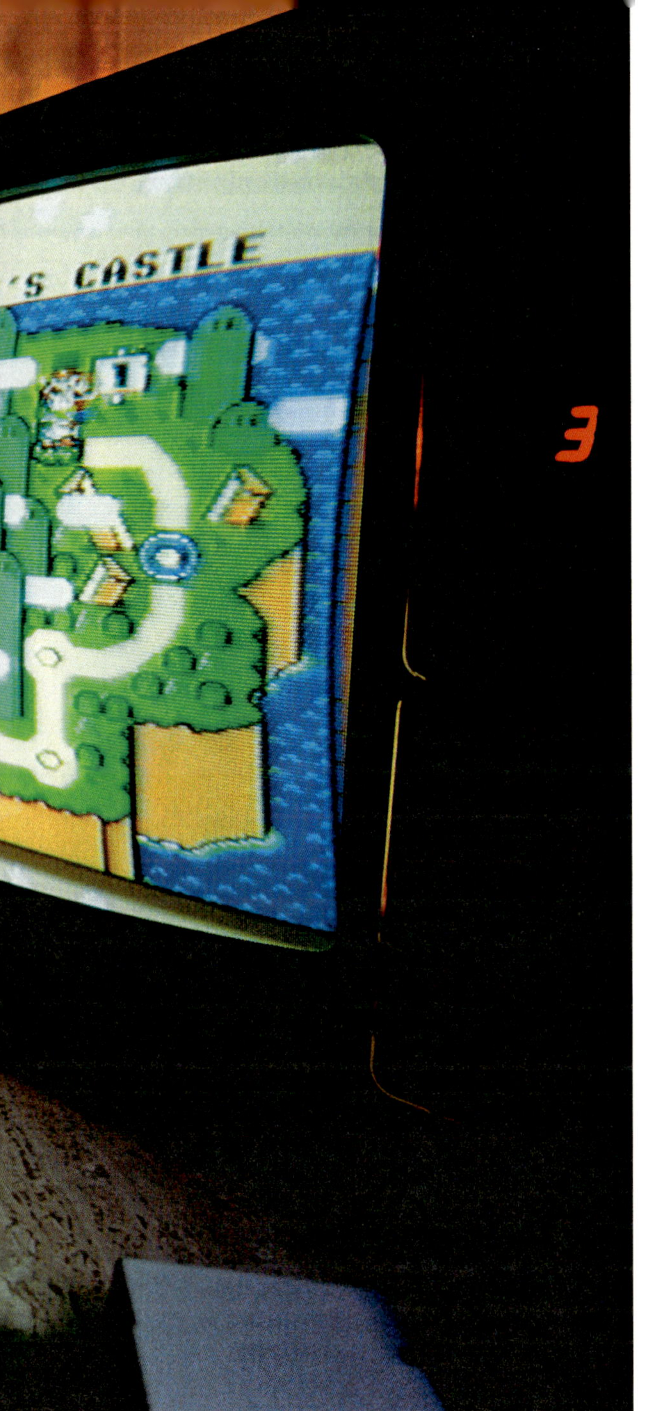

"This was it?! This is what we thought was good enough?" That being said, I do have new understandings of that work. The balance in that game is what it needed to be at that time. It really was. And so, even seeing all the limitations, I'm very happy with what we created and I wouldn't change it.

One of the things I've read is that the magic mushrooms in the Super Mario games come from myths about enchanted food. Is that true?

Whether or not this is actually a factor or not, we're not really sure. But this whole idea of mysterious foods that have mysterious properties comes from a lot of the European folk tales. Of course, you see foods like that in Alice in Wonderland. I'm not really sure if the Japanese folk really knew what we were referencing. But that was sort of kind of where it was coming from. At least I think that's what it came from.

I think the fantasy elements in the Legend of Zelda games are obvious, but were there other folklore or mythology elements that inspired parts of Mario's world and his universe?

Yeah, like you said, Zelda, of course, does have elements of fantasy folk tales with goblins and whatnot. You can see those right away and they are easily recognizable. With Mario, however, it's more surrealism. You'd see blocks floating in the middle of the air, doorways just appear out of nowhere. That kind of look draws on the work of René Magritte.

There's that sort of surrealistic element of just giving people the freedom to draw — where the drawing is playing the game — and not really being worried about facing it in reality. Players are artists who create their own reality within the game. So that's sort of Mario. Creating new and surrealistic things rather than being based on anything else.

The typical structure of a Mario game is kind of a mythological journey. There's an overworld and an underworld. And it's interesting how the games themselves have been passed through generations, like old stories used to be. With that in mind, how do you feel about maybe those stories moving to another medium again? Like new TV or movie adaptations?

When we're creating a game, we have the world that's there but, really, it's up to the user to fill in the spaces of things that aren't explained or laid out for them. Our job as the game creators or developers — the programmers, artists, and whatnot — is that we have to kind of put ourselves in the user's shoes. We try to see what they're seeing and then make it and support what we think they might think.

So, if we're playing, we think, "Well, the players would probably want to do something like this or maybe they're going to do something like this." The games need to be flexible enough to hit all of the different users and support all of those possible ideas of what they think might be out there.

Whereas with a book or a movie, you're basically explaining to people, this is what's here, we're showing you what's here. And for us, it's sort of the opposite.

There have been lots of homages to *Super Mario Bros.* over the years, in games like *Braid* or *Super Meat Boy*. *Super Meat Boy* even has the same initials as *Super Mario Bros.* How do you feel about that formula, that recipe, being reinvented? Have you liked any of "the riffs," the improvisations on the formula?
I haven't actually played any of them! But I'm assuming they're done pretty well. I think we were just lucky. *Super Mario*, of course, is sort of the pioneer of that side-scrolling, action-game style, and we're just lucky to be in that position.

Right. It could have been somebody else whose game caught on and became one for the ages.
It could have been somebody else. And even when we go into 3D with *Super Mario 64* or whatnot, we revert back to that side-scrolling style so often. If people like it and want to use it, that's great, isn't it?

Do you feel that there is a group of designers at Nintendo who can't wait to get on to the next thing in terms of technology? Who see new processors and things like that as they move forward and want to explore the possibilities? Do you personally feel that way?
We are always looking at and evaluating new technology. That being said, we're pretty much looking at some of the same technologies as every other company, you know. But rather than the technology being the only driving force, we also think about how can we use it.

What can we do with it is where we put our focus. There's something to be said about taking an idea and the value of that idea [in conjunction with technology]. What's important is the ability to take that idea and make it more than itself. You can use a lot of different technologies to create something that doesn't really have a lot of value.

How does it make you feel to know that these games you've helped produce are something that families connect over or share with each other? Not everybody who makes a game is lucky enough to be in that position. Do you feel honored? Or is there a responsibility?
Well, yeah, there's a bit of responsibility. I'm a player too. So I'm always thinking about the player and how the player is enjoying their experience in the game. The goal is something that's accessible to all ages, of course, and all experience levels.

How are we appealing to the consumer? Because we're gamers as well. And, personally, I want to create something that makes me look cool while I'm playing it. When I'm playing as Link in a Legend of Zelda game, that's something where I feel like I'm cool because I'm that guy.

You're going to celebrate the 25th anniversary with hundreds of people here in the United States. What does their devotion to Mario mean to you personally?
I'm obviously very appreciative. A lot of things that come out of Japan are sort of segmented or taken as, "This is from the Orient. This is East Asia."

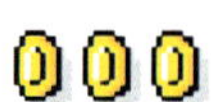

HOW ARE WE APPEALING TO THE CONSUMER? BECAUSE WE'RE GAMERS AS WELL. AND, PERSONALLY, I WANT TO CREATE SOMETHING THAT MAKES ME LOOK COOL WHILE I'M PLAYING IT.

Right, they're looked upon as exotic.
Right. Exotic. Where Mario is different . . . I don't think people need to recognize it as something out of Japan. He's become sort of this worldwide easily accessible idea. People like it. That's great. To learn about kids or see kids dressed up as Mario on Halloween is something I'm very grateful for.

Seeing as how we're at the 25th anniversary of *Super Mario Bros.*, what would you like to see in the next 25 years? Mario is obviously very connected to you. How would you like to see the torch passed on? Is the idea of other people creating Mario something you think about?
Whoa, I'll still be here in 25 years! [*Laughs*] I mean, there are a lot of people at Nintendo who really get Mario. A lot of people I'm working with really understand who and what Mario is. Because Mario, as we've spoken about earlier, evolves with technology, it's hard to say where he's going to be in 25 years.

You may not be able to imagine what's possible in the future?
That's right. I can't imagine it. I'm confident, though, people will still be playing as Mario!

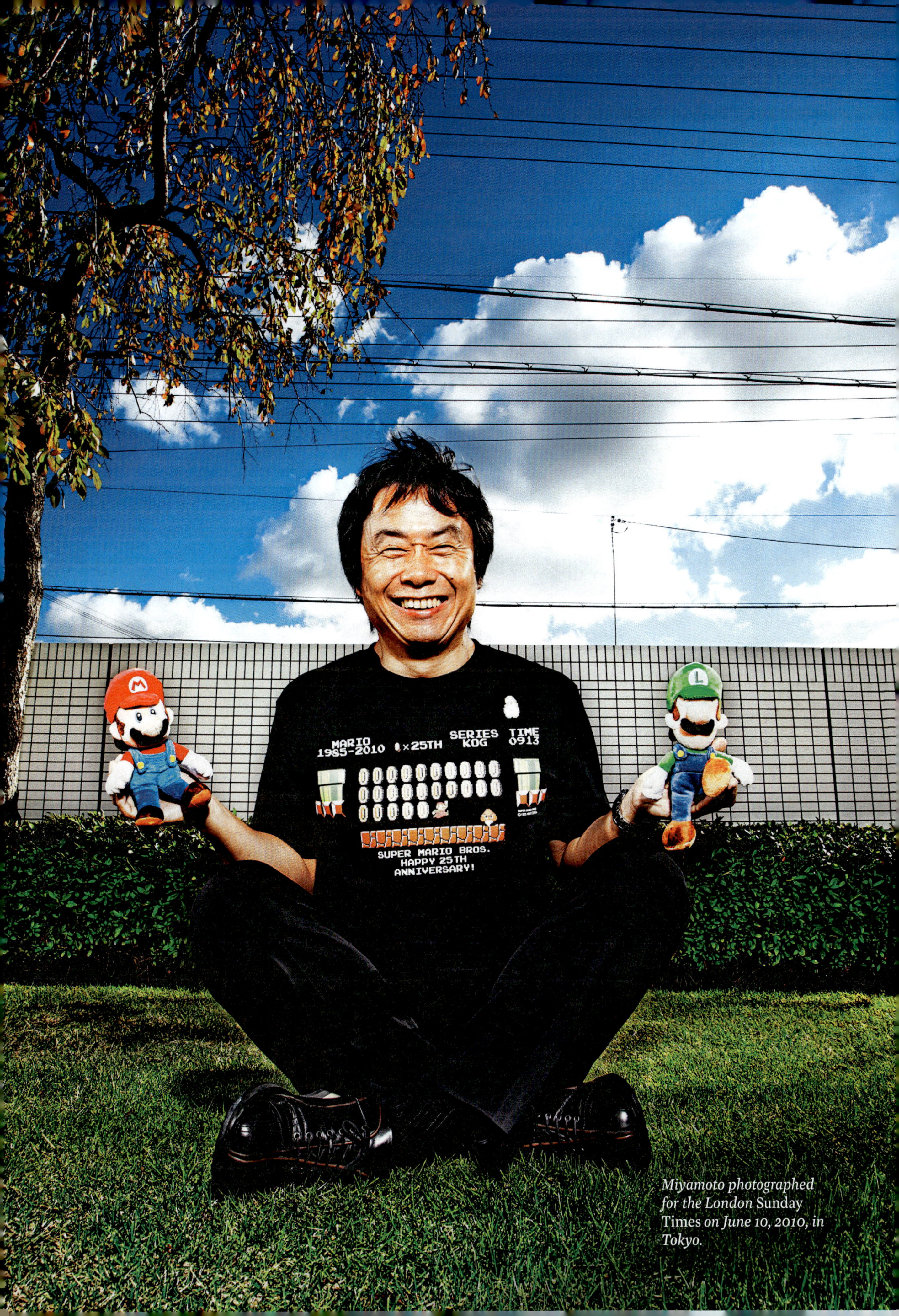

Miyamoto photographed for the London Sunday Times *on June 10, 2010, in Tokyo.*

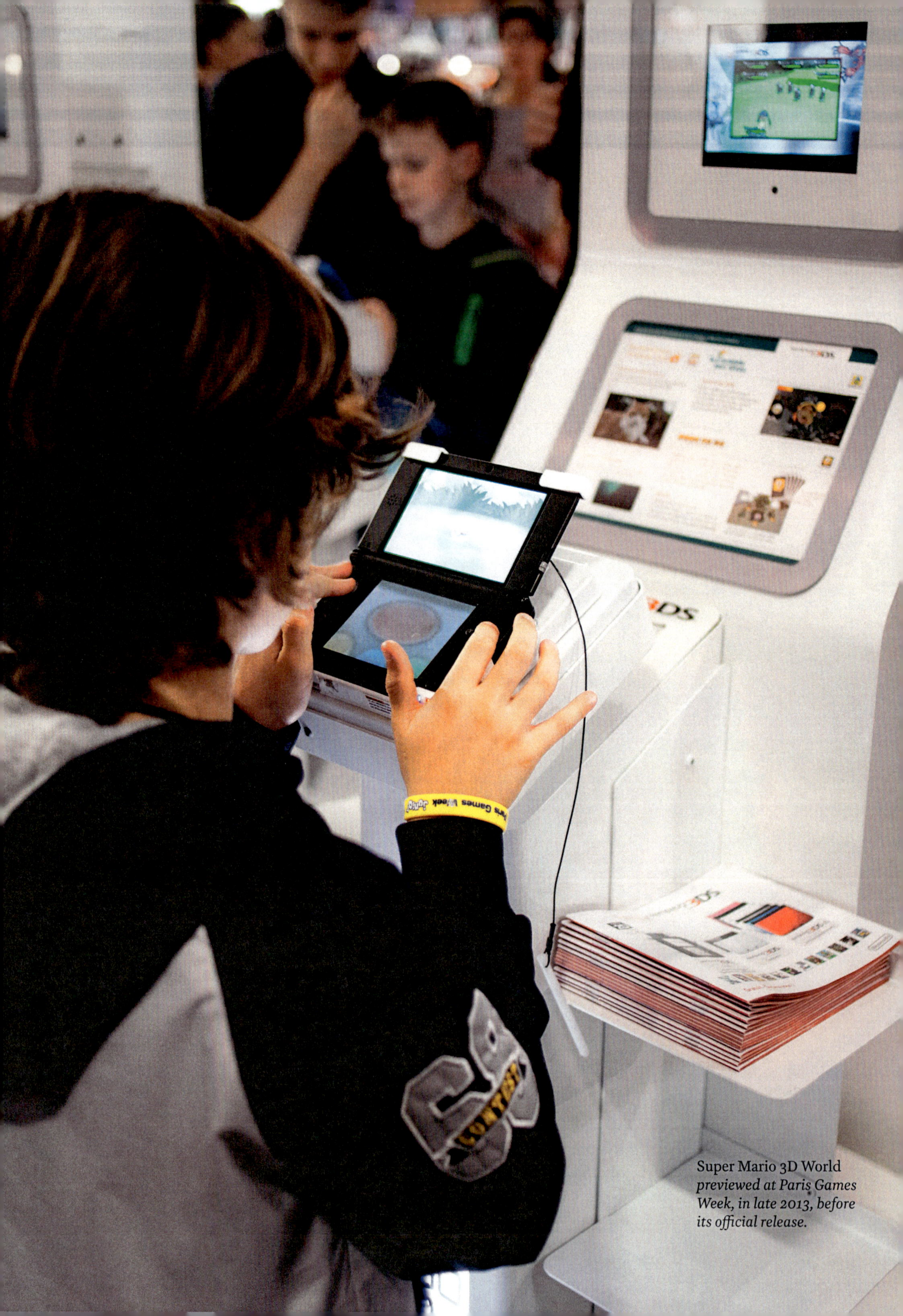

Super Mario 3D World *previewed at Paris Games Week, in late 2013, before its official release.*

HIS 3D TRANSFORMATION

In 2013 Nintendo reached into its library and remade series mainstays in a new way. That year, TIME spoke to the developers on that process.

BY MATT PECKHAM

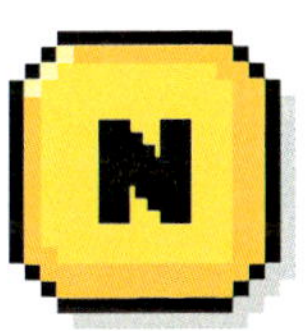

INTENDO'S NEXT BIG MARIO GAME for Wii U, unveiled at the 2013 Electronic Entertainment Expo (E3), turned out not to be strictly a Mario game at all: *Super Mario 3D World* reaches back to the Nintendo Entertainment System's halcyon days, when we were smitten with a little something called *Super Mario Bros. 2*.

Super Mario 3D World supports up to four players at once, handing you control of Mario, Luigi, Toad, and even the series' perennial abductee, Princess Peach. The twist? Everything's fully 3D, and you can play either cooperatively or competitively.

As in *Super Mario Bros. 2*, Mario, Luigi, Peach and Toad each have unique abilities, so for instance Peach can hover in the air when jumping, and Toad can sprint faster than his companions. Oh, and there's the cat suit, which — no, that's not just a yellow Tanooki suit — lets you scratch enemies, climb up walls and even scurry up those precious end-level flagpoles.

Developed by the same team behind *Super Mario 3D Land* for 3DS and the Wii's *Super Mario Galaxy* series, *Super Mario 3D World* for Wii U arrives this December. I spoke with the game's director, Koichi Hayashida (*Super Mario Sunshine*, *Super Mario Galaxy*, *Super Mario 3D Land*), and producer, Yoshiaki Koizumi (too many to list). Here's what they had to say about some of their design choices.

Why the choice not to support online multiplayer in *Super Mario 3D World*?

MR. HAYASHIDA: I think that we've always wanted to focus on being able to see the other players around you. I always thought that was fun.

MR. KOIZUMI: The first *Super Mario Bros.* on the Nintendo Entertainment System had two controllers, so you could play multiplayer with someone right next to you. I think that we wanted to accomplish the same kind of feeling in a 3D Mario game for the first time.

MR. HAYASHIDA: I've always really enjoyed playing games with my children. In *Super Mario Galaxy*, we had the "assist play mode" that was available, but this is the first time that we've implemented a real multiplayer where the second player is moving a character around on screen in a 3D Mario game. And so I'm really happily looking forward to the experience of playing that with my kids.

How co-op/multiplayer-centric is *Super Mario 3D World* if someone wants to play it as a single-player game? What's the single-player experience like by comparison?

MR. HAYASHIDA: Yes, we spent a lot of time thinking about the single-player experience in this game, particularly when you're using the GamePad while playing it, which is my personal choice as well. You can use the touch screen on the GamePad to interact with hidden coins and blocks and reveal them. Or you can activate the gyro camera controls on the touch screen, which you can use to look around in the game, much like you would look around in *Super Mario 64* or *Super Mario Sunshine* with the camera controls in that game. I feel like we've gotten to the point where it's feeling really good. And looking around in the 3D world is very important not just for navigation but also for being able to explore and to enjoy the fun of finding things that were hidden.

Will the player operating the Wii U GamePad have an advantage over other co-op players?

MR. HAYASHIDA: I think the person who is going to be using the GamePad is in all likelihood the person who owns the game and the Wii U and perhaps has had a few friends over to play the game. And so they're in a really good position to, let's say, stop enemies using touch screen for these other players just to make it a little bit easier for them because they know where the enemies are. Likewise, they can reveal hidden blocks and coins for the other players. These are just little nice things they can do as the person using it. Now I don't think people are necessarily at a disadvantage for using the Wii Remote, but if you are the sort of person who prefers the feeling of a stick for controlling movement in a 3D game, we will be supporting the Wii U Pro Controller, which does have analog stick controls.

MR. KOIZUMI: Yes, I really like to think of the person who has the GamePad as the one who is in the best position to help out other players, not necessarily that they are the leader of this particular expedition but just that they have the ability to do a lot for the other players.

How do the competitive elements of gameplay, like hurling your friends to their doom, compare to the cooperative ones?

MR. HAYASHIDA: Of course people are free to play however they like, and that's going to look different from one person to the next. But ultimately we envision everyone working together to finish a stage. But along the way there are certainly lots of opportunities for a little bit of friendly conflict here and there.

MR. KOIZUMI: I'd like to point out that you can pick up and carry other players. At first it might seem like this is something that you would do to help carry someone through a difficult part of a stage. But that's not necessarily the case, because you can also throw them, which in certain situations is definitely not helpful and cooperative. So I think this is the kind

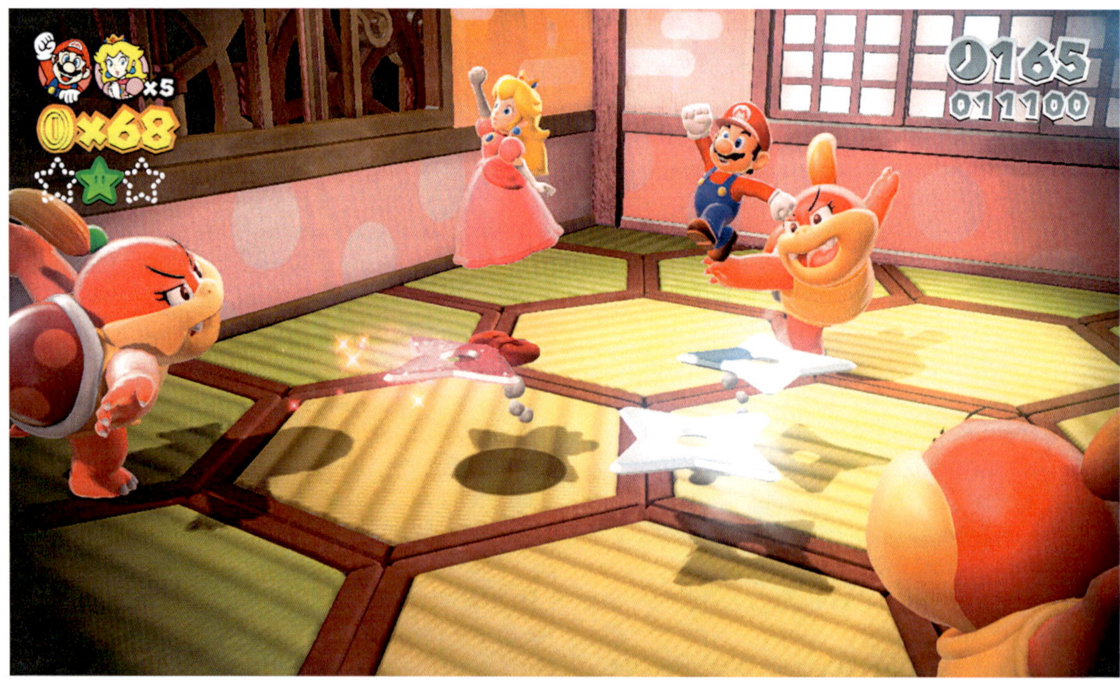

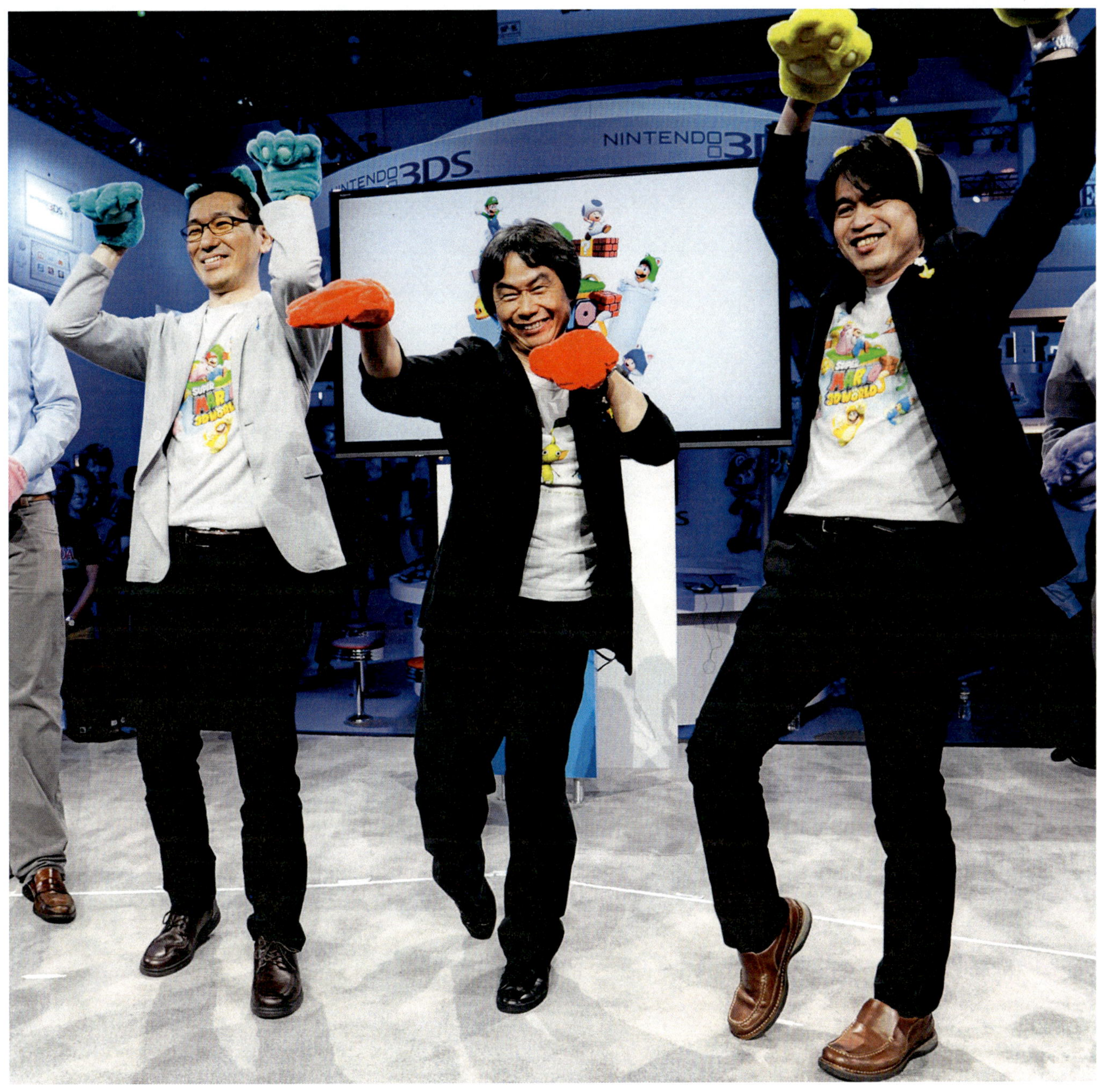

Shigeru Miyamoto (center) joined fellow developers Yoshiaki Koizumi (right) and Koichi Hayashida (left) in highlighting Cat Mario in Super Mario 3D World, *June 11, 2013, in Los Angeles.*

of game play that really brings out the personality of each individual player.

I have had a lot of similar experiences playing *New Super Mario Bros.* with someone when suddenly they did something I wasn't very fond of and I was like, "What?!"

Which came first in the design process: the idea of including a cat suit or the gameplay mechanics of climbing walls, scratching, and pouncing on enemies?

MR. HAYASHIDA: Well I think the first thing we thought of was, What kind of new experiences can we create? What's really important to that is the feeling of the control when you're playing through a new gameplay mechanic. So we always spend a lot of time testing out new ideas. I think the first test that came in this particular design was Mario running on all fours like an animal.

Once we started testing that out, we realized it felt really good. The next thing we did was trying out his ability to stick to a wall: What if Mario could jump and then just attach himself like that? And that test went well also. Only after that did we add climbing walls and start to put all of those different pieces together. Then we began to think about how best to express this as a new power-up. And that's when we hit upon the idea that a cat would be best.

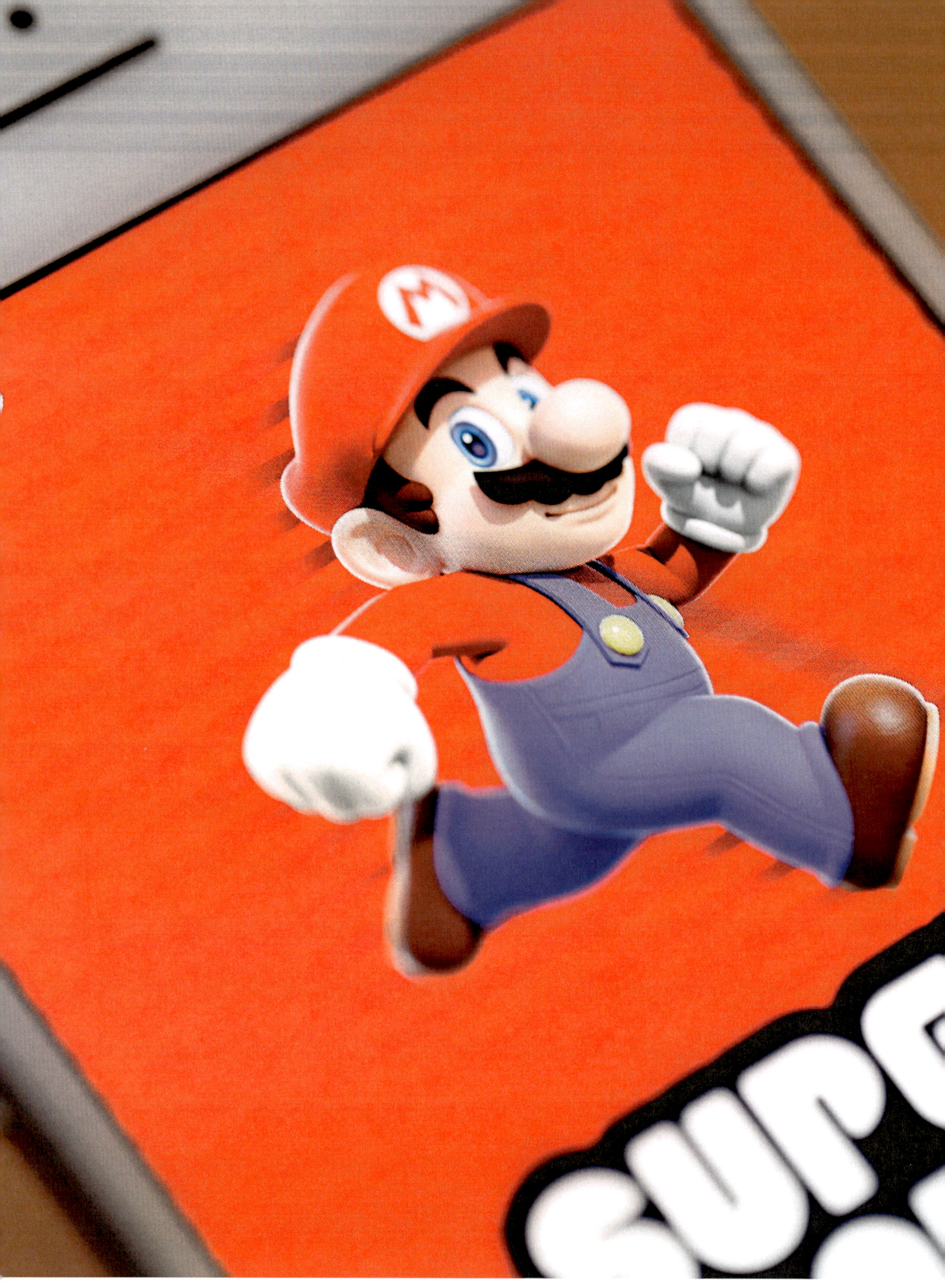

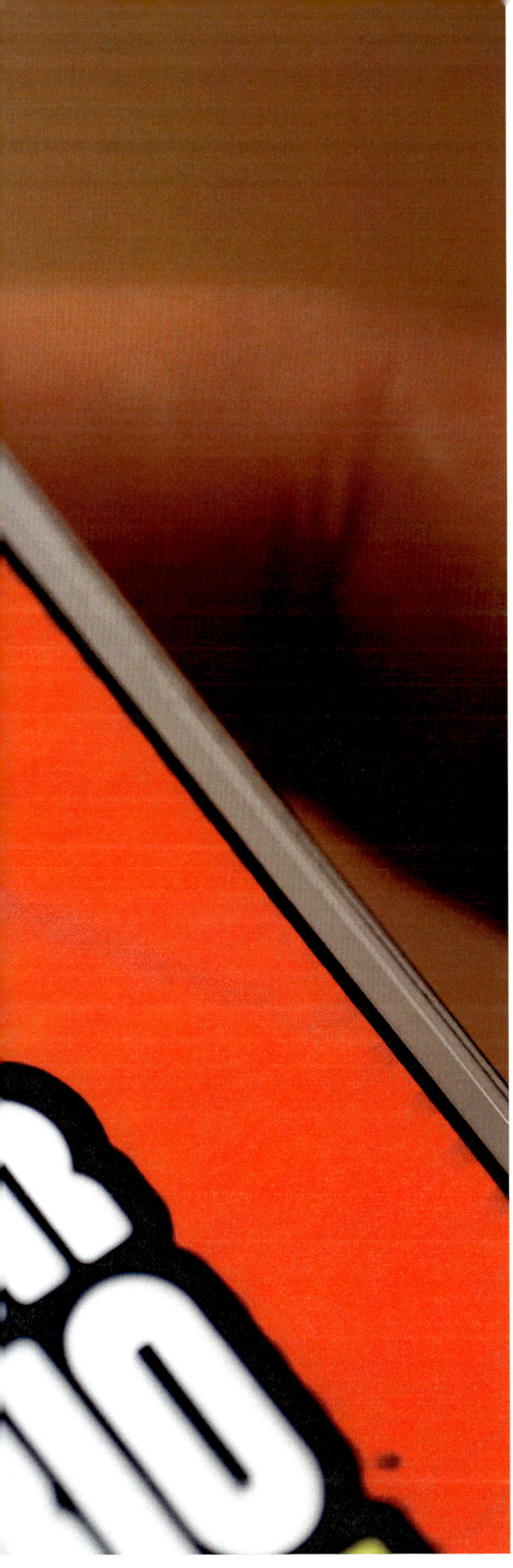

WHEN MARIO WENT MOBILE

In 2016, ahead of a landmark new Mario game, TIME spoke with the character's famed creator on the transition.

BY LISA EADICICCO

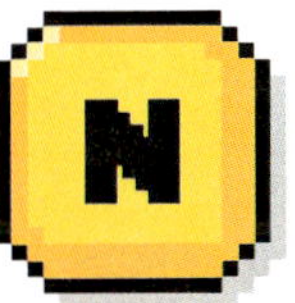

NINTENDO VIDEO GAME DESIGNER Shigeru Miyamoto has spent his career developing some of the world's most iconic and cherished games, from the *Super Mario* franchise to *Zelda* and *Donkey Kong*. As video game consoles have changed over the years, so have the ways in which people play them: The Wii heralded motion controls, Wii U introduced a dual-screen experience for the first time, and the 3DS handheld system brought *Mario* and others to life in 3D.

In 2016, Nintendo began to venture into a widely lucrative yet untapped territory for the company: mobile gaming. December 15 marked the launch of *Super Mario Run* for the iPhone and iPad, the first time the legendary plumber made his way to a mobile device. TIME spoke with *Mario* creator Miyamoto about the challenges that come with bringing *Mario* to a new platform, and more.

This is the first time *Mario* is coming to the iPhone. What were some of the challenges that came with bringing *Mario* to a new medium?

I've been using smartphones myself for many years,

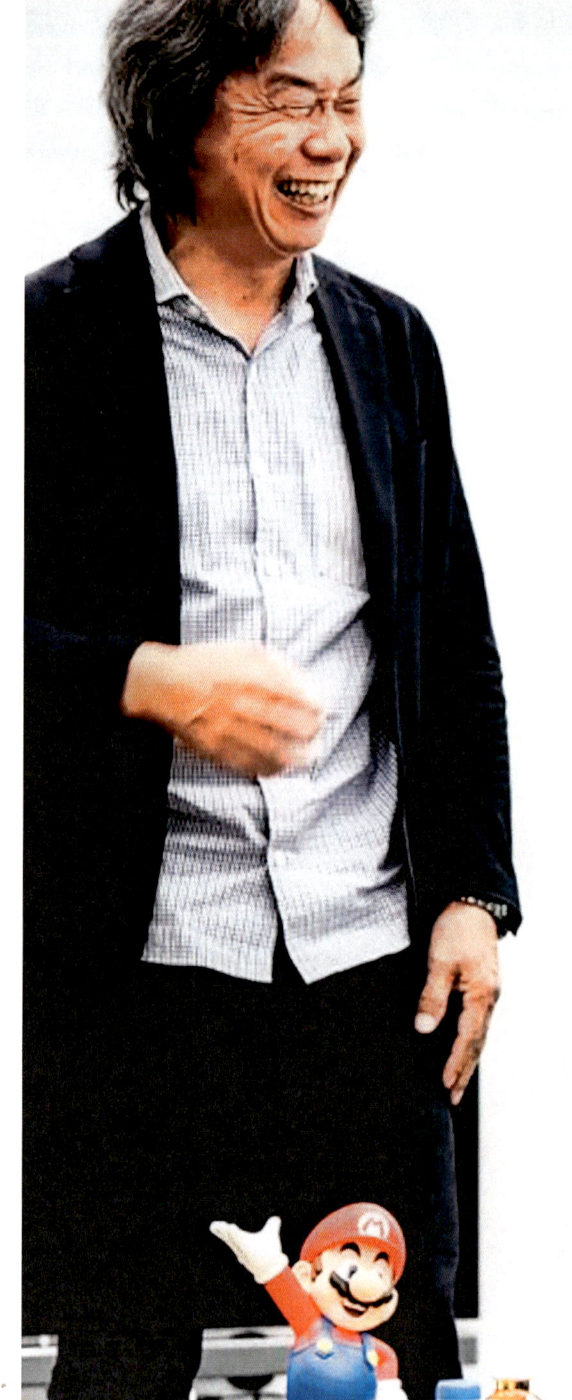

so I had a good idea in mind for what would be a good way to bring *Mario* to smartphones.

But I think for us, the biggest challenge was really in zeroing in on those core elements of *Mario* that would be best suited for play on smart devices. We had, during the Wii and 3DS days, experimented with ideas where Mario ran automatically and you would play by making Mario jump. And after doing some of those experiments we felt that would probably be the best way to bring Mario to iPhone, where you're just playing with one hand, just controlling the jumps. And once we zeroed in on that it became relatively straightforward for us in terms of the game development.

And then in terms of actual development challenges, Nintendo has always focused its development on a single platform at a time. And of course we're designing the hardware and the games. And so when we designed our hardware for gaming we're doing it in a way that offers very stable performance for gaming. But because smartphones are a multiuse device, we had some challenge in trying to get the performance out of the system that we wanted. But just working through development and with the team we were able to get it to where we were able to get the performance we wanted from iPhone to offer a stable gameplay experience.

Nintendo has always been great at using hardware in creative ways that complement gameplay. We saw that with Wii U with *Super Mario 3D World*: The player sometimes has to interact with elements on the tablet screen to progress through the level on the TV screen. What was it like bringing that mentality to the iPhone?

One of the challenges in game development is the very first time you make a new game, you generally design it so that as broad of an audience as possible can play.

But then gradually as you make more and more sequels, you start to make the game more complex and more challenging for the fans that have played the series. And you gradually get to a point where it becomes more difficult for beginners to be able to get into the game. So this has been sort of a focus of ours during the DS and the Wii days, where we've sort of tried to go back to the roots of the original gameplay and reset so that it has an easier entry point for people. And that was a very important thing for us with *Super Mario Run* as well.

We didn't think about bringing an existing *Mario* gameplay to iPhone and just porting over something that you controlled with buttons before. We really focused on, What is the best *Mario* experience for what you get with iPhone?

Of course one of the advantages or one of the things about interactive entertainment that people like is the ability to completely control everything themselves. But even if you have some automatic support structures built in, it can still be fun for people to interact with what's on the screen.

And with *Mario* games in particular, it really is that sense of satisfaction that you get when Mario gets to

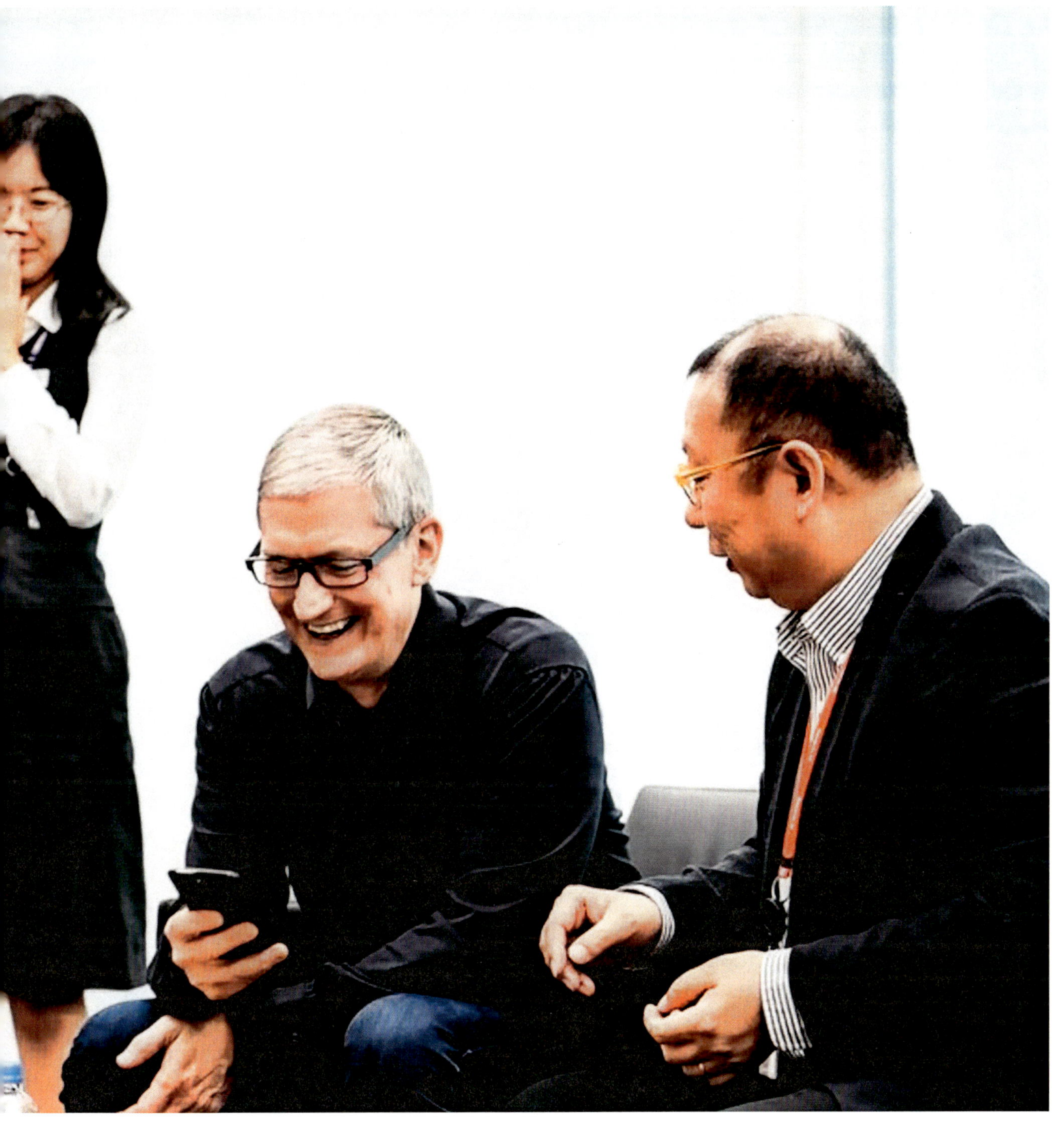

While on a visit to Japan, Apple CEO Tim Cook, center, met with Miyamoto, far left.

the flagpole at the end. But I also think that one of the most entertaining elements of interactive entertainment is that you as the player are able to look at what you've done and what's coming ahead of you.

And it's really fun to think about 'Oh, I should have done this a different way' or 'This is coming and now I have to adjust to that.' By playing these levels and replaying *Super Mario Run*, I think people will find a lot of fun just in slight changes to the timing of their taps in order to get all of the colored coins or maximize their score.

How did you pick and choose which gameplay elements are right for the iPhone and which are not? I noticed, for example, that I didn't see any of the power-ups in the console games other than the mushroom in *Super Mario Run*. Is that something we'll eventually see in a mobile *Mario* game?

I think with this being our first *Super Mario* game on iPhone, we've designed this both in what's the best experience but also with a long road ahead of us in terms of what else we can do on iPhone. So perhaps you can look forward to some of that at some point in the future. But one thing we have done this time is that you'll be able to play not just as Mario, but after going through the game and unlocking some things and meeting some conditions you'll be able to play as some of the other characters as well.

In previous console-based *Mario* games, playing with different characters can give you various gameplay advantages. Will this carry over to *Super Mario Run*?
It's less on having those characters to achieve or accomplish specific tasks, and more of giving players a tool to unlock more of their gameplay creativity. Even if you're trying to collect the same group of colored coins, doing so with a different character will require you to do it in a different way. So that can be fun for the players to explore.

This is one of the first mobile games Nintendo is releasing. We saw the launch of *Miitomo* earlier this year, which is more of a social app, and *Pokémon GO*, which is a geolocation app. What other genres are interesting to you?
There are a number of other areas that we're looking at. But in the near term, the ones that will be coming out are a *Fire Emblem* game and *Animal Crossing*. And then of course each of these different games appeal to slightly different audiences. We see that a lot of parents often buy *Mario* games for their kids. From a pricing and payment structure, we felt it was important that parents would just pay once and then their kids can play to their hearts' content. So what we'll do with each of these games is look at who's the main audience playing and we'll devise a pricing structure for each game that's applicable for each audience.

An app like *Super Mario Run* is more condensed than a Wii U title. How did you balance incorporating a variety of characters and level types?
Just because of the history of the franchise, we have a lot of assets to choose from. Actually for us, one of the biggest challenges was deciding what doesn't go

Bowser's Bob-ombing Run (or World 6-4) is the 24th level overall in Super Mario Run *(opposite). It is the final normal level in the game and unlocks Princess Peach as a playable character.*

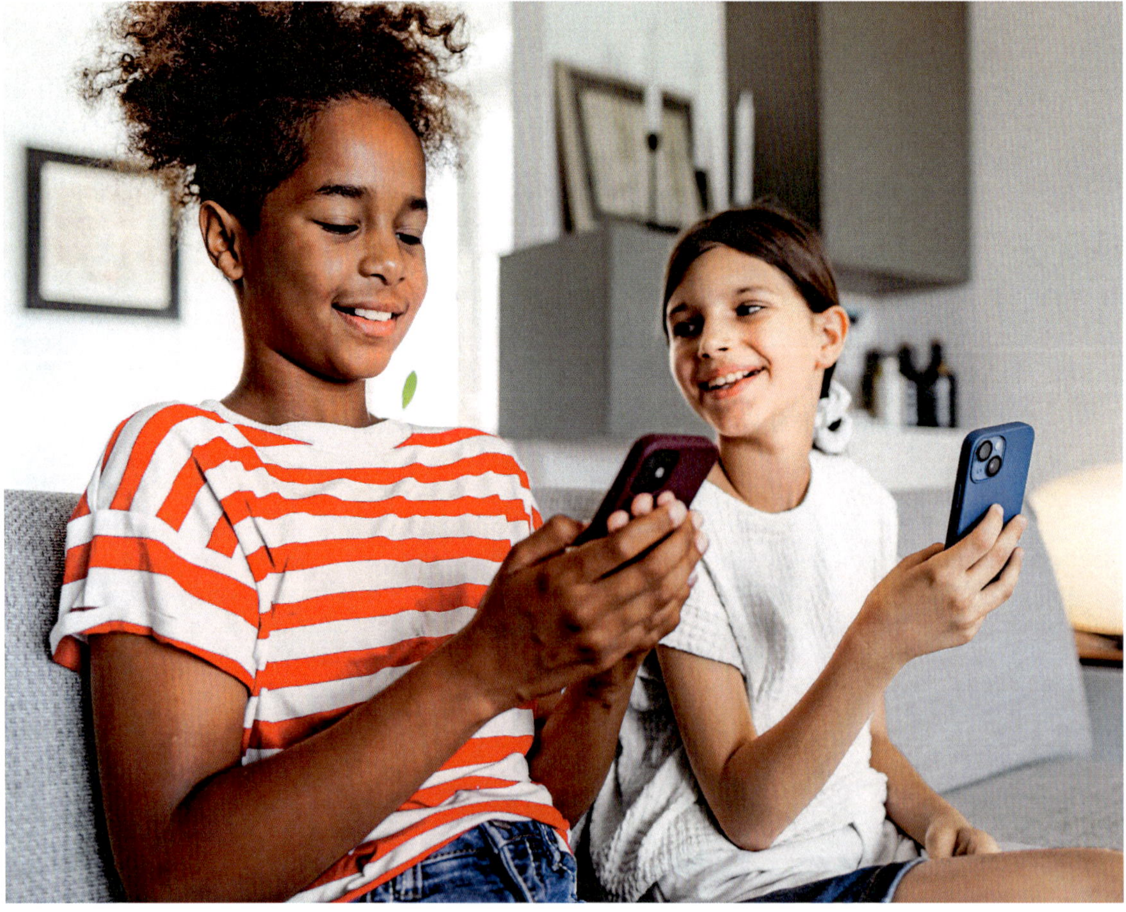

in, because we were very quickly able to fill it up with content. Our approach was really to focus in on what are the right enemies for a game when Mario runs automatically. What are the right course styles? Those were the decisions that we were making, zeroing in on those types of elements. But what that means is we still have a lot of ingredients left over that we can continue to cook with, so to speak.

A few things that we did, for example, is we took the Bullet Bill characters that usually come at you from the direction that you're heading and we changed them and made them red, and now we have them coming at you from behind. The spiny characters with spikes on their shells are also little bigger so they're easier to see.

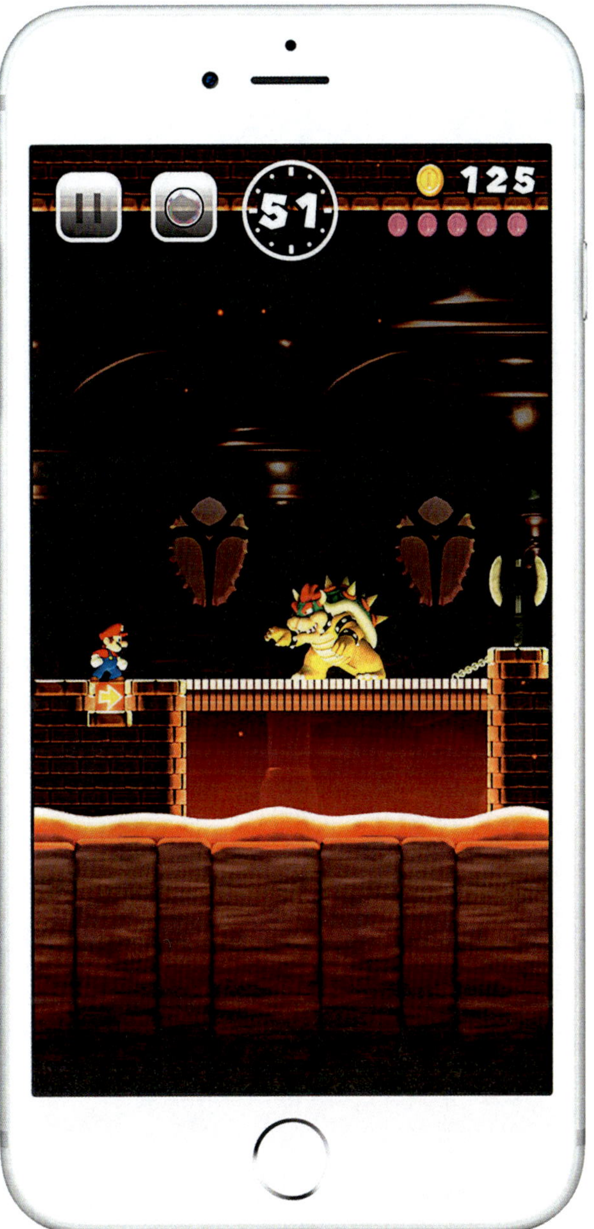

The Kingdom Builder mode is a relatively new concept for *Mario* games. What made you decide to include that in *Super Mario Run*?

There are a couple of reasons. One is there is actually a game in Japan that I've been playing on a smartphone with my wife called *Neko Atsume*. It's sort of a cat collecting game. From that, I really got the sense that having this thing on your phone that you interact with on a regular basis, and then grow and build from there, is a very compelling feature. And certainly Nintendo has had games that have done this in the past on our own platforms.

The other reason behind it, typically with the *Super Mario* games, what you're really doing is you're sort of strategizing and working your way through individual levels. And we wanted to have a method for you to save the accomplishments that you get in each of those levels and have a place where those accomplishments can kind of build up. And that's where the idea for the Kingdom Mode came from.

Why is this the right time to bring Mario to the iPhone?

A big factor is that over the past few years smartphones have just gotten more and more powerful to the point where the performance that we're able to get out of the device is finally on par with what we expect from the gameplay performance and response for our games.

And then I think also there was a period, certainly for many years, our devices were the first sort of computing or interactive entertainment devices kids came into contact with. And that would be the first place where they experienced games. But now as more and more parents are giving hand-me-down phones to their kids, kids are oftentimes coming into contact with games on smart devices at earlier and earlier ages. We wanted to be able to reach those kids on those devices so that they'll be able to experience our games and those characters there, but then when they want to play a more in-depth experience they'll gravitate toward our devices to do that.

And then also I think we've seen this with *Pokémon GO*, there are a lot of adults that, as they've gotten older, they've gravitated away from even purchasing gaming machines but they're carrying a smartphone around with them. And all of a sudden, with *Pokémon GO*, they're reconnecting with Pokémon and playing Pokémon again.

Our hope is with *Super Mario Run* that we'll be able to reconnect with a lot of people that grew up playing *Mario* and that they'll come back and want to play some more of our games on our platforms as well.

Super Mario Run: The Best Way to Play

The game is unique among other franchise entries. You can play with one hand, and it all comes down to your taps.

BY LISA EADICICCO

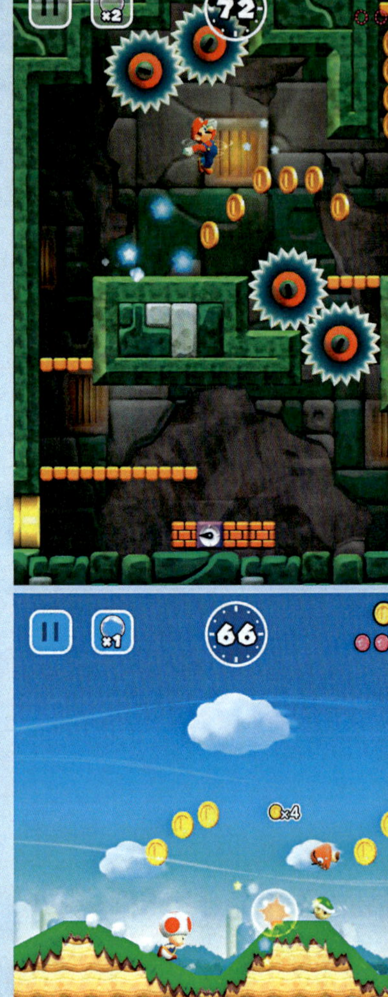

With *Super Mario Run*, the buttons are gone. Start the game and Mario begins to move automatically, zipping through otherworldly obstacle courses without input from the player. Gamers tap the screen to make him jump, or press and hold to make him leap higher.

In a mobile game, sometimes called an "endless runner," the main character dashes automatically across the screen as the player taps to perform jumps or other maneuvers. In classic Nintendo fashion, *Super Mario Run* feels as versatile and satisfying as the Mario games for Nintendo's own platforms. Understanding how to play is simple and the gameplay remains rich and addictive, but true mastery takes plenty of practice.

Rather than focusing on where Mario moves or in which direction he runs, it's how players orchestrate his leaps that gets him to the flagpole at the end of each stage, unlocking new challenges. Simply letting him beeline from one point to another doesn't accomplish much. It's the timing and longevity of taps and longer presses that boost Mario to his goal.

Mario automatically vaults over enemies as they approach, for instance, but tapping the screen at the top of these hops gives him extra height and allows him to collect coins. In many cases, players have to use these jumps in creative ways to advance through a level or snatch a special coin. During my demo, I found myself ricocheting off walls, bouncing on the backs of Koopas, or grasping a ledge to avoid falling. Timing is everything in *Super Mario Run* — a carryover from prior Mario games that's employed in novel ways here.

Players can choose from three different modes in *Super Mario Run*: World Tour, Toad Rally and Kingdom Builder. World Tour is essentially the game's story mode, wherein players progress through levels and unlock different worlds. Toad Rally, by contrast, is a competitive mode in which players compete to collect more coins and impress as many "Toads" as possible. To access this mode, gamers must collect Rally Tickets, which can be obtained by completing levels in the World Tour mode and collecting coins.

The bigger a player's Toad following, the more he or she will be able to build up their kingdom. A player has to collect coins by playing through levels and coerce Toads to live in their kingdom by impressing them in Toad Rally mode, in order to acquire new buildings and structures in Kingdom Builder mode. Some of these additions are purely ornamental, but others unlock related features. A tiny house with a white roof and a red star includes a bonus game, for instance, while adding Luigi's home to a player's kingdom will introduce him as a playable character. (Toad and Yoshi can be unlocked in the same way.) But beware: Toads can leave a player's side as quickly as they have joined the player. Losing a run to another player in Toad Rally mode can result in Toads leaving.

A big part of what's made previous Mario games so addictive is the hidden challenges folded into various levels, for example, the stars and stamps sprinkled throughout *Super Mario 3D World*. In the same way, Nintendo has embedded goodies in *Super Mario Run*'s World Tour mode that make levels worth replaying, such as collecting pink coins scattered through a game level. In most cases, reaching these coins requires a skillful tap that involves strategically timing a hop or springing off an enemy.

In some situations, Nintendo's made it easier to grab these coins or avoid an adversary by planting a red block in Mario's path, which stops him in his tracks to give the

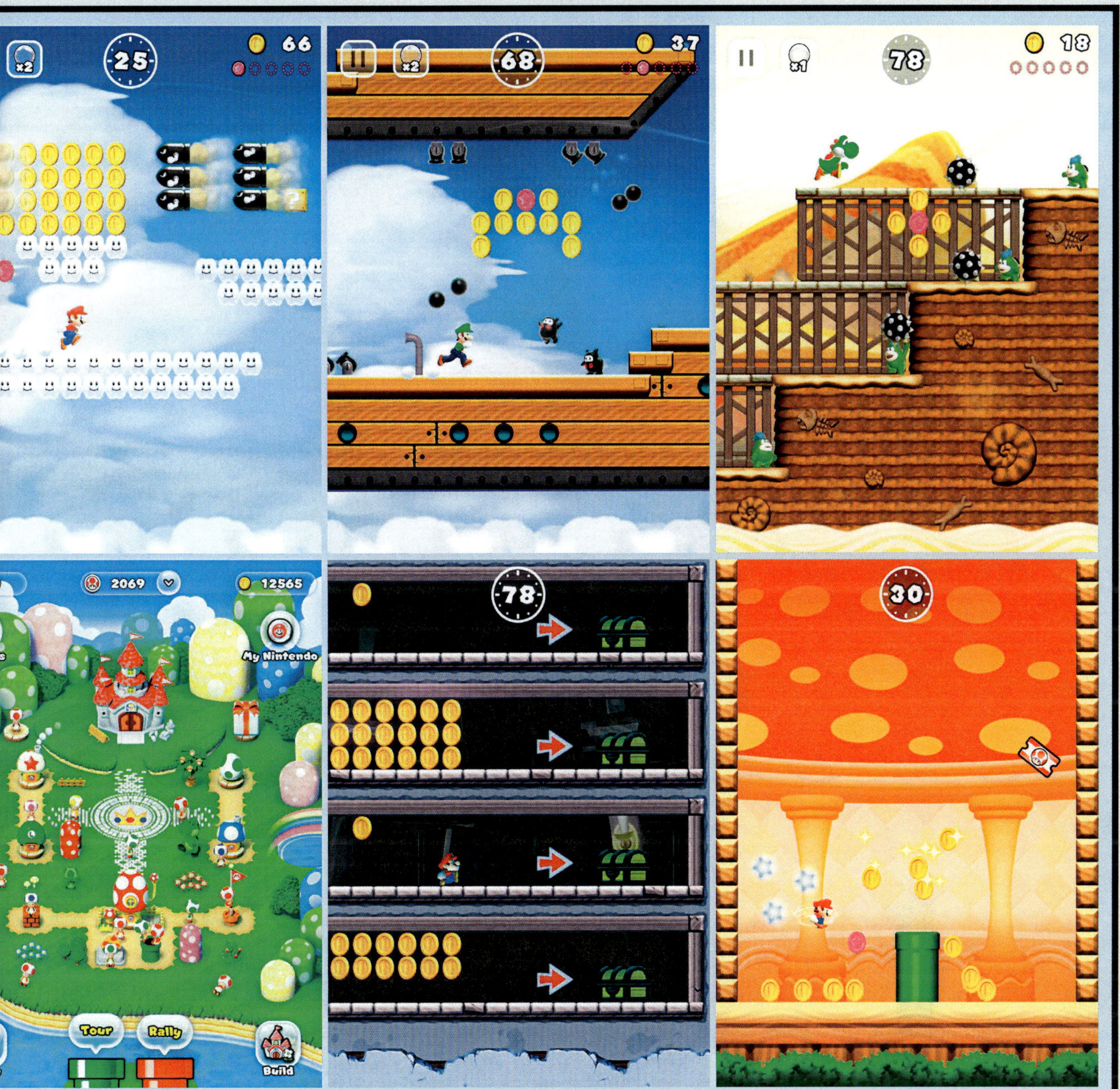

Throughout Super Mario Run*'s many courses, Mario automatically runs from left to right and jumps on his own to clear small gaps or obstacles. In Toad Rally game mode, players can challenge "ghost" versions of other players' prerecorded playthroughs of levels.*

player time to adequately plan a jump. Once a player gathers all of the pink coins in a level, they then progress to the next challenge, where they must collect purple coins before progressing to a black coin phase. These coin-based mini-missions, combined with all the incentives to build an expansive kingdom, suggest that *Super Mario Run* should have plenty of replay value.

The new touch controls aside, the game's levels will feel structurally familiar to anyone who's played the arcade or console games. Familiar foes like Boos, Koopas and Goombas will thwart Mario's progress. Some puzzles include choosing the right door to proceed to the next section of a level, just like in previous games, which helps *Super Mario Run* feel more like a traditional Mario game and not just another endless runner. Some characters have also been tailored to better suit the game's mobile-centric controls. Bullet Bill, for example, no longer charges at Mario, but instead follows the mustachioed plumber as he sprints across a stage.

Super Mario Run is also more polished and rich than most mobile titles I've encountered. Nintendo wonks have waited years for Mario to move to mobile, and his appeal translates well to a smartphone. By bringing some of its biggest franchises to the mobile universe, Nintendo is keeping its games relevant, enlarging its celebrated brands, and setting the table for future mobile maneuvers.

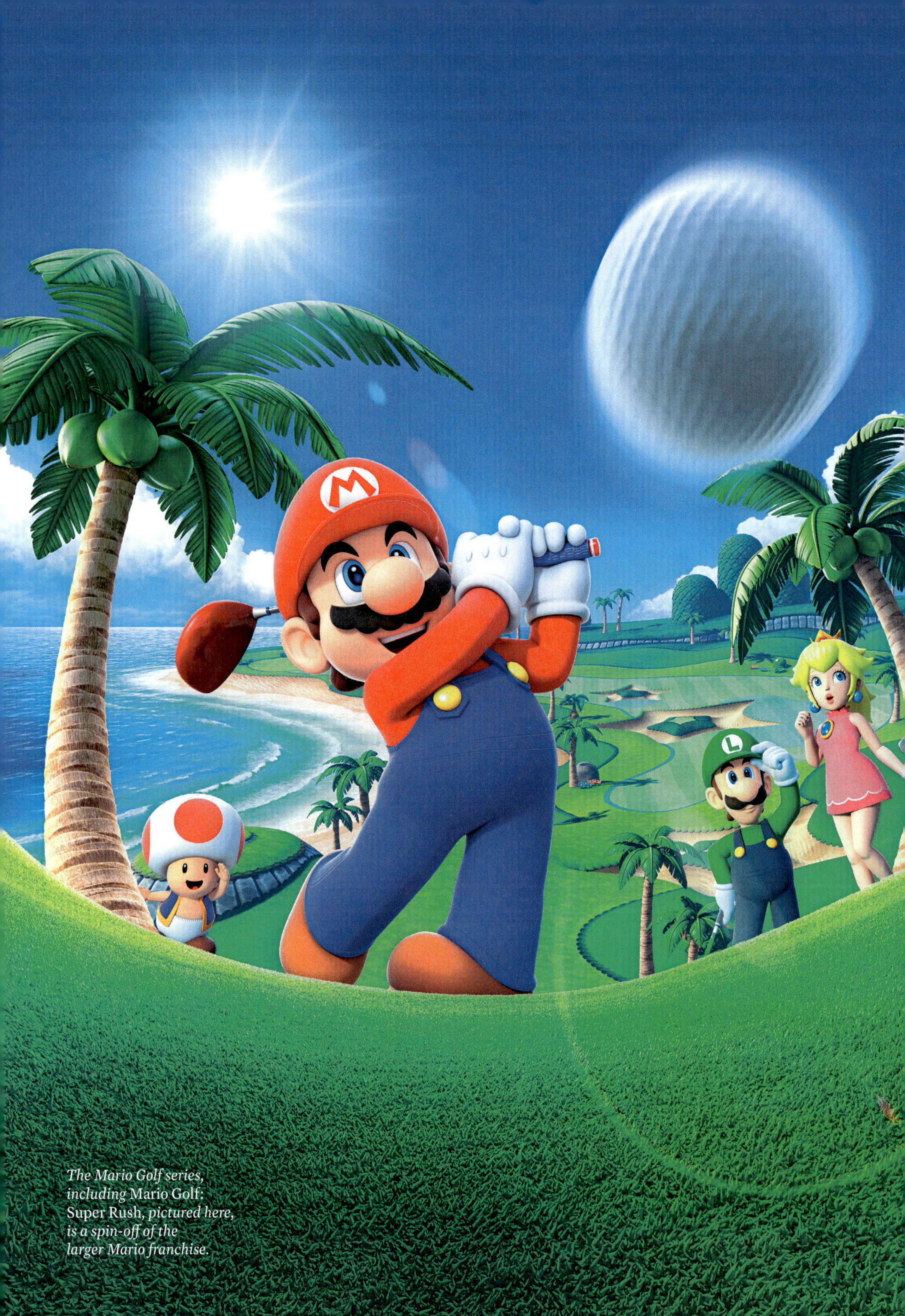

The Mario Golf series, including Mario Golf: Super Rush, *pictured here, is a spin-off of the larger Mario franchise.*

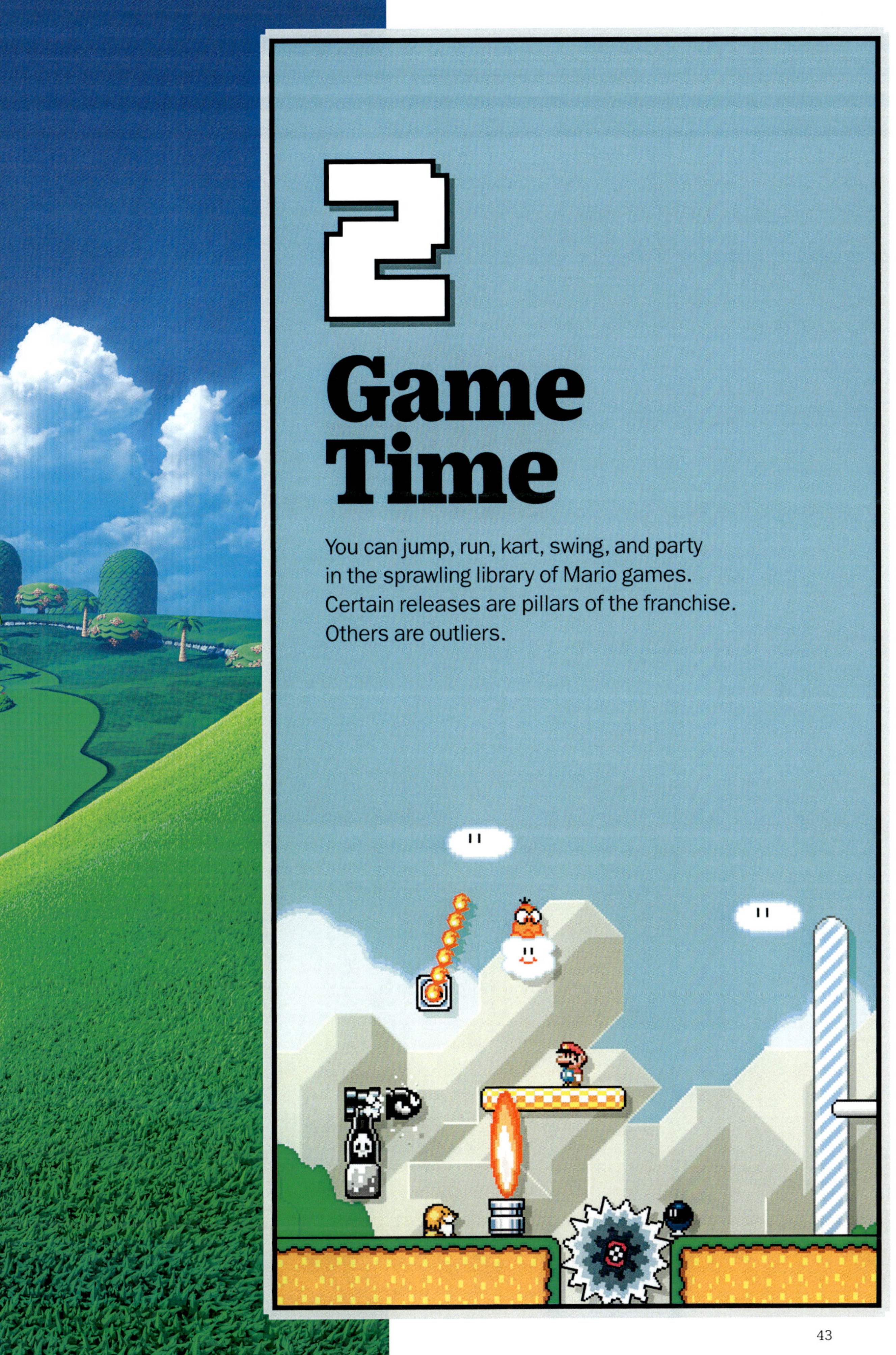

2

Game Time

You can jump, run, kart, swing, and party in the sprawling library of Mario games. Certain releases are pillars of the franchise. Others are outliers.

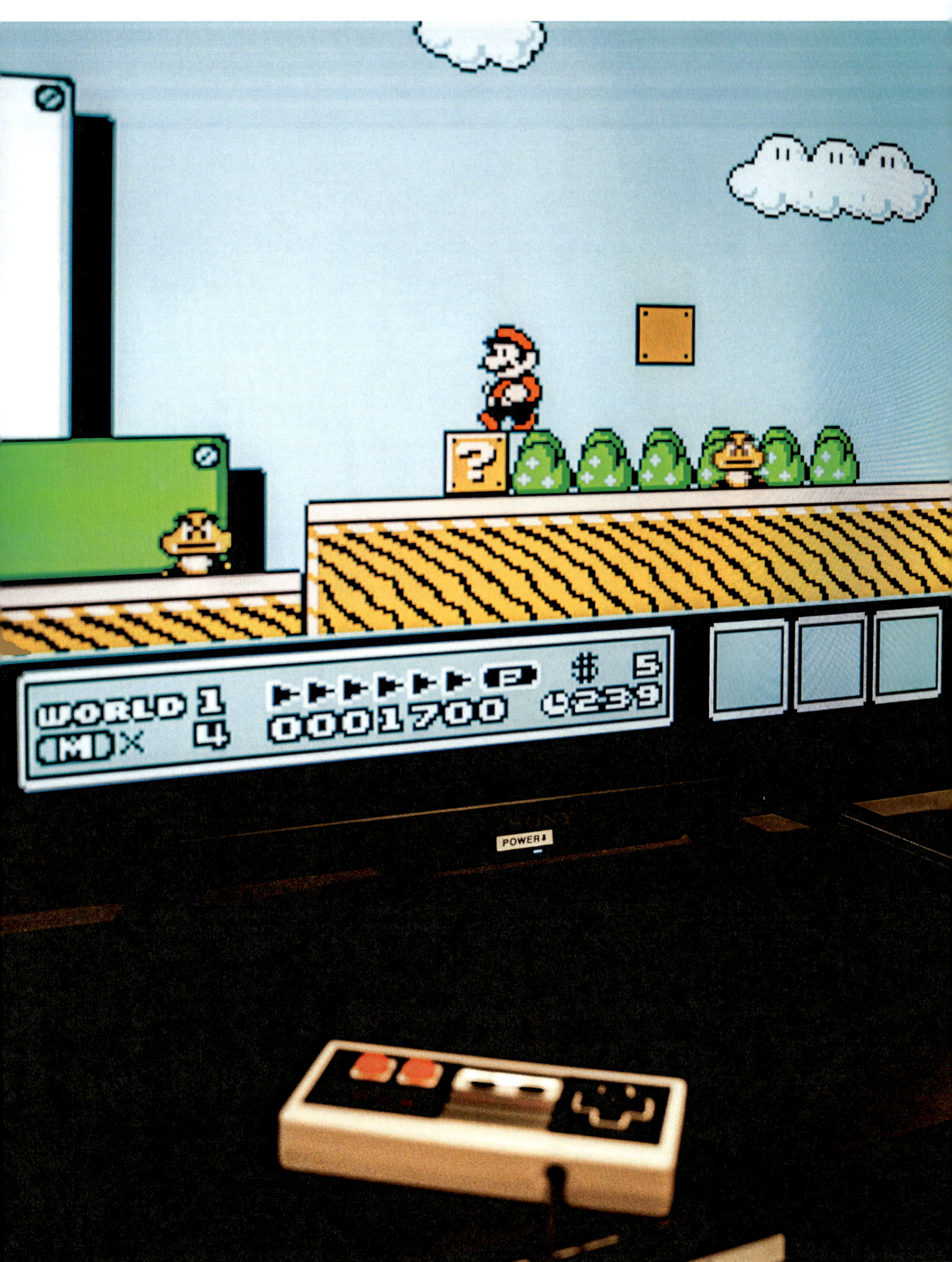
WORLD 1
M × 4
P
5
0001700
239
POWER

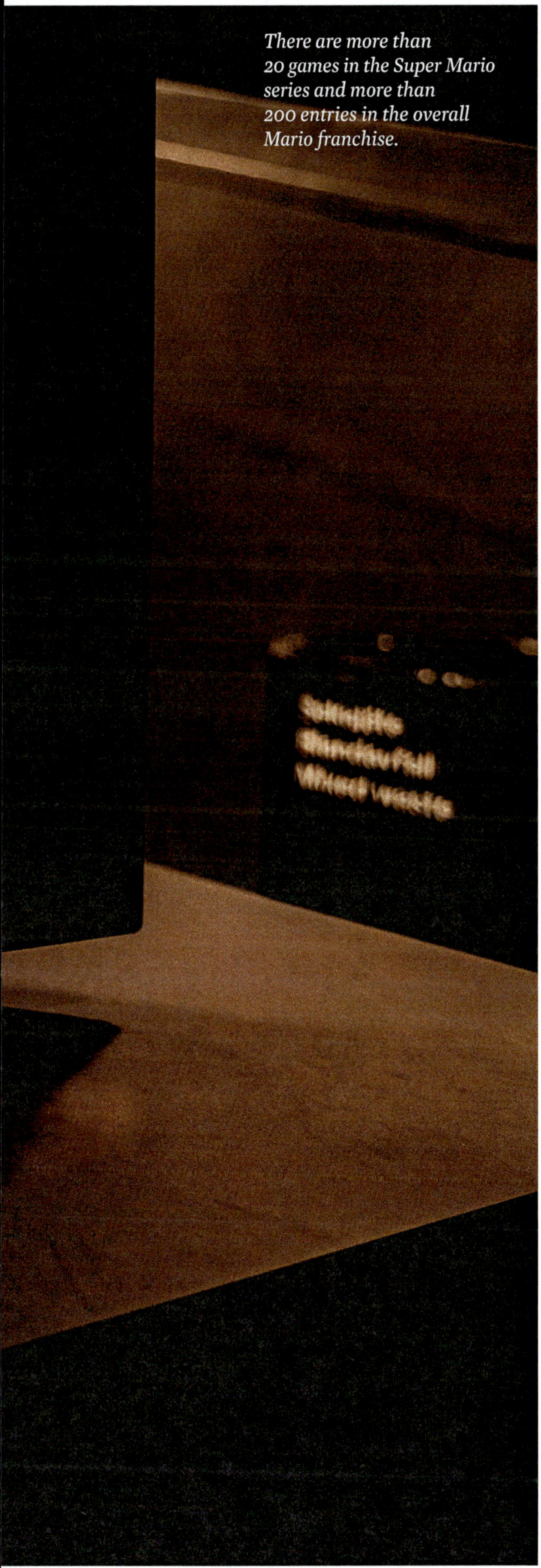

There are more than 20 games in the Super Mario series and more than 200 entries in the overall Mario franchise.

THE BEST GAMES

A lifelong gamer weighs in on the must-plays—and some you can skip.

BY DANIEL HOWLEY

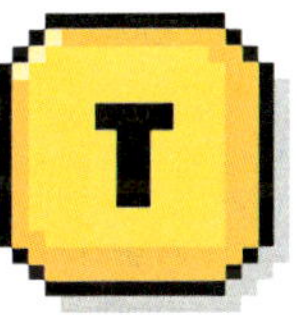

HE MARIO FRANCHISE IS THE quintessential gaming series. It's always evolving, full of surprises, and, above all, fun. It's why Mario has flourished for so long when other video game mascots have fallen by the wayside.

I've been playing Mario games for as long as I can remember, from the Nintendo Entertainment System and Game Boy to the Wii, Wii U, and Switch. My goal, from an early age, was to write about games for a living. And I've managed to do just that. I've reviewed everything from first-person shooters to action adventure titles and role-playing games; traveled to E3, the defunct yearly games conference; and currently cover the business of games as the tech editor at Yahoo Finance. Throughout it all, Mario has been one of my favorite franchises. And based on how popular Mario continues to be, chances are it's one of your favorites too.

But not every Mario game is like another. From the very first *Mario Bros.* game to the latest and greatest, *Super Mario Bros. Wonder*, what follows are the Mario game essentials, the games to play with friends, and the games you can skip.

Must-Plays

MARIO BROS.

Let's start with the O.G. of Mario games: *Mario Bros.* The first title in the long-running series, 1983's *Mario Bros.* took Mario from his original role as the main character in *Donkey Kong* into his own world. The game introduced a number of series staples, including Mario's brother, Luigi, turtle enemies, coins, and the famous pipes the plumbers regularly use to traverse their world.

Though it doesn't get the same amount of love as its successor, *Super Mario Bros.*, *Mario Bros.* is absolutely worth playing if for no other reason than to appreciate the series' roots and recognize how far it's come.

SUPER MARIO BROS.

The game that supercharged the Mario franchise and turned Nintendo into a gaming powerhouse, *Super Mario Bros.* is a must-play for gamers young and old.

Challenging if you want to go for a high score and easy enough for a casual playthrough, *Super Mario Bros.* brought along the Goombas; Bowser, otherwise known as King Koopa; and power-ups, including Fire Flowers and Super Mushrooms.

I'll never forget unwrapping the Nintendo Entertainment System and playing *Super Mario Bros.* with my brother, jumping across gaps and finding hidden Warp Tunnels. If there's one game that represents the juggernaut that Mario would become, it's *Super Mario Bros.*

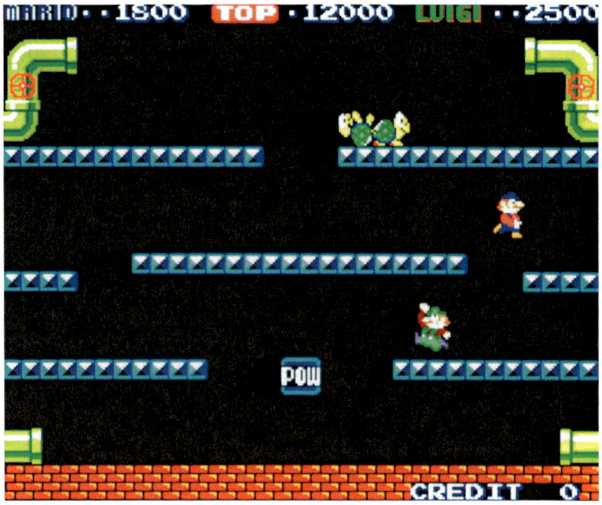

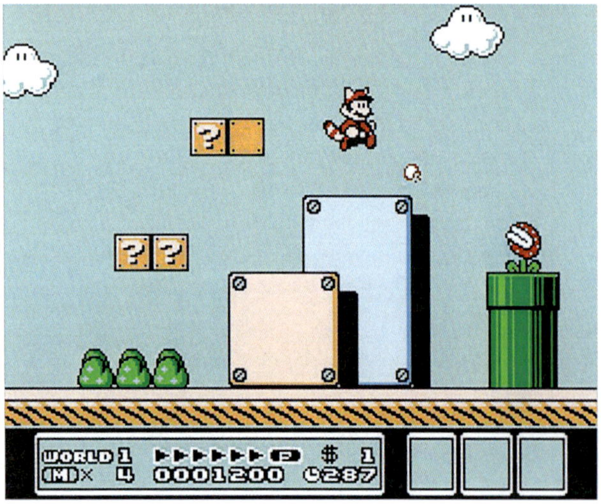

SUPER MARIO BROS. 3

This iteration of *Super Mario Bros.* was the game that started to make Mario interesting. If you don't count the fever dream that was *Super Mario Bros. 2*, that is. More on that later. *Super Mario Bros. 3* introduced the Super Leaf power-up that gave Mario a raccoon tail and the ability to fly short distances. Few things were as exciting for NES gamers at the time than seeing Mario zip across the screen and take off.

SUPER MARIO WORLD

No one can ever accuse Nintendo of failing to innovate. For *Super Mario World*, the gaming giant added a variety of new gameplay elements, including everyone's favorite egg-laying friend: Yoshi.

Super Mario World expanded on the formula of *Super Mario Bros. 3*, opening up the world to more than 70 new levels with various themes and enemies. You still have to take down Bowser, but *Super Mario World* felt like the first time Nintendo understood that players wanted a vast selection of game lands to explore and experience. In fact, it's that very element of never knowing quite what the next world will throw at you that makes each new Mario game exciting.

SUPER MARIO 64

If you're my age, closing in on 40, you probably stayed up all hours of the night during sleepovers at your friends' houses playing *Super Mario 64* until the sun came up. Mario's first 3D adventure, *Mario 64*, established what 3D platformers could be.

Whether you're flying as Mario, thanks to his Wing Cap, or turning into Metal Mario by donning his Metal Cap, *Super Mario 64* brought about a whole new world of powers and abilities for the portly plumber.

It's impossible to deny how influential *Super Mario 64* was to 3D gaming in general. From its rotating camera (really a Lakitu, a longtime enemy type)

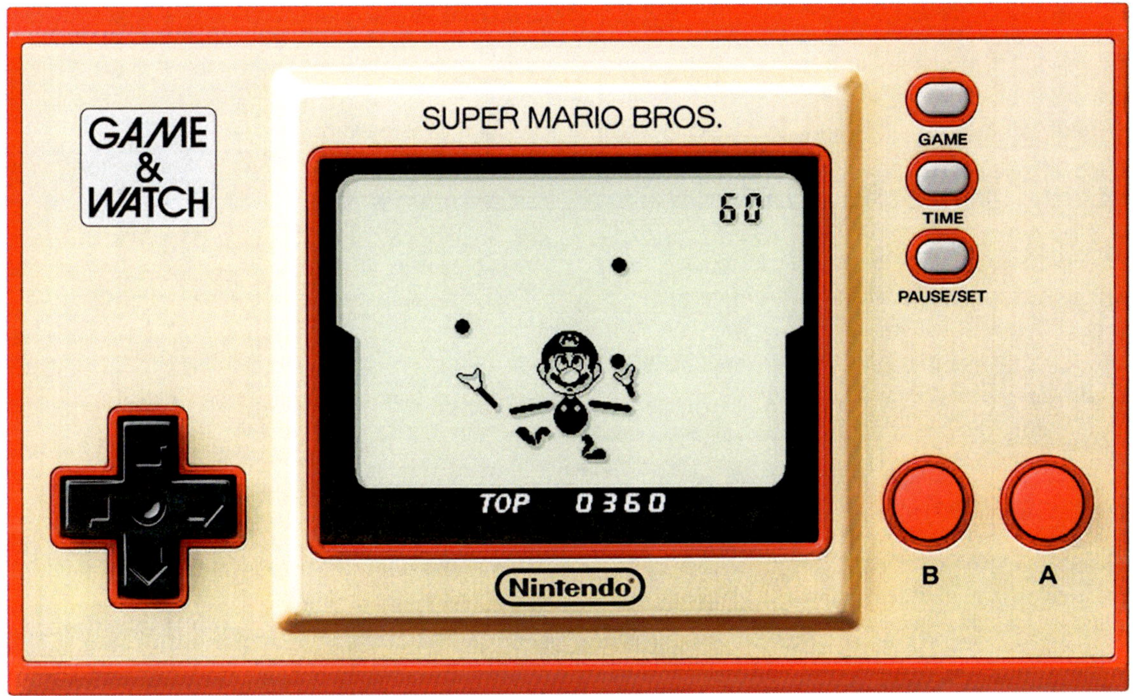

Mario the Juggler, *above, was the last Game & Watch game released in the New Wide Screen series, in 1991. Opposite: The 1983* Mario Bros. *arcade game (top) birthed a franchise that led to* Super Mario Bros. 3 *(bottom), among many others.*

to the swimming system and more, *Super Mario 64* is easily one of the best Mario games of all time. And after nearly 30 years, it's still as fun to play as ever.

SUPER MARIO RPG

Nintendo has taken Mario in many different directions over the years, but dropping him and his friends into a traditional role-playing game was certainly the most unexpected. In *Super Mario RPG*, Mario teams up with Peach and Bowser, as well as new characters Mallow and Geno, to fight a group known as the Smithy Gang and find seven star pieces to repair the Star Road. Yep, it's as silly as it sounds.

But what makes *Super Mario RPG* so fun is the fact that despite its odd premise, it's an exceptional role-playing game in the vein of RPGs like *Final Fantasy*. You don't fight enemies by simply jumping on them or throwing fireballs but rather through turn-based battles that wouldn't seem out of place in a game like *Pokémon* or modern titles like *Persona 5*.

Super Mario RPG also uses a unique isometric camera angle, a means of making a 2D game appear as if it's 3D by changing the player's view. Add in some great gameplay and fun characters, and it's easy to see why Mario's first entry into the RPG genre is so impressive.

SUPER MARIO GALAXY

This game is among Nintendo's most inventive. Mario is tasked with saving Peach and stopping Bowser from creating a galactic empire and taking control of the universe. That's largely par for the course when it comes to Mario games, but what *Super Mario Galaxy* does so well is play with physics, not to mention tackle stages in new and exciting ways.

Released for the Wii in 2007, *Super Mario Galaxy* also includes a spell spin attack that you can activate by shaking the Wii's motion controls. You'll traverse galaxies with planets featuring their own gravitational pull and settings complete with wild power-ups that turn Mario into a bee, a Boo, a spring, and more. Want to ride a manta ray? You'll do it in *Super Mario Galaxy*. Ah, and then there's Rosalina, the protector of the starlike Luma people and cosmos.

Rosalina is now a mainstay in the Mario franchise and appears in everything from *Mario Kart* to mainline Mario games.

SUPER MARIO ODYSSEY

Mario's big debut for Nintendo's best-selling Switch console, *Super Mario Odyssey* takes everyone's favorite plumber on a tour of the world, including a stop in the Mario universe's stand in for New York City, New Donk City. And *Odyssey* introduces a new character—Cappy.

Mario's hat is a living character and allows him explore otherwise unreachable areas of the map and throw his consciousness into a T. rex, Bullet Bill, or even a tank.

Of course, your goal is to save Peach from Bowser. And to do that, you'll need to collect Power Moons to move from area to area. Along the way, you'll find new outfits from Mario's different eras, including his original 2D style.

The entire game is a celebration of all things Mario, which makes it a standout title in the series' long-running history.

SUPER MARIO 3D WORLD

I've played *a lot* of Mario games, but I've easily put the most time into *Super Mario 3D World*. The sequel to 2011's *Super Mario 3D Land* for the Nintendo 3DS handheld console, *3D World* combines the 2D side-scrolling gameplay of the original Mario games with the free-form 3D platforming of later titles, to create something wholly unique.

The change in perspectives makes exploring levels all the more exciting, allowing you to find better positions to jump onto Goombas or reach distant platforms. Four-player co-op means you and friends and family can each play at the same time.

And with the Double Cherry power, you can clone your characters and then clone their clones, filling your TV with more Marios, Peaches, and Toads than you can handle.

Toss in the Super Bell power-up that turns you into a house cat with sharp claws for climbing and swatting your foes and an incredible number of extra worlds and levels, and *Super Mario 3D World* will leave you wanting for nothing.

SUPER MARIO WONDER

A psychedelic kaleidoscope version of Mario and friends' classic side-scrolling adventure, *Super Mario Wonder* takes the 2D Mario formula and adds a touch of . . . wonder. *Wonder* lets you play as virtually all of Mario's best pals, including Luigi, Princess Peach, Princess Daisy, Yoshi, and more, as you try to stop Bowser's quest to take over the Flower Kingdom.

Grabbing a Wonder Flower power-up changes the game world in a slew of ways, including pipes turning into wormlike creatures that crawl along the ground

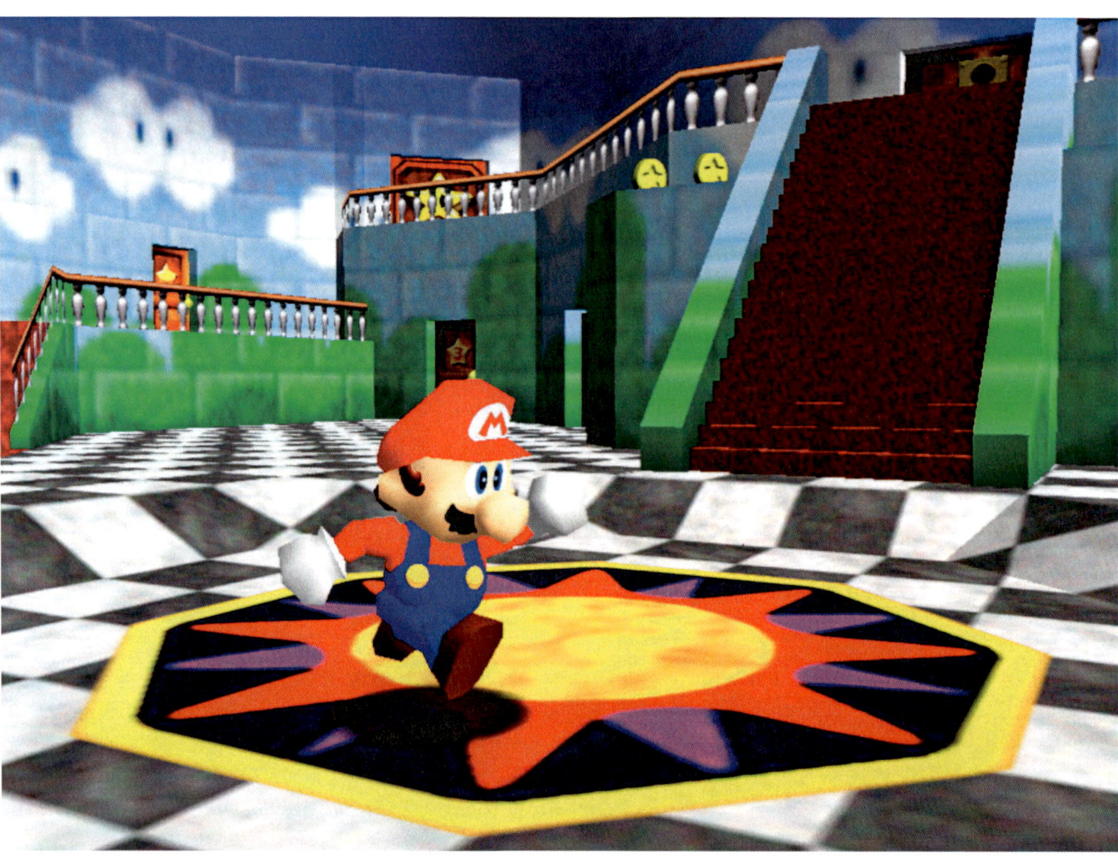

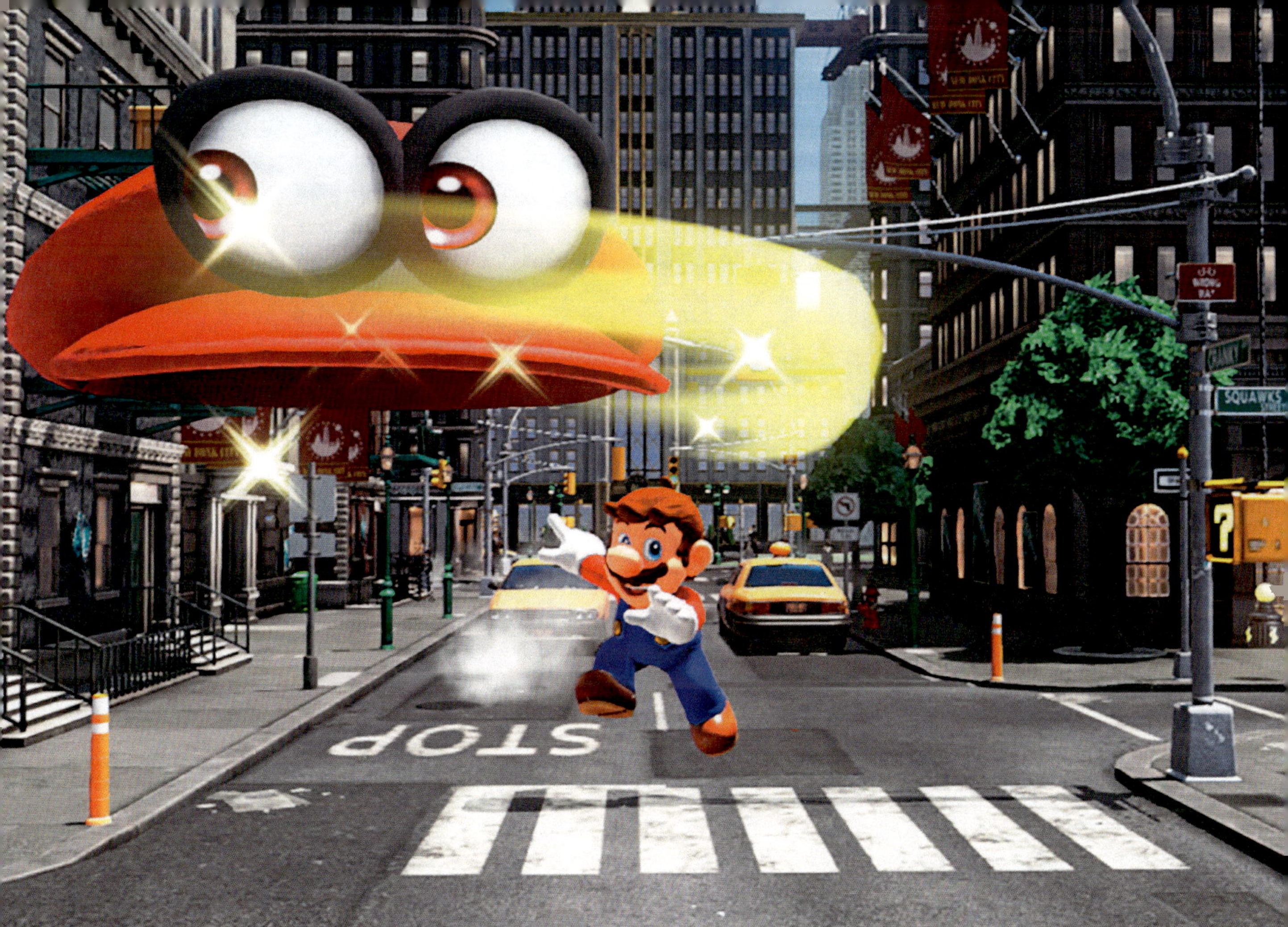

It didn't take long for Mario to leave his 8-bit realm for a 3D world. Nintendo released Super Mario 64 *(opposite) in 1996 and took Mario far from the Mushroom Kingdom in 2017's* Super Mario Odyssey *(above).*

and parts of the level transforming into playable musical notes. *Wonder* is an excellent throwback to the days of 2D Mario with the kind of excitement that makes Mario's adventures so endearing.

Party Games

SUPER MARIO PARTY JAMBOREE

The latest edition of the long-running Mario Party franchise, *Super Mario Party Jamboree* is exactly what you want in a party game. Grab a seat on the couch with your friends and family and dive into a slew of ridiculous minigames, win stars, scramble to collect as many coins as possible, and, above all, leave your competitors in the dust.

My friends and I still play *Party Jamboree* every few weeks just to test our relationships. Yes, you're essentially trying to screw over the people you love, but isn't that what every good game is about?

Choose from your favorite Mario series stars, including Luigi, Peach, and Mario, as well as other franchise favorites — Waluigi, Donkey Kong, Monty Mole, and more. *Jamboree* also brings a host of new minigames and levels, which should keep players coming back over and over again.

MARIO KART 8 DELUXE

Hit the track with Mario and his crew in a race to see who's the Mushroom Kingdom's fastest kart driver. *Mario Kart 8 Deluxe* brings back a variety of tracks from older games in the series — titles for the Game Boy Advance, SNES, and N64.

I can't tell you the number of times I've been in last place only to grab a Bullet Bill and come screaming back into the pack. I've also had fewer opportunities to be hit with a blue turtle shell, something that only happens to the first-place driver, to knock them out and let others grab the lead.

I'm not saying I'm the worst, but I'm not the best. Even so, every time I fire up *Mario Kart* is a joy. And with special features that keep your kart from leaving the track and moving forward, first-timers and new gamers can join in on the action. And if you're looking for more of a challenge, take the time to

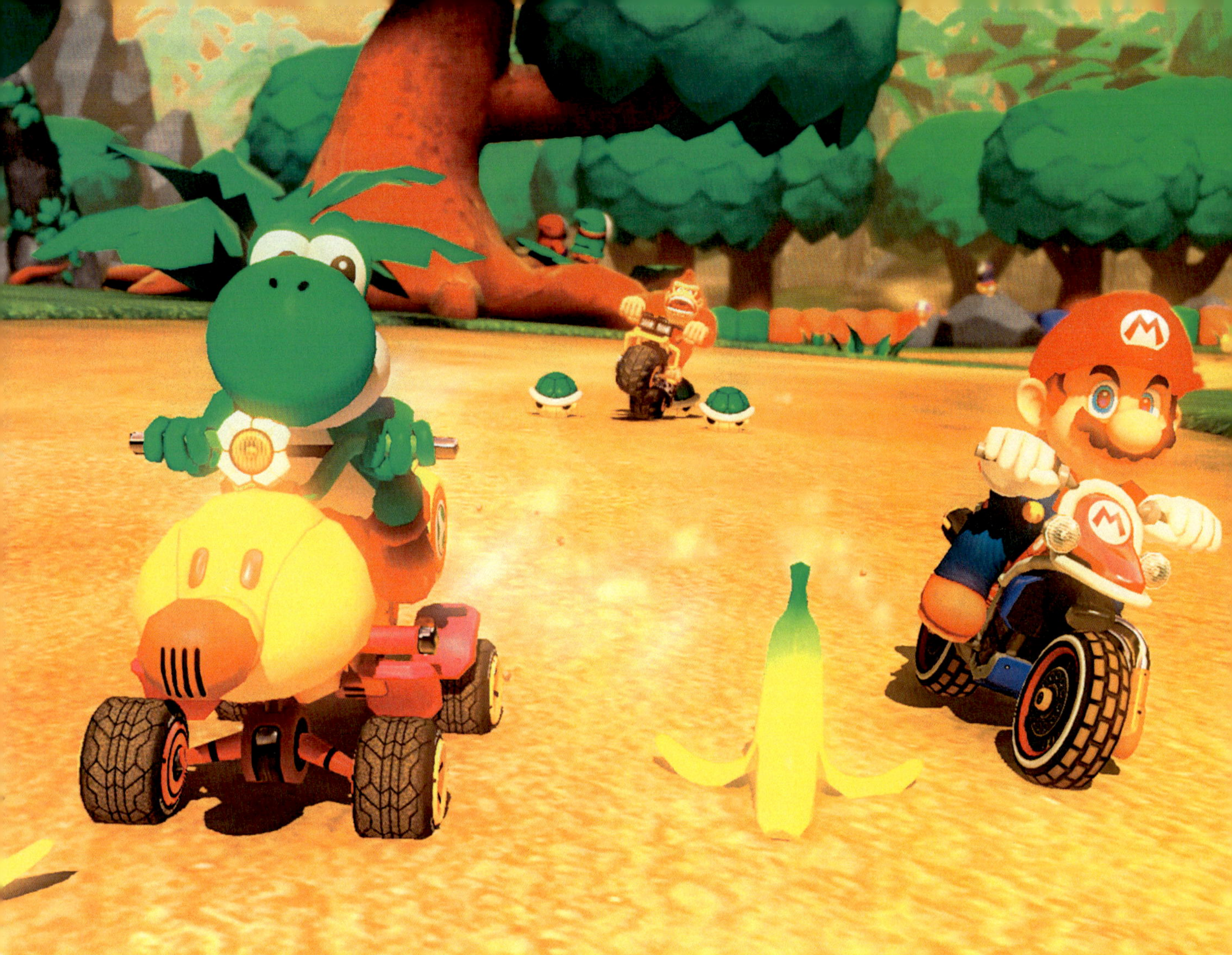

The beloved racing series Mario Kart *(above) has nearly a dozen distinct entries. 2014's* Mario Kart 8 *was rereleased in a deluxe version on the Nintendo Switch in 2017. Opposite,* Super Mario Sunshine *shook up the standing mechanics with Mario's water-cannon backpack.*

learn which karts, wheels, and gliders provide the best speed, traction, and acceleration. It's a game for everyone.

MARIO GOLF

It turns out Mario is more than just a plumber with a mustache and some ups. He's also a world-class athlete. From baseball and soccer to tennis and even events in the Olympics, Mario and his friends have played and participated in them all. But the best and most beloved Mario sports game has to be *Mario Golf* for the Nintendo 64.

And while the title takes place in the Mario universe, *Mario Golf* is in fact a shockingly competent golf simulator in its own right. You'll need to adjust for the wind, avoid bunkers, and more. While it's not a traditional party game like *Mario Party*, the multiplayer elements, like mini golf, make it a fantastic title to throw on with friends for a few quick rounds.

SUPER SMASH BROS.

One of the strangest and most successful Mario crossover titles ever, *Super Smash Bros.* is a fighting game that pits Mario and a slew of Nintendo and Nintendo partner characters against each other in a no-holds-barred tournament. Mario, Donkey Kong, Pikachu, Link, Samus, and others fight across a variety of multilevel stages, trying to knock each other off of platforms in order to win each round.

Each character gets their own unique attacks and abilities that make them worth trying at least once. And when you're looking to take on your friends, you can throw down in an epic four-player match to see who's the best.

What makes *Smash Bros.* and its successors so fantastic is the fact that, despite being incredibly approachable thanks to a relatively simple control scheme, it also offers room for players who want more technical gameplay. Master your favorite character's skills, learn the ins and outs of the various stages, and you can become unstoppable. Few things are more fun than sitting around with your pals, pounding Doritos and playing *Smash Bros.* for hours.

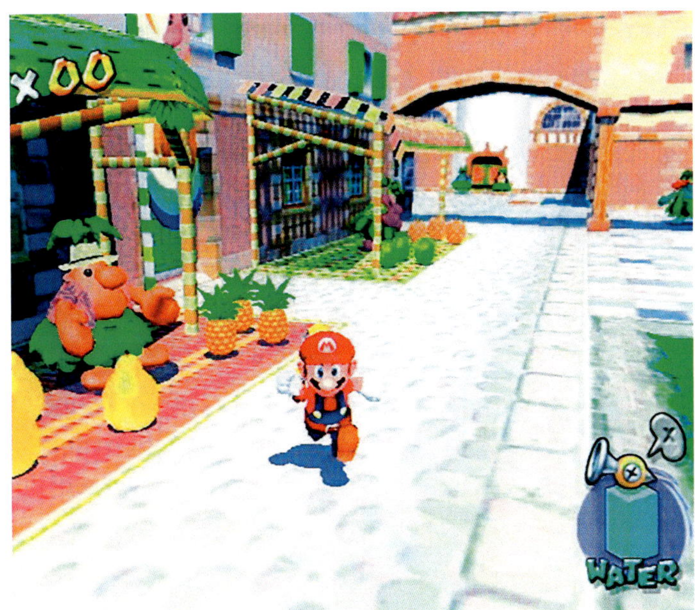

Skippable Entries

SUPER MARIO BROS. 2

This is a controversial take, but this bizarre entry in the Mario universe, while influential in terms of characters and gameplay, is easily skippable. *Super Mario Bros. 2*, at least the U.S. version, didn't start out as a Mario game. It's a remade version of the game *Yume Kōjō: Doki Doki Panic*. Nintendo had already developed a *Super Mario Bros. 2* game for its Japanese domestic market, but the company didn't think it would pass muster with U.S. audiences at the time and instead dropped Mario characters in *Yume Kōjō: Doki Doki Panic* and released it as *Super Mario Bros. 2* for international audiences.

The game allows you to play as Mario, Luigi, Peach (known as Princess Toadstool in the United States when the game debuted) and Toad. It also introduced characters like Birdo and the Shy Guys.

It introduced aspects of characters that have continued throughout the franchise, including Mario's overall balanced approach to running, jumping, and power; Luigi's high jumping ability; Peach's ability to glide on her dress; and Toad's relatively high strength. But as far as Mario games go, this one just didn't capture the same sense of wonder as the original.

SUPER MARIO BROS. 2: THE LOST LEVELS

Okay, remember the Japanese version of *Super Mario Bros. 2* I mentioned earlier? Well, this is that game. And there's one reason to skip it: It's frustratingly difficult. Nintendo kept this version of *Super Mario Bros. 2* in the Japanese market because it was too similar to the original game but with a difficulty level cranked up to 12.

It's less about enjoying the world of Mario and more about becoming an expert Mario player. That's the antithesis of the Mario formula, which tries to bring everyone in while still providing a depth that hardcore players will want to master. If you want to complete your Mario collection, or just want a punishing challenge, then this is a game for you. For everyone else, fire up the original *Super Mario Bros.* or dive into *Super Mario Bros. 3*.

NEW SUPER MARIO BROS.

This Mario title for the Nintendo DS handheld was a return to the side-scrolling style of old. Released in 2006, the game is fun but largely forgettable. It includes original and new power-ups and updated graphics that made it feel exciting at the time of its debut, but I've never had the desire to go back and replay it like other Mario titles.

It's not that this is a bad game; it is enjoyable. I remember playing it in the car while my brother drove me home from GameStop and loving being reminded of the first *Super Mario Bros.* game. But beyond that, it's tough to recommend this as a must-play.

SUPER MARIO SUNSHINE

Nintendo's big follow-up to *Super Mario 64* has Mario wrongfully convicted of vandalizing Isle Delfino and forced to clean up a goopy mess with a specialized backpack called the Flash Liquidizer Ultra Dousing Device, or F.L.U.D.D. Mario can not only use the backpack to get rid of the ooze on the island, but to hover as well.

Sunshine has a bright, colorful style that is eye-catching, but it doesn't feel as revolutionary as its predecessor. To be fair, that was a tall order to begin with, but not impossible.

The very best Mario games, like *Odyssey* and *Wonder*, make it feel like anything is possible and that there's no telling what will come next. *Sunshine*, while a solid game, just doesn't do that for me.

HOW *SUPER MARIO* CHANGED PLATFORMER GAMES FOREVER

Mario brought arcade games into our living rooms with his approachable style, endearing character, and zest for exploration.

BY LISA EADICICCO

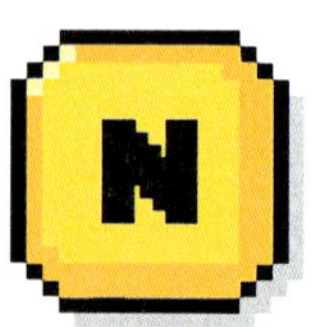

NICOLAS DOUCET, THE CREATIVE director for the hit 2024 PlayStation game *Astro Bot*, has a special relationship with *Super Mario Bros.* — and not just because it was his first console game. As a child, Doucet remembers, he spent weeks diligently searching for a secret invisible mushroom hidden in one of the first levels.

But he just couldn't find it.

So he enlisted help from his mother, who finally picked up the controller after he kept insisting that she try the game. While Doucet kept unknowingly running past the hidden mushroom, his mother accidentally stumbled upon it by jumping in the right place at the right time.

"Invisible becomes visible, which is the ultimate magic trick," Doucet said when describing *Super Mario Bros.*' influence on platformer games, a video game category in which the primary gameplay mechanic involves running and jumping on different surfaces. Everything from classics like *Super Mario Bros.* and *Sonic the Hedgehog* to modern blockbusters like *Astro Bot* are platformers.

Secrets like the one Doucet remembers from his

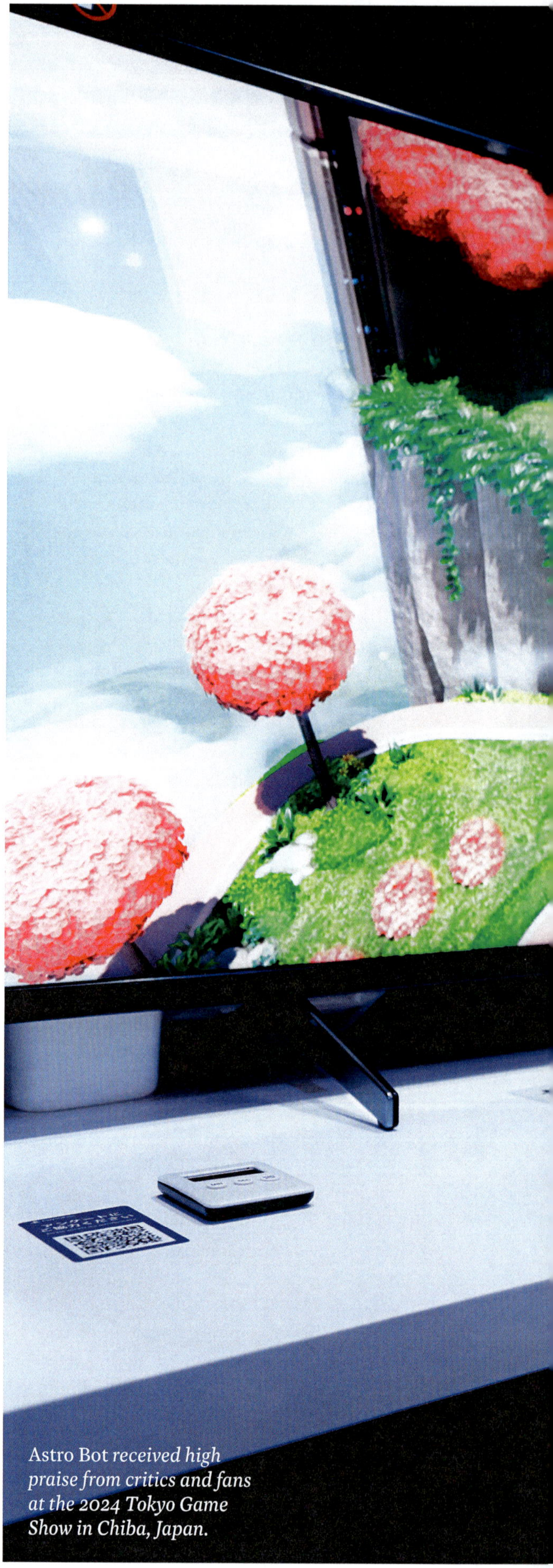

Astro Bot *received high praise from critics and fans at the 2024 Tokyo Game Show in Chiba, Japan.*

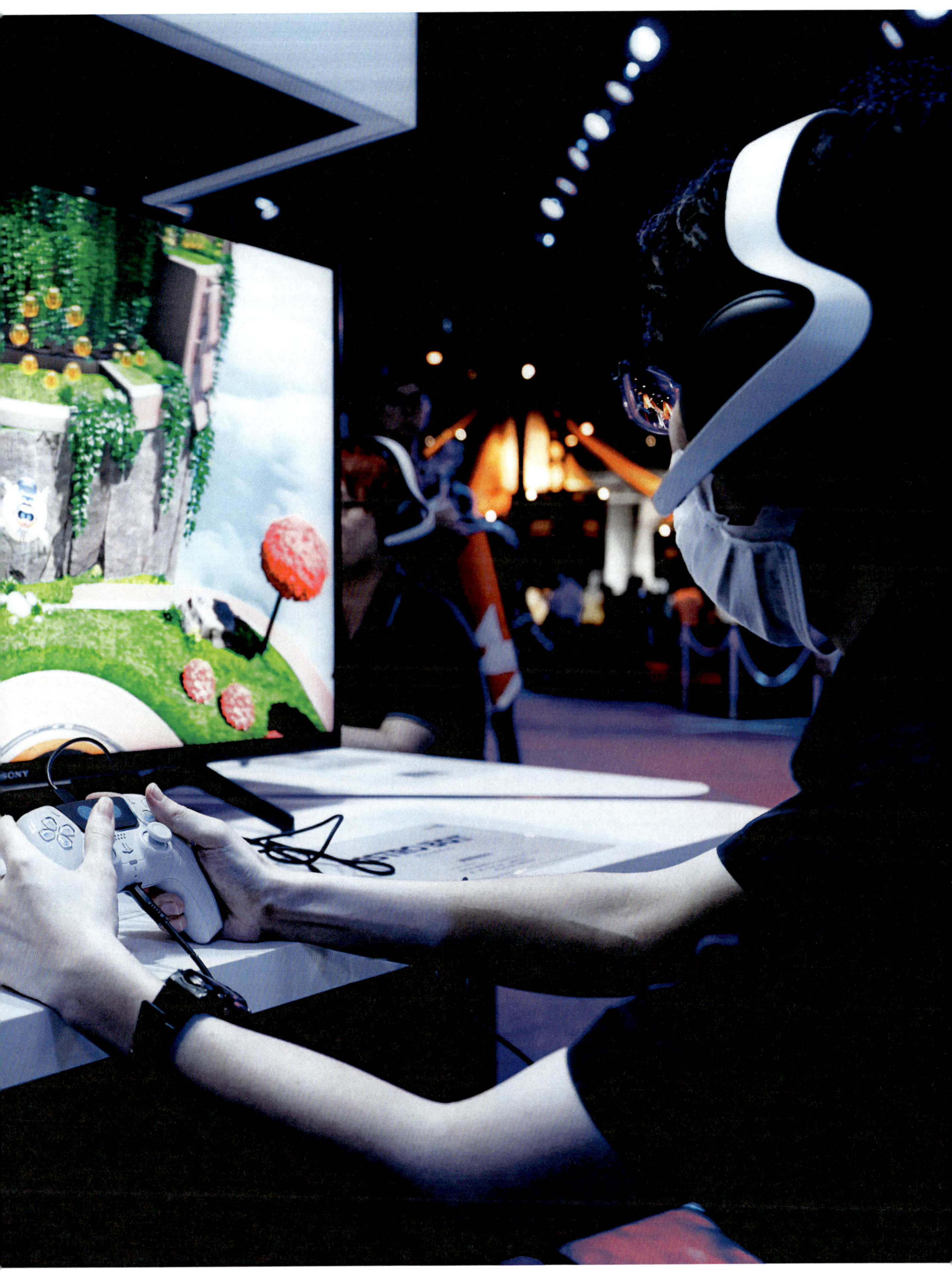

childhood perfectly sum up why *Super Mario Bros.*, which debuted on the Nintendo Entertainment System in 1985, has such an important place in video game history. It's not Mario's first appearance, nor was it the first platformer game. But *Super Mario Bros.* elevated both the Mario franchise and the genre as a whole by encouraging players to explore, not just rack up a high score. It's this approach, combined with *Super Mario*'s world building and accessible gameplay, that sparked a whole wave of beloved platformers for decades. "*Super Mario Bros.* really set the template for what [an] offline, single-player adventure game is," said Frank Cifaldi, founder and director of the Video Game History Foundation. "[It set] the stage by saying that a video game can essentially be an interactive movie, something that has a storyline and a goal and can be completed."

Adventure and story-driven games existed before *Super Mario Bros.*; these themes just weren't prominent amongst platformer games specifically. To grasp the impact of *Super Mario Bros.*, it's important to understand what the platformer gaming landscape was like before 1985.

Early titles like *Space Panic* (1980), *Pitfall!* (1982) and even *Donkey Kong* (1981), in which Mario makes his first appearance, as Jumpman, were all about reaching an endpoint while avoiding enemies and hurdles, whether they be aliens, barrels plummeting from above or gaping pits in the ground beneath you. They were difficult but straightforward games.

In *Space Panic*, for example, players climb ladders and traverse platforms to ensnare aliens by digging holes, earning points for each creature they trap. In *Donkey Kong*, the player is tasked with ascending platforms to reach the princess. Points are accumulated by jumping over or destroying obstacles like barrels and fireballs along the way.

Pitfall! — which launched on the 1977 Atari 2600 home video game console — was a bit different. Gameplay entailed moving the character from the left side to the right side of the screen across a jungle-themed backdrop, a departure from the single-screen platform-centric gameplay found in games like *Donkey Kong*. But like other platformers at the time, gamers have one main job in *Pitfall!* — avoid hazards and adversaries at all costs. Players jump over rolling kegs, use oscillating vines to swing over giant pits in the ground, and hop on the heads of crocodiles to make their way across swamps.

These games were influential in their own right, but they were designed to encourage players to consistently feed coins into arcade machines or remain glued to their consoles. Even the original 1983 *Mario Bros.*, the first game to feature Mario's name in the title, was based on this type of arcade-minded game-

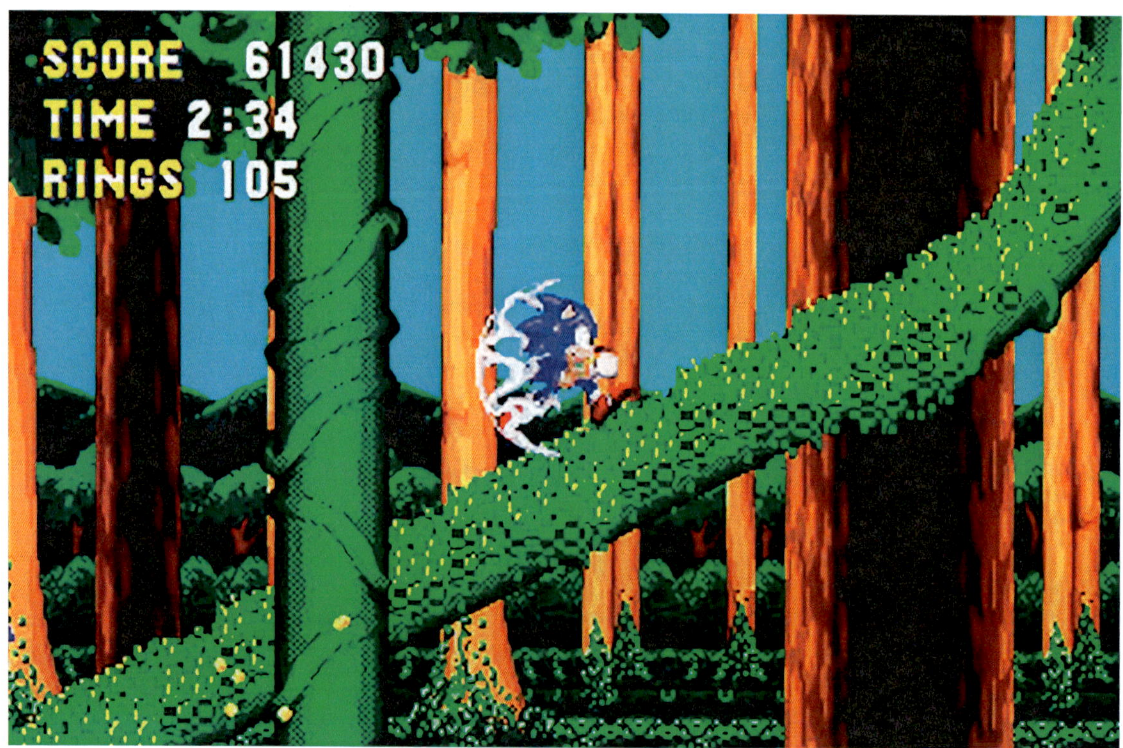

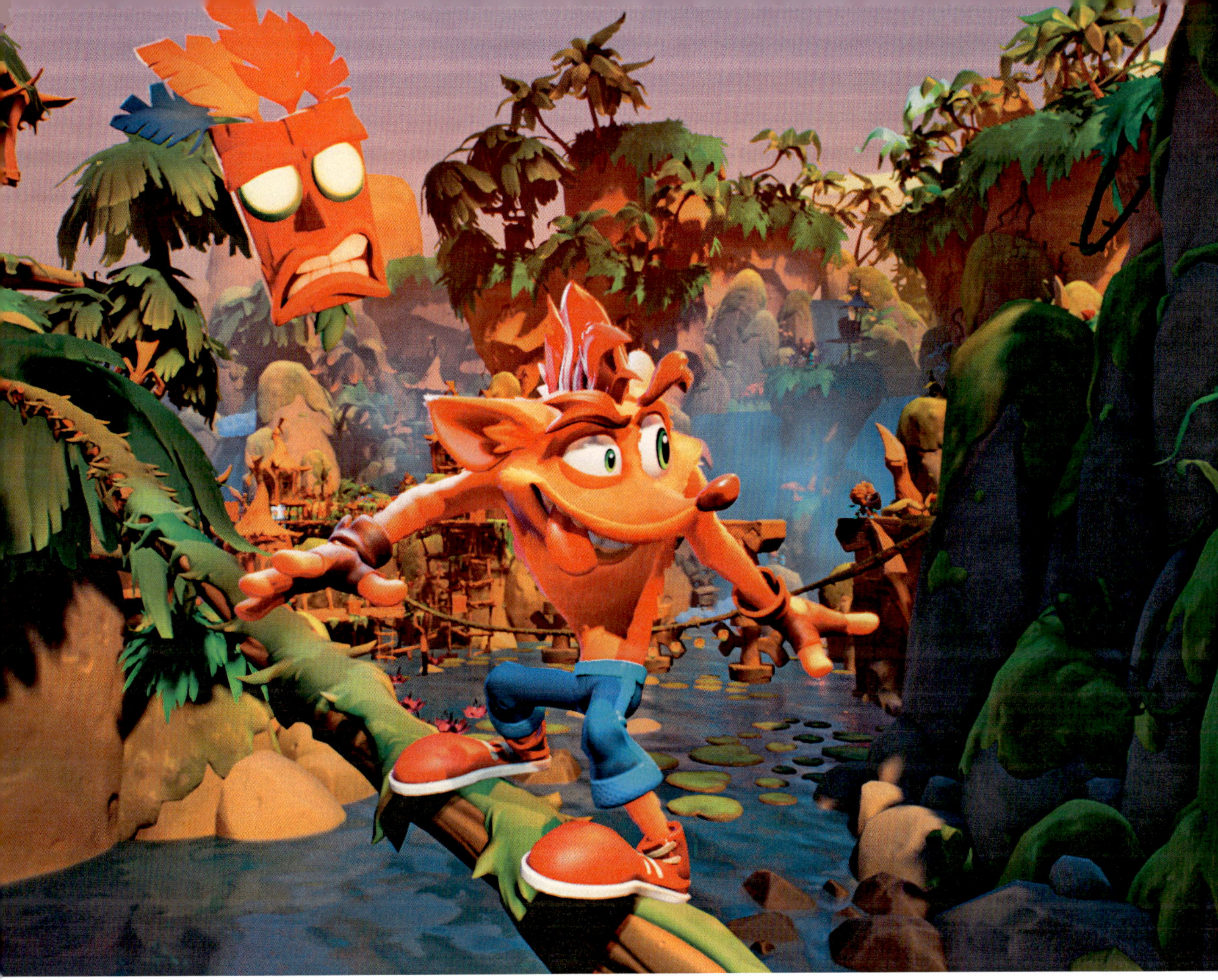

Crash Bandicoot *(above) and* Sonic the Hedgehog *(opposite), both highly successful platformer franchises, follow in* Super Mario's *8-bit footsteps.*

play. And that approach was evident in the style and aesthetics of those games, compared to *Super Mario Bros.* "The background was black and very grim and institutional," said Jeff Ryan, author of the book *Super Mario: How Nintendo Conquered America*, in reference to the visual differences between *Super Mario* and arcade games. "And it fit in with the arcade, because arcades were these dark, foreboding, cool places. And Mario was so sunny."

EARLY GAMES LACKED many of the traits found in platformers that have come to define the category over the last three decades: spunky and sometimes cute main characters (think Sonic the Hedgehog and Spyro the Dragon), robust worlds filled with secrets, environments begging to be investigated, and story-driven plots.

So what exactly did *Super Mario Bros.* do differently? In the game, completing a level isn't always linear. You're rewarded for being curious and following your instinct to check every single question mark–branded box, just in case there's a power-up, or attempt to descend a pipe because there's a chance it'll take you somewhere new and different. Players learn this from the very outset, in World 1-2, which includes a secret Warp Zone area hidden at the end of the stage.

Most of the time, breaking the brown bricks found throughout most *Super Mario* levels does nothing more than free up more space for Mario to jump. But every once in a while, something special happens. Hitting one of these nondescript blocks in World 2-1, for example, causes a vine to grow, which Mario can climb to reach a secret area in the clouds filled with coins.

This interactive approach to gameplay not only rewarded eagle-eyed and inquisitive players, but also made *Super Mario Bros.* accessible in a way that many arcade games weren't. Instead of punishing players for losing, *Super Mario Bros.* taught gamers

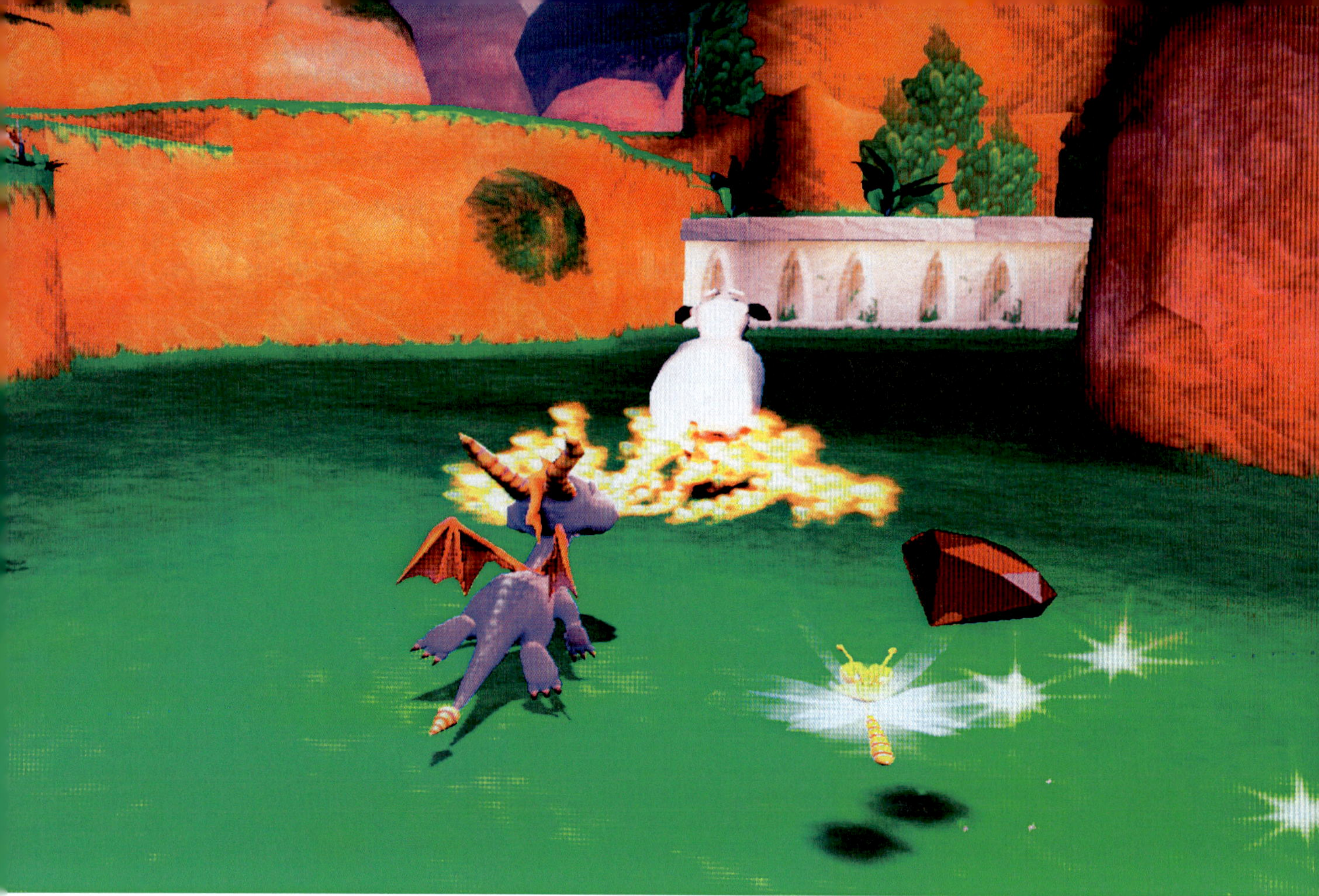

Elements of Super Mario 64 *informed the design of the 3D platformer* Spyro the Dragon, *including having levels with extended views of architectural landmarks.*

techniques they could apply to future levels to defeat upcoming foes and discover hidden gems.

For example, the first time you encounter a Koopa Troopa (turtle-looking creatures that walk upright on two legs), you quickly learn that stomping them doesn't eliminate them. Instead, it just prompts them to hide in their shells, which you can then launch at other enemies by jumping on them. That can make it easier to contend with and use them to your advantage next time.

Super Mario Bros. is full of elements that make the world feel alive in ways other game worlds don't, from the bright and sunny backdrop Ryan mentioned earlier to the animations and the way players are treated to extra lives after jumping on a Koopa Troopa's shell multiple times in a row.

Touches like these left an impression on game designer Derek Yu, known for the popular indie platform game *Spelunky*, in which players fight their way through randomly generated underground levels using anything at their disposal to fend off monsters. "It's a really important aspect of game design, because these simple interactions are connected directly to the player's button presses and they're happening all the time," Yu said, over email. "Even if we don't notice it, we definitely feel it."

Spelunky is just one of the many platformer games to draw influence from the ideas pioneered in *Super Mario Bros. Mario* kickstarted the era of the mascot platformer, or platformer games helmed by feisty, goofy, adorable characters designed to leave an impression rather than just serve as pixels to be piloted to an endpoint.

WHAT FOLLOWED THROUGHOUT the 1990s wasn't an onslaught of *Mario* ripoffs but a number of creative games led by endearing characters that, like Mario, pushed the boundaries of platformers in their own ways. *Mario* provided the formula for other developers to iterate upon and make their own, proving that the character's success wasn't just a fluke. "These are mechanics that technically existed prior to *Super Mario Bros.*, but that's really the game that demonstrated to the world that it is kind of like the template that people are looking for," Cifaldi said.

Sonic the Hedgehog may be the most famous video game mascot other than Mario. When the sassy blue hedgehog arrived on the Sega Genesis in 1991, he made a name for himself by being everything that

Mario wasn't. "As a character, he was expressly built to showcase Nintendo's weaknesses," Ryan wrote when describing Sonic in his book. "Mario was jolly; Sonic was rude. Mario was happily unrushed; Sonic's express purpose was to rush."

Of course, the approach to gameplay in *Sonic* is decidedly different from the *Mario* games; you could argue *Sonic* is just as much a racing game as it is a platformer. But Sega's determination to compete with Nintendo undoubtedly contributed to *Sonic*'s creation and success. As Ryan also notes in his book, Sega attempted to promote its consoles with other mascots that just didn't click before landing on Sonic, such as Alex Kidd, who starred in the 1986 platformer *Alex Kidd in Miracle World*. "He was totally forgotten because a much cooler person showed up afterward," Ryan said in reference to the iconic blue hedgehog.

Not to be outdone, Sony's PlayStation division needed a mascot platformer of its own. Enter Crash Bandicoot, the zany (and often clueless) orange marsupial that, along with *Super Mario 64*, helped usher platformers into the 3D era of the mid-1990s.

Like Sonic games, Crash Bandicoot games put a different spin on platformer gameplay compared to Mario. (Quite literally, one of Crash's signature moves is a spin attack that's performed by pressing the square button.) Instead of traversing along a flat, 2D surface like Mario, Crash runs forward from the player's perspective.

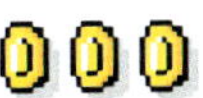

SUPER MARIO BROS. IS FULL OF ELEMENTS THAT MAKE THE WORLD FEEL ALIVE IN WAYS OTHER GAMES DON'T.

But Mario's influence is undeniable. Like Mario, Crash hops atop enemies to defeat them and jumps on boxes — some of which are punctuated with a question mark — to retrieve extra lives and Wumpa fruit, the game's fictional fruit that looks like a cross between an apple and a peach. Like the coins Mario collects, gathering 100 Wumpa fruit earns Crash a one-up. The level select area is even known as the Warp Room in certain Crash games, akin to *Super Mario*'s Warp Zone.

Sonic and Crash may be two of the most iconic mascot platformers to debut in Mario's wake, but they're far from being the only ones. Don't forget about Kirby, the lovable pink blob that made his debut on the Game Boy in 1992. Similar to the way Mario gains new abilities by finding power-up items hidden throughout levels, Kirby learns new attacks by inhaling enemies (although that trick wasn't present in the original Kirby game).

Spyro the Dragon, the 1998 PlayStation game in which the titular purple hero must rescue his fellow dragons from being transformed into statues, also takes some cues from *Mario*. *Spyro*, like *Crash* and *Sonic*, also pushed the platformer category forward in its own way. The game helped popularize open-world environments at a time when linear levels like those found in *Crash* and *Mario* were generally considered the norm.

But Spyro games wholeheartedly embraced the idea of curiosity and adventure that Mario previously established. A core element of the gameplay involves visiting every nook and cranny of a level to discover a concealed treasure chest, a hidden dragon in need of rescuing, or a sneaky thief with a stolen dragon egg in its clutches.

Mario set the stage for what would become one of the most prominent styles of gaming for years to come. That's true even today, as evidenced by the success of *Astro Bot*, which won the prestigious Game of the Year title at the annual Game Awards. *Astro Bot* embodies platform gaming at its best, with bubbly environments, innovative gameplay mechanics, hidden rewards and an unbelievably cute main character.

Like many of the great platformers that came before it, *Astro Bot* inherits many of the staples that *Super Mario Bros.* established but with its own twist. While the controls in Mario games tend to be very focused on momentum (i.e., making sure you gain enough speed and height to reach the top of the flagpole at the end of a stage), *Astro Bot*'s control's are more about precision. "In *Astro*, we try to move away from inertia, to actually give perfect pinpoint control, because we feel like this is what modern audiences need," Doucet said.

But Mario's reach extends beyond platformers. As Cifaldi points out, *Super Mario* is fundamentally a game about exploring the world around you, a key tenet that guides many beloved modern games. "It's hard, if not impossible, to find any adventure-style game today that doesn't have things off the path that you can go find and be rewarded for," he said. "And I think all of that points back to the pipes in *Super Mario Bros.*"

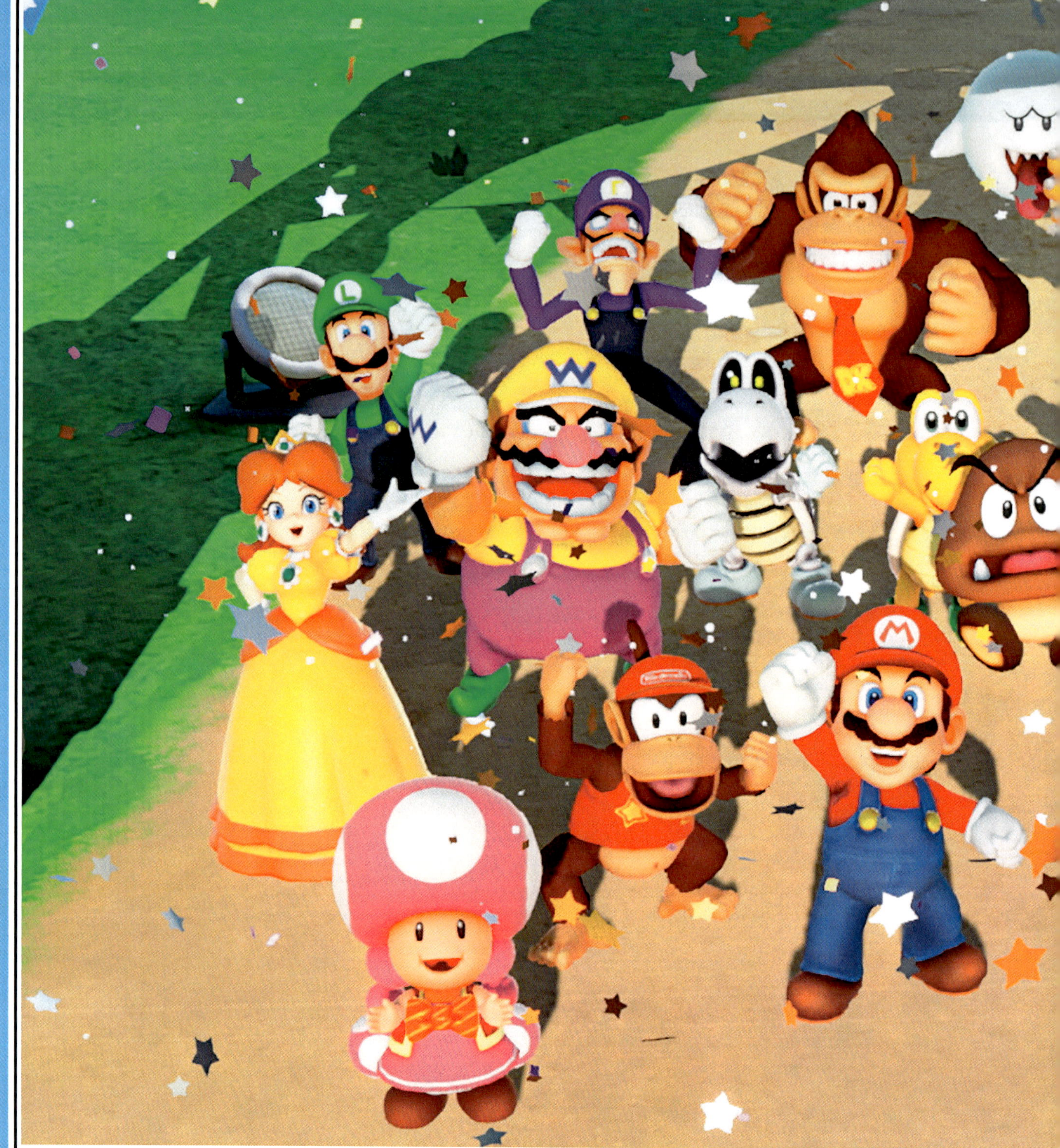

THE EXPANDED UNIVERSE

There's more than Mario in the Mushroom Kingdom. A lot more.

BY COURTNEY MIFSUD INTREGLIA

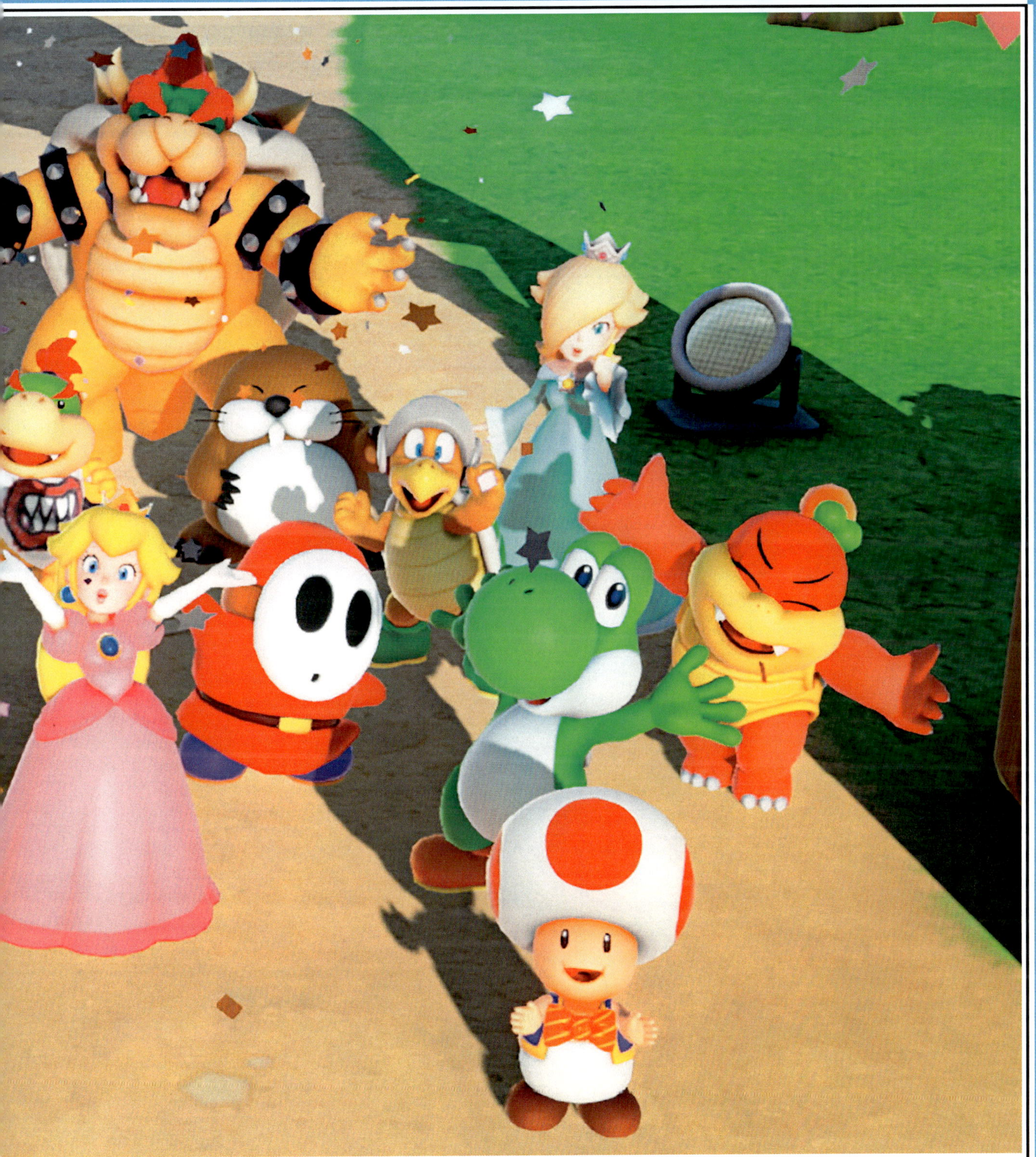

AS ONE OF THE MOST SUCCESSFUL video game franchises of all time, Super Mario is about more than the primary plumber. Nintendo created an extensive cast of recurring characters, villains, and sidekicks to fill out the Mushroom Kingdom. Some, like Luigi, have their own games and franchises spun off from the original Super Mario universe. Plus, Nintendo leverages closely linked partner enterprises, in the form of spin-off series and crossover games. The long-running multiplayer fighter series Super Smash Bros. features well known characters from various Nintendo franchises duking it out with unique powers. Here's a nonexhaustive breakdown of the main players throughout Mario's world, and a few friends they made along the way.

Primary Protagonists

LUIGI

As Mario's slightly younger twin, Luigi has always gotten the short end of the stick. Even though he's quite a bit taller, he's always existed in his brother's shadow. Instead of residing in Peach's Castle, Luigi is relegated to a gauntlet of haunted mansions.

When Gunpei Yokoi set out to produce 1983's *Mario Bros.*, he took inspiration from the arcade game *Joust*. He and Shigeru Miyamoto wanted to incorporate a competitive and cooperative two-player gameplay into their project. While *Joust* had stork-riding Player 2, *Mario Bros.* had Luigi, a color-palette-swap version of Mario.

Since his initial conception, Luigi has been portrayed as clumsy, cautious, timid, and, for the most part, cowardly. He'll show some heroic moments (when necessary), but he is easily startled. Much of this characterization came when, in 2001, Nintendo released the first entry in the Luigi's Mansion series. Originally released on GameCube, these games feature Luigi as the main star. Players explore haunted mansions through his avatar, gobbling up ghosts through a special vacuum cleaner, and ultimately rescue Mario.

PRINCESS PEACH

The benevolent and elegant ruler of the Mushroom Kingdom made her debut in the 1985 Nintendo Entertainment System title *Super Mario Bros.* She has been kidnapped by Bowser and his minions in nearly every game in the long-running Super Mario series. The main female character often wears long pink ball gowns, and is known for her flowing blond hair (although early NES games depicted her as a brunette).

Throughout the games Princess Peach has a few unique moves and weapons. In *Super Mario RPG: Legend of the Seven Stars*, she can use healing abilities Therapy and Group Hug. In *Super Smash Bros. Melee*, Peach attacks with the Peach Bomber: She lunges her body at opponents and blasts them in an explosion.

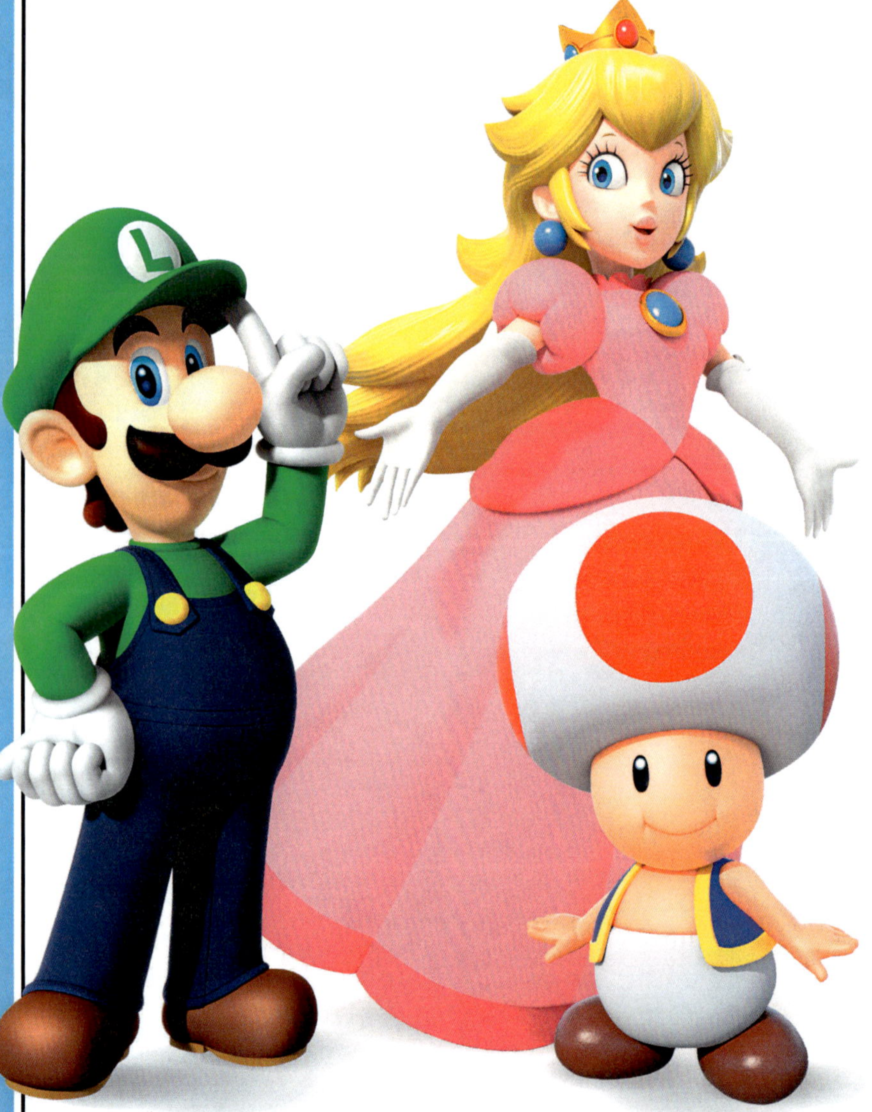

TOAD

The speckled-headed sidekick is small in stature but serves as a big helper throughout the series. Toad represents the larger Toad species, which are the primary denizens of the Mushroom Kingdom. Although there were Toads in the original *Super Mario Bros.*, Toad the individual did not debut until 1988's *Super Mario Bros. 2*.

It can be hard to discern Toad from Toad, so in 2004's *Mario Power Tennis* Nintendo set the singular Toad apart from the rest. While most of his kind have spots that match their vests, Toad's speckles are largely depicted as red while his vest is blue. *Super Mario Odyssey* is one notable exception and features all Toads in the game with red spots and blue vests, outside of the Toad Brigade.

Toad is portrayed as a lightweight character, which translates to some powers related to speed and endurance, and Toad has Power Squat Jump ability in *Super Mario Bros. 2*.

YOSHI

Like Toad, Yoshi is both the name of a main character in the Mario franchise and the dinosaur-like species to which the character belongs. Yoshi's functionality for the player depends on which game

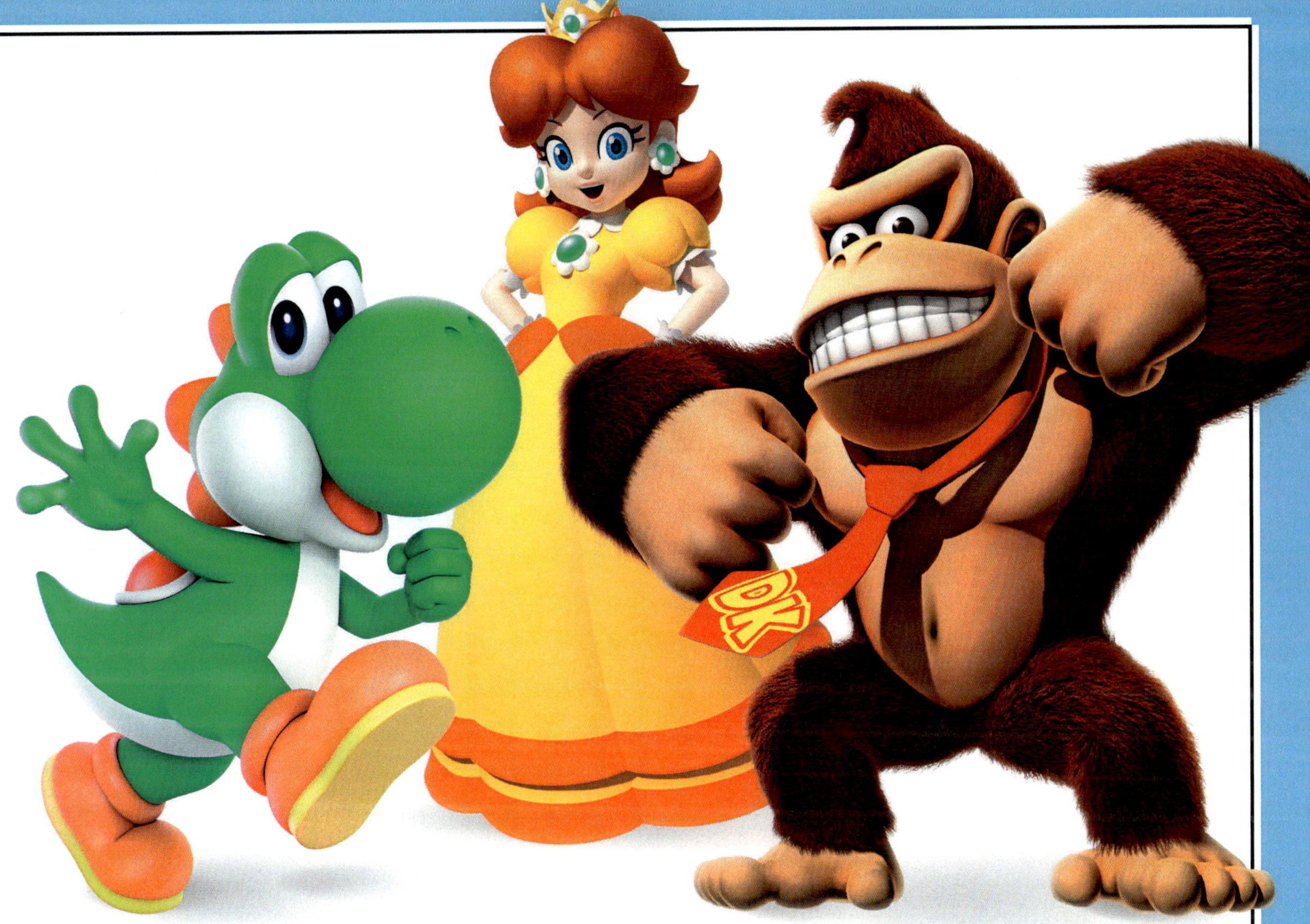

series he's a part of. In the Super Mario series, Yoshi is a rideable character for the players. In spin-off series, such as Mario Kart and Mario Party, Yoshi is a playable character himself.

Nintendo spun Yoshi into his own franchise in 1991 with the puzzle game *Yoshi* for the Family Computer and NES. Inspired by *Tetris*, players must stack two indentical Super Mario enemies on top of each other in order to clear them. A 2D platformer scrolling game series, *Yoshi's Island*, began with 1995's *Super Mario World 2: Yoshi's Island* (and features Mario and Luigi as babies). The most recent franchise entry, *Yoshi's Crafted World* was released on the Nintendo Switch in 2019 and features a handcrafted-art style — every level looks like it could have been created in a child's art class.

PRINCESS DAISY

The princess of Sarasaland, Daisy, is depicted as more of a tomboy than her best friend, Peach. Like Peach, the world met Daisy as a damsel. She debuted in the 1989 Game Boy game *Super Mario Land*, in which she was kidnapped by the missile-wielding alien Tatanga after he had taken over her kingdom. Daisy has long auburn hair, and she wears a yellow-orange gown.

She has consistently been presented as Luigi's love interest, in the same way that Nintendo suggests that Mario and Peach are a romantic pair. In both *Mario Party 5* and *Mario Party 6*, their team name is Steady Sweeties, and Daisy acts as Luigi's caddie in 1991's NES *Open Tournament Golf* — just as Peach caddies for Mario.

Many of Daisy's powers throughout the games lean into her association with flowers. She can perform Bloom Blast in *Mario Tennis Aces*, where she walks over a trail of summoned daisy petals before hitting the ball. Daisy confuses opponents with her special Flower Ball in *Mario Superstar Baseball* and *Mario Super Sluggers*.

DONKEY KONG

The hulking ape goes by a few monikers: DK, Donkey, Kong, and sometimes even D. Kong. While he's a major character in the Super Mario franchise, he's the main star of his own, which began as a series of arcade games in 1981 and has since sold more than 65 million units across various platforms.

Shigeru Miyamoto, who created the character, has repeatedly affirmed that he used the word "donkey" to convey a sense of stubbornness and the name Kong to invoke the image of a gorilla. Through his many adventures, the burly ape tries to stop his nemesis King K. Rool from stealing his valuable Banana Hoard.

"Donkey Kong" is as much of a title as it is a name. Cranky Kong, DK's relative, originally bore the Donkey Kong title in releases prior to 1994's *Donkey Kong Country*. Both DK and Cranky Kong were the first Mario antagonists, chucking barrels at the mustachioed hero.

Supporting Stars

TOADETTE

The cheerful pink Toad with bouncing pigtails was first introduced as Toad's companion in *Mario Kart: Double Dash!!* She is the most regularly recurring female Toad throughout the Mario franchise, appearing as a supporting character and playable hero. She's shown as happy and upbeat, while also being childish and forgetful.

It's known that Toad and Toadette are close friends, but some games hint they may be more than that. The ending photo in *Mario Kart Wii* shows the two of them holding hands, and the opening of *Super Mario Galaxy* shows the pair sitting in the grass observing shooting stars. (Some official guidebooks from Prima Games declare the duo to be siblings.)

Toadette utilizes many power-ups throughout the franchise, including the Invincibility Mushroom and Super Pickax. In 2019's *New Super Mario Bros. U Deluxe*, she can transform into a Peach clone called Peachette, who can double jump and float in a similar fashion as the original Mushroom princess.

DIDDY KONG

The best friend and smaller sidekick to Donkey Kong was introduced in *Donkey Kong Country*, in 1994. Diddy Kong is a playable character in nearly every Donkey Kong Country game, having more appearances than the big DK has in his own franchise. Diddy Kong pairs up with his girlfriend, Dixie Kong, and has a series of spin-off racing games that began on the Nintendo 64 in 1997.

Throughout the Mario universe, Diddy Kong is playable in such games as *Mario Golf: Toadstool Tour*, *Mario Power Tennis*, and the *Mario Kart* entries. He makes a brief cameo in the *Super Mario Bros.* movie, cheering on Donkey Kong during a fight scene.

Quick and nimble in nearly every game appearance, Diddy Kong is a foil to Donkey Kong's brute strength. He cartwheels to attack opponents and jumps farther and has a special dashing ability called Chimpy Charge, as seen in 1999's *Donkey Kong 64*.

ROSALINA

The recurring, powerful sorceress first appeared in 2007's *Super Mario Galaxy*. She lives in space with her adoptive children, the Lumas, and traverses the universe on the Comet Observatory, protecting the cosmos. She has long, blond hair like Peach and wears a turquoise gown.

Throughout the games Rosalina can generate force fields, surrounding the Observatory for protection. She levitates, teleports from earth to space, and can use her wand to manipulate gravity and launch stars. Rosalina's story is central to *Galaxy*, as players unlock tales about her from the Comet Observatory's Library throughout the game's nine chapters. Because of this mechanic there's a good amount of lore regarding her history and parentage — unlike Mario and Luigi's canon history, which is rather thin. Rosalina's story begins when she meets a young Luma in a rusted spaceship. She embarks on

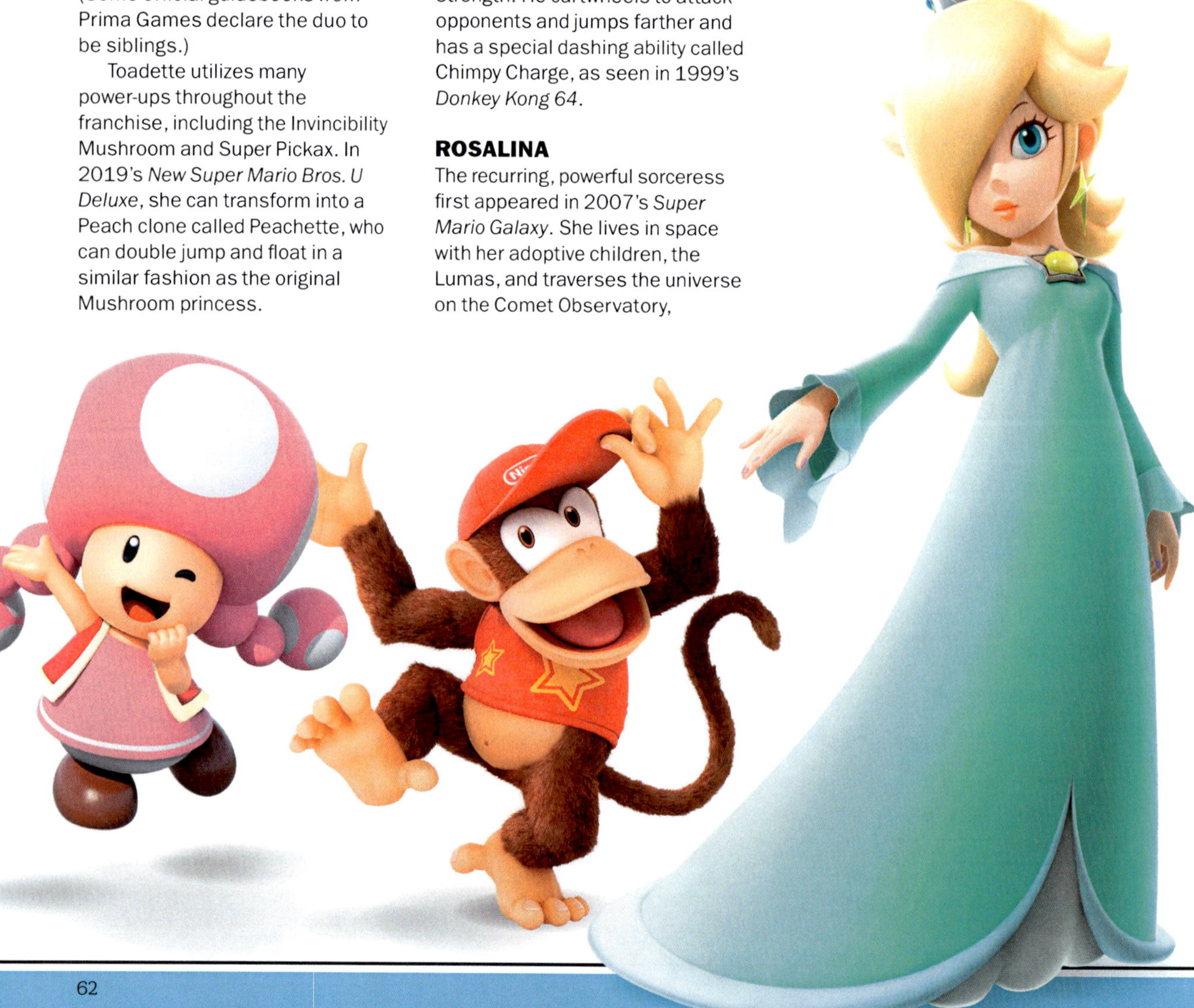

a quest to rebuild the vessel and search for the Luma's mother, and makes centennial visits to the Mushroom Kingdom on Mushroom Earth.

BIRDO

The world met Birdo in *Yume Kōjō: Doki Doki Panic*, a Japanese-only video game that was released in 1987. Nintendo of America remade the game with characters from the Mario franchise but kept the enemies and bosses of the original. The remake is known as *Super Mario Bros. 2* in America. Like her friend Yoshi, Birdo, a bright-pink dinosaur, can fire eggs as projectables.

Although Nintendo avoids commenting on it, Birdo is considered to be one of the first transgender characters in video games. The English manual for *Super Mario Bros. 2* describes Birdo as a character who "thinks he is a girl" and would prefer to be called Birdetta, thus inspiring some video game media to interpret the character as transgender. (In subsequent printings of the English manual, mention of Birdo's being male was omitted).

Largely, Birdo's status as a transgender icon has been welcomed by the game community, as part of an ongoing conversation on inclusion and representation in games.

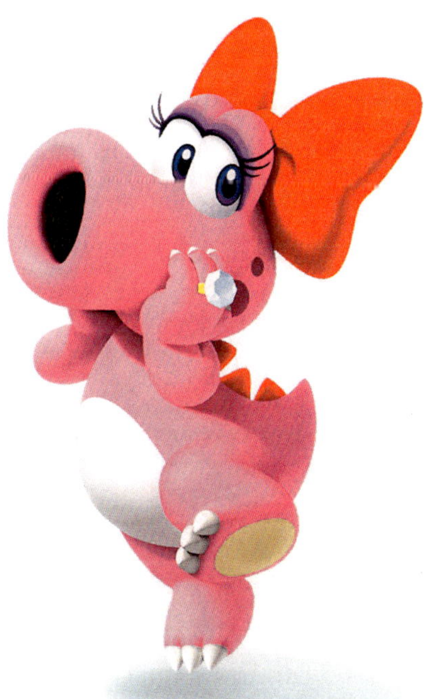

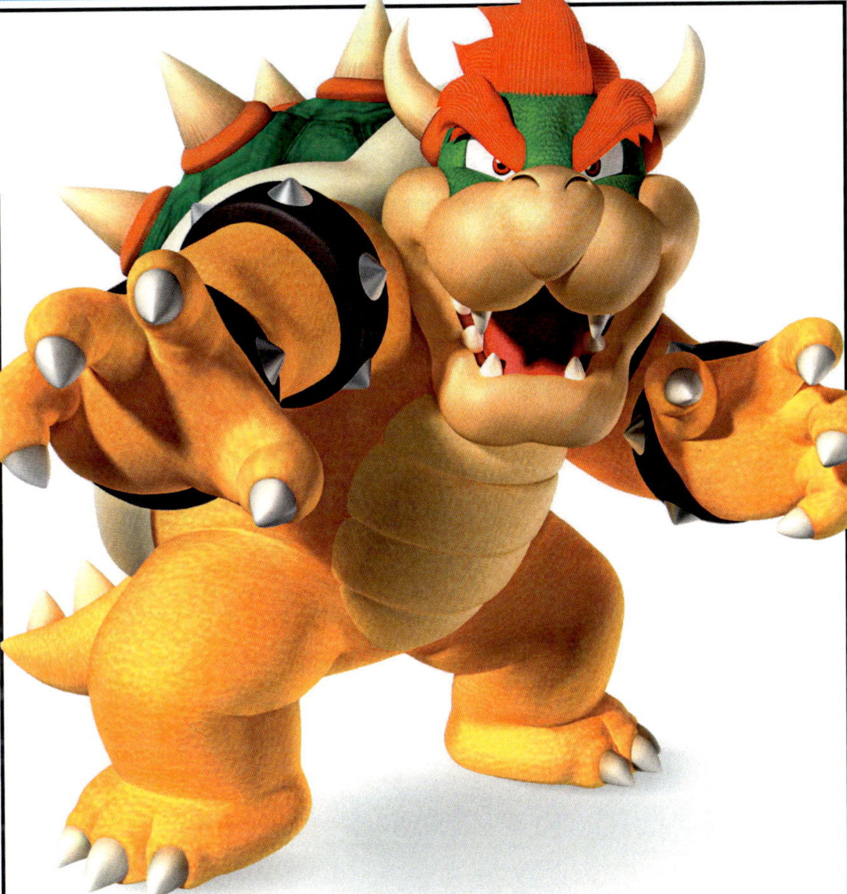

Recurring Villains

BOWSER

Immensely strong, filled with fiery wrath, and obsessed with Peach, Bowser is the archnemesis of Mario and the King of Koopa Kingdom. Bowser was created as the villain of *Super Mario Bros.* and tentatively had the name Boss Creeper — a reference to Shellcreepers from the *Mario Bros.* arcade game.

Bowser's spoiled son, Bowser Jr., aids him in his campaigns for world domination (and princess kidnapping). The villain's size varies from game to game, but he's consistently pictured as twice the height of Mario. Although he's a merciless brute in games in which he's an antagonist, there are some games in the franchise that feature Bowser's more heroic and gentle side. The game *Mario & Luigi: Bowser's Inside Story* showed that, while Bowser is tyrannical to his troops, he has a soft side. He rescued imprisoned soldiers who served him, got enraged when he learned that the evil scientist Fawful had kidnapped his men, and went as far as to forgive three traitors. The Paper Mario series also shows that Bowser's troops follow him out of respect rather than fear.

For the initial run of games, Bowser's continual kidnapping of Princess Peach was largely unromantic. But at the turn of the millennium, the Koopa King's unrequited feelings began to bubble to the surface. In *Paper Mario*, released in 2000 for the Nintendo 64, Peach finds Bowser's secret diary, which contains proclamations of love for the Mushroom Princess.

In the 2023 *Super Mario Bros.* movie, Bowser's infatuation with Peach is one of the funniest plot points; he even sings an '80s-style ode to her.

KOOPALINGS

Sometimes known as the Koopa Kids or Bowser's Minions, the seven-member troupe of recurring villains do Bowser's bidding. Made up of Larry, Morton, Wendy, Iggy, Roy, Lemmy and Ludwig, the group first appeared in 1988's *Super Mario Bros. 3*, in which Bowser ordered them to use airships to conquer various parts of the Mushroom World. Each of the Koopa Kids would

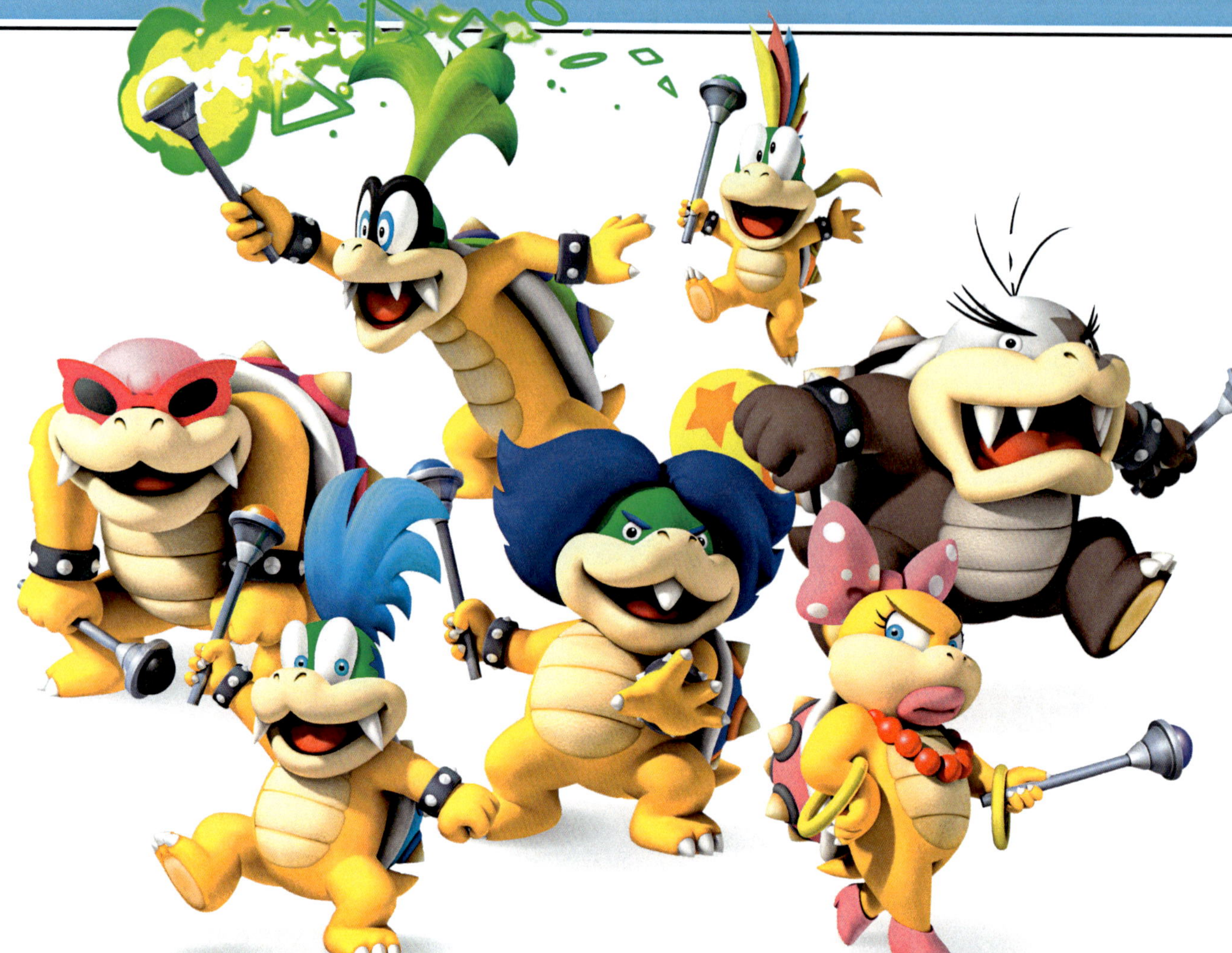

conquer a kingdom, steal that king's scepter, and transform the sovereign into an animal.

Having appeared in various games throughout the Mario franchise, and in *Yoshi's Safari* (Jewelry Land was their mark this time), the Koopalings are unlockable playable characters in *Mario Kart 8*.

The Koopalings are childlike and love mayhem. Their individual personalities are not too distinct from one another, and they have very similar powers. They use their shells as offensive attacks and for defensive measures. They spit fireballs, and have their own unique spells.

KING BOO

Many of the franchise's bad guys first made Mario their nemesis; after all, he's the hero. But King Boo initially antagonized Mario's cowardly brother, Luigi, in the spook-filled Luigi's Mansion game series. The first installment was released in 2001 on the Nintendo GameCube.

There are a few pillars of any Luigi's Mansion game: He'll stun ghosts with his flashlight and suck them up with Professor E. Gadd's latest Poltergust vacuum. All paths lead to King Boo in this series, as he's the ultimate antagonist. He's mastered the elements with fire, lightning, and ice attacks, and traps Mario in a painting.

Outside of the Luigi's Mansion franchise, King Boo is an avid karter who appears in *Mario Kart: Double Dash!!* and *Mario Kart Wii* as an unlockable racer. His last spin-off appearance is in *Mario Kart 8 Deluxe*, exclusively on the Nintendo Switch version.

The spectral sovereign appears as a frequent minigame boss throughout the Mario Party series and reigns supreme over his own board, called King Boo's Haunted Hideaway, in *Mario Party 8*, released on the Wii in 2007.

WARIO

Perhaps no introduction to Mario's alter ego is more telling than the one on Nintendo's website, which states that "this rude and crude fellow likes to toot . . . his own horn."

Designed as both the evil doppelgänger and rival of Mario, the recurring character is hot-tempered and muscular, with a distinct chin and rosy nose. Not to be outdone by his enemy (OK, he's largely outdone by Mario), Wario has gone on to become the protagonist of his own franchise, including games such as the Wario Land series and the WarioWare series.

His adventures mainly center around collecting treasure or reclaiming loot from villainous thieves who plundered it from him. An automobile connoisseur, Wario has many at his disposal: the Wario Car from the Wario Land series, the Wario Bike in the WarioWare titles. He owns a plane called the *Bulldog*, which appears in *Mario & Wario* and *Wario's Woods*.

The WarioWare series establishes that, when he is not thieving, Wario's day job is running a microgame production company, WarioWare, Inc., where employees create super short minigames that last for only a few seconds.

WALUIGI

While many of the heroes and villains listed here were first introduced in mainline platform games, Waluigi is an outlier. The world first met Luigi's lanky purple rival with a racket in his hand, as a playable character in *Mario Tennis* on Nintendo 64. His long arms and legs give him an edge in the various sports Mario characters enjoy.

In his debut game, Waluigi was partnered with Wario, and the duo's relationship has been on unsteady ground ever since. Originally depicted as siblings, 2008's *Mario Super Sluggers* depicted them as just friends. The following year, in *Mario & Sonic at the Olympic Winter Games*, there are several claims that they are unrelated.

Charles Martinet, who voices Mario, Waluigi, and Wario (among many others) describes the pair as "two nice, evil guys who found each other," in a 2008 interview with gaming website Kombo.

BOWSER JR.

The pint-sized prince is packed with trouble. Known in Japan as Koopa Jr., Bowser Jr. is the son of King Bowser and heir to his throne. He dons a bib, decorated with fangs, that he'll wear as a mask if he's feeling menacing. Bowser Jr. made his debut in the Nintendo GameCube's *Super Mario Sunshine*, in which he is seen assuming the alter ego Shadow Mario to get the hero arrested so that Junior can kidnap Peach. The princess is just trying to enjoy Isle Delfino, but Junior believes Peach is his biological mother, based on his father's lies. Despite Bowser's misdirection, Junior serves him faithfully throughout future games, fighting Mario on his behalf and commanding the King's troops.

Like any fictional prince, Bowser Jr. is bratty and spoiled, throwing tantrums if he doesn't get his way and commanding the Koopalings with arrogance and disrespect.

Junior has at times been so beside himself that he needs to ask for help from unlikely sources. In the Bowser's Fury mode of *Super Mario 3D World + Bowser's Fury*, Junior is an ally and a playable character. He beseeches Mario's help to save his father.

KAMEK

When it comes to Bowser's confidants, one Koopa stands out from the rest. Kamek is a Magikoopa, a wizardlike Koopa who wields a wand and advises their king. He's a secondary antagonist throughout the Super Mario games, like Bowser Jr., but an archnemesis in the Yoshi franchise. Kamek first appeared in 1995's *Super Mario World 2: Yoshi's Island*, and was the caretaker of Baby Bowser (the infant form of Bowser, not Bowser Jr.). He still looks after Bowser even though he's fully grown.

Kamek can teleport, create several copies of himself, and fire magical blasts from his scepter. The Magikoopa can also fly on a broomstick.

He's almost as brawny as he is brainy. In 2014's *Yoshi's New Island*, Kamek can wield a giant hammer several times his size with seemingly no effort.

In the Mario Party series, Kamek acts as a host for the boards, triggering certain events and often causing grief for players.

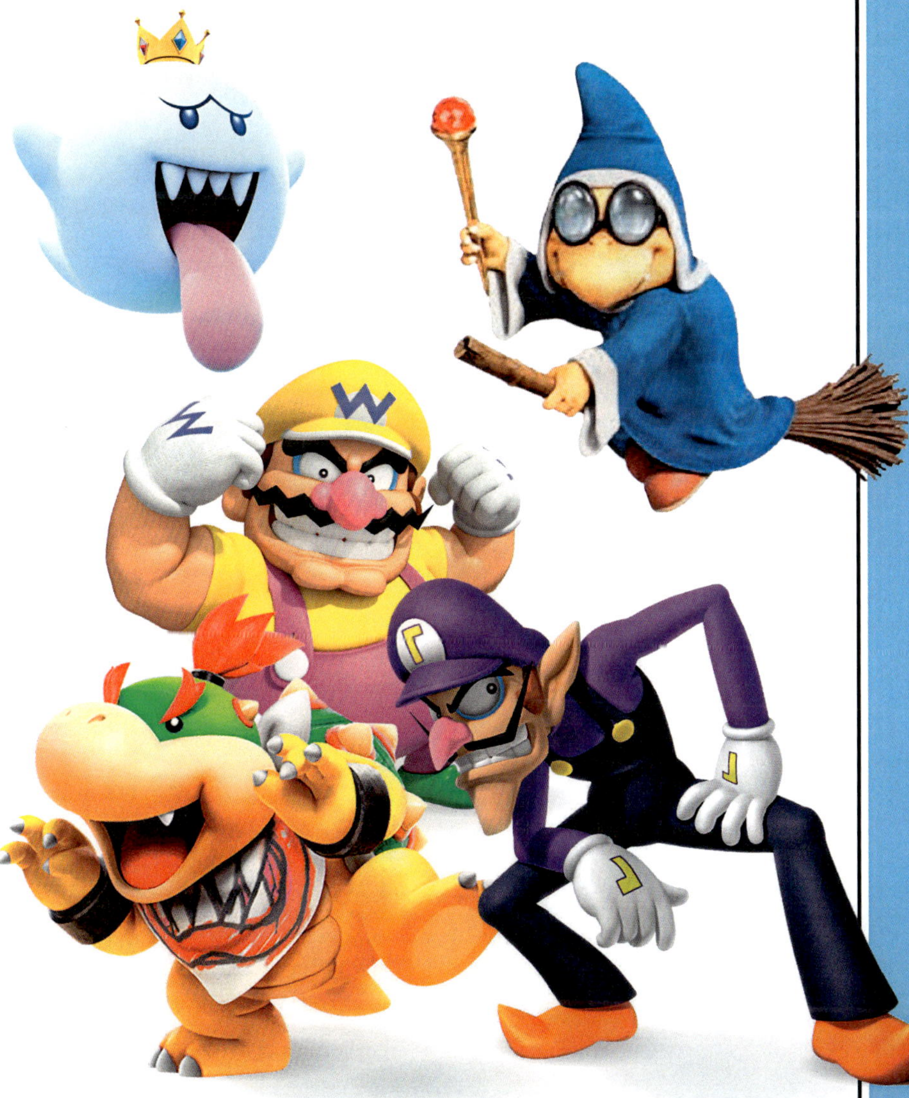

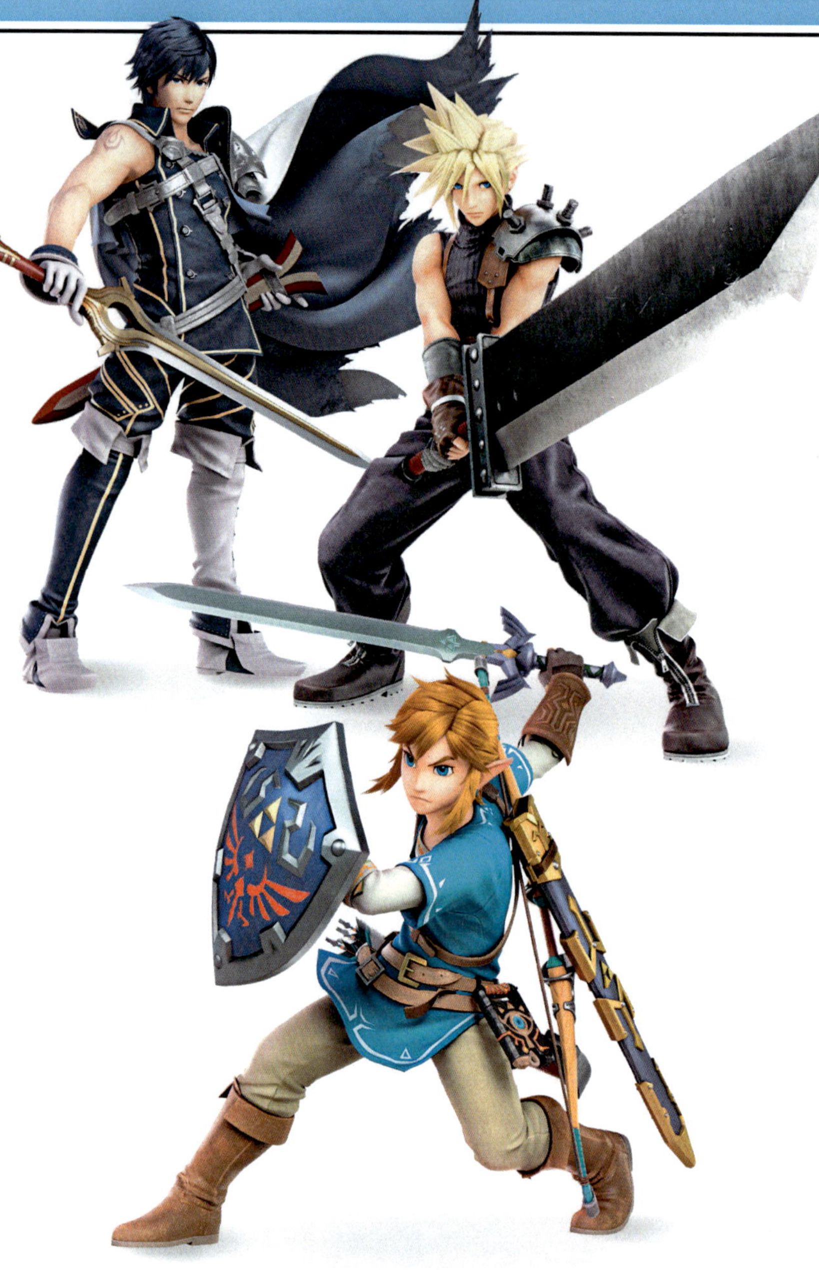

Friends of the Franchise

LINK

The Legend of Zelda is a creation of Shigeru Miyamoto's, the legendary Mario creator, so it's not surprising that the two franchises' main protagonists would cross paths from time to time. In 1992 Link first found himself in a Mario game, in *Super Mario Bros. & Friends: When I Grow Up* (a digital coloring game for the Microsoft Disk Operating System). Link also makes a small cameo in *Super Mario RPG: Legend of the Seven Stars*, released in 1996 on the SNES. He's found sleeping in a bed at the Rose Town inn, but since Link is generally a silent protagonist, talking to him triggers a *Legend of Zelda* melody instead of dialogue.

Mario and Link most frequently trade jabs in the long-running Super Smash series, in which Link (like Toon Link and Young Link) is a playable character, along with heroes from the wider Nintendo library.

CLOUD STRIFE

Clouds are common enemies in the Super Mario universe. In *Hotel Mario*, clouds appear to obscure the player's view, and in *Mario Kart* a Thunder Cloud sunders opponents into miniature versions of themselves. Cloud Strife is the main protagonist of *Final Fantasy VII*, developed by Square Enix. Cloud rubs elbows with Mario and friends in the Super Smash arenas. He is a downloadable character for *Super Smash Bros.* for Nintendo 3DS and *Super Smash Bros.* for Wii U, and an unlockable hero in *Super Smash Bros. Ultimate*. Players who purchase Cloud from the Nintendo e-shop also get Midgar, a stage based on the *Final Fantasy VII* setting.

CHROM

Players were first teased with the *Fire Emblem Awakening* protagonist in certain background scenes of *Super Smash Bros. 4*. Chrom was later included as Roy's echo fighter in *Super Smash Bros. Ultimate* in 2018 on the Nintendo Switch, facilitated by a wave of popular demand in Japan.

The sword fighter also dips his toes into the Warioverse, appearing in the WarioWare series through 5-Volt's aptly named microgame *Fire Emblem Awakening*. In the microgame the player controls Chrom in his quest to defeat Victor, an enemy boss character in the original game.

SONIC

Sonic is the protagonist of the SEGA-owned Sonic the Hedgehog series and appears in crossover titles alongside Mario in the Super Smash Bros. series and the Mario & Sonic series. The latter is a run of crossover sports games that began with *Mario & Sonic at the Olympic Games*, in 2007, tied to the Beijing 2008 Olympics.

Since the series began, the duo has faced off for every Olympic Games until the 2018 Winter Olympics in Pyeongchang, South Korea. The companies partnered up again for *Mario & Sonic at the Olympic Games Tokyo 2020* on the Nintendo Switch, which is the final entry in the series.

Although he doesn't physically appear in these games, scanning the Sonic amiibo onto the NFC touchpoint for *Mario Kart 8 Deluxe* and *Yoshi's Woolly World* unlocks aesthetics based on the speedy hedgehog.

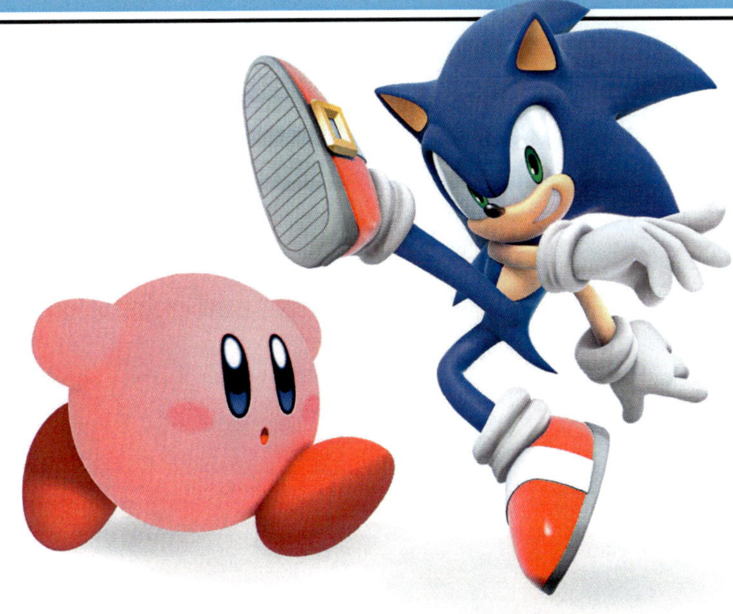

KIRBY

This plump hero lives in the kingdom of Dreamland on the Planet Popstar. Kirby's first appearance in the Super Mario franchise is in volume 5 of the manga series Super Mario-kun. When Mario and his friends are being chased by Boos, Mario and his allies mistake the round character for a sinister Boo, but after realizing their mistake they team up with Kirby to suck up their enemies.

Like many of the heroes on these pages, Kirby enters the Marioverse through the Super Smash Bros. games. Having debuted in the original Nintendo 64 version, Kirby utilizes jumping abilities to avoid attacks. He has a special Inhale move where he can suck up opponents and copy their abilities. Kirby makes a miniscule cameo in the original version of *Mario & Luigi: Superstar Saga*, released in 2003 on the Game Boy Advance. The player finds a poster at the Yoshi Theater advertising a movie called *Kirby Story*, with artwork featuring the titular character riding a Warp Star.

POKÉMON

Nintendo tied two of their most profitable IPs together starting with some of the earliest entries. In 1996's *Pokémon Red and Blue* there's a blink-and-you'll-miss-it Mario cameo in Saffron City. Checking a certain TV in the city triggers the player character to say that there's a game with Mario wearing a bucket on his head. The reference was kept in two years later for *Pokémon Yellow*. In 2015's *Mario Maker*, players can use a Mystery Mushroom to unlock various costumes for Mario. Nine of them are based on Pokémon.

A slew of Pokémon have joined the Super Smash Bros. roster over the years, including Ivysaur, Pikachu, Charizard, Pichu, and Squirtle. In some of the entries the player characters hero is the Pokémon Trainer and the individual Pokémon can be swapped in and out throughout the gameplay.

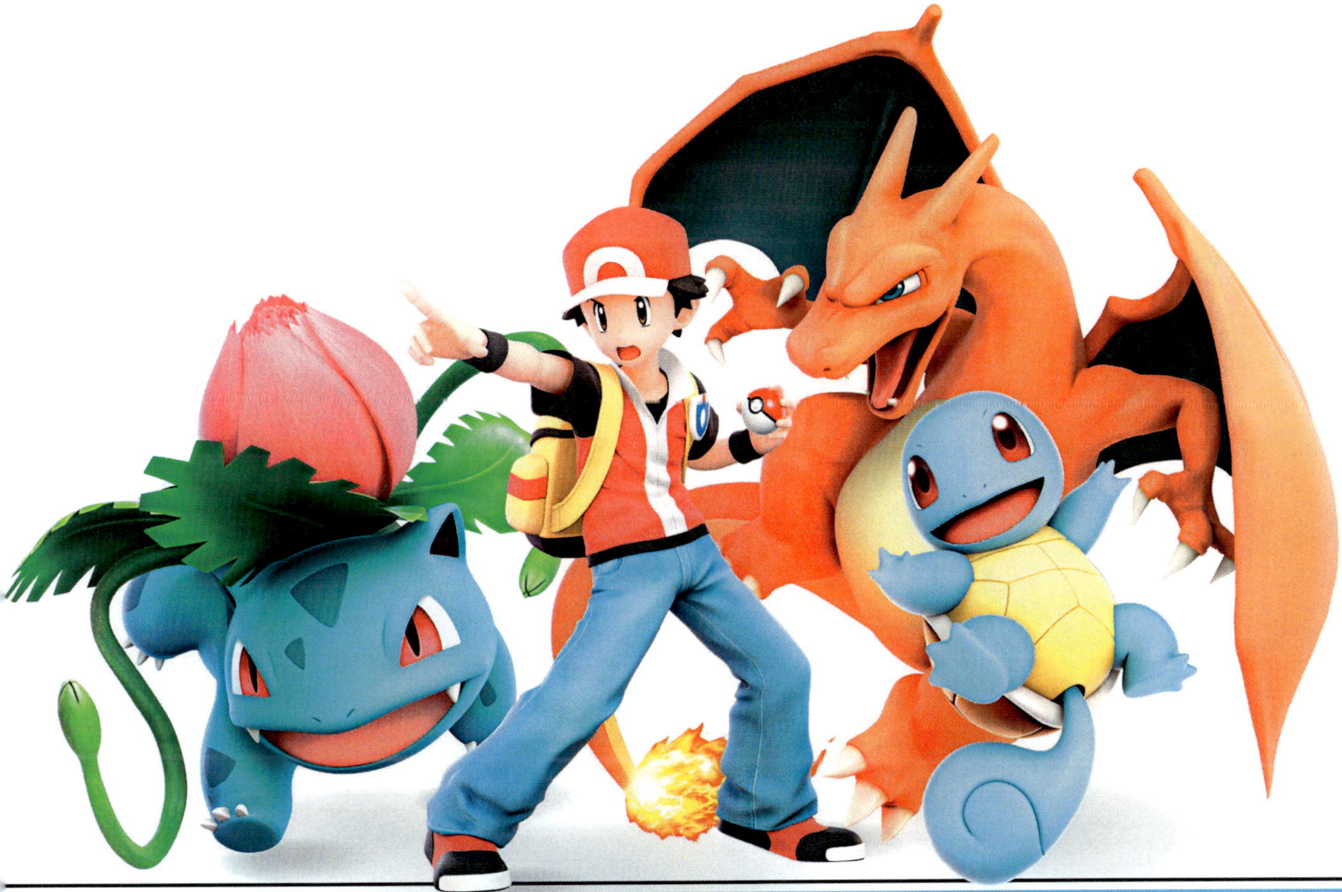

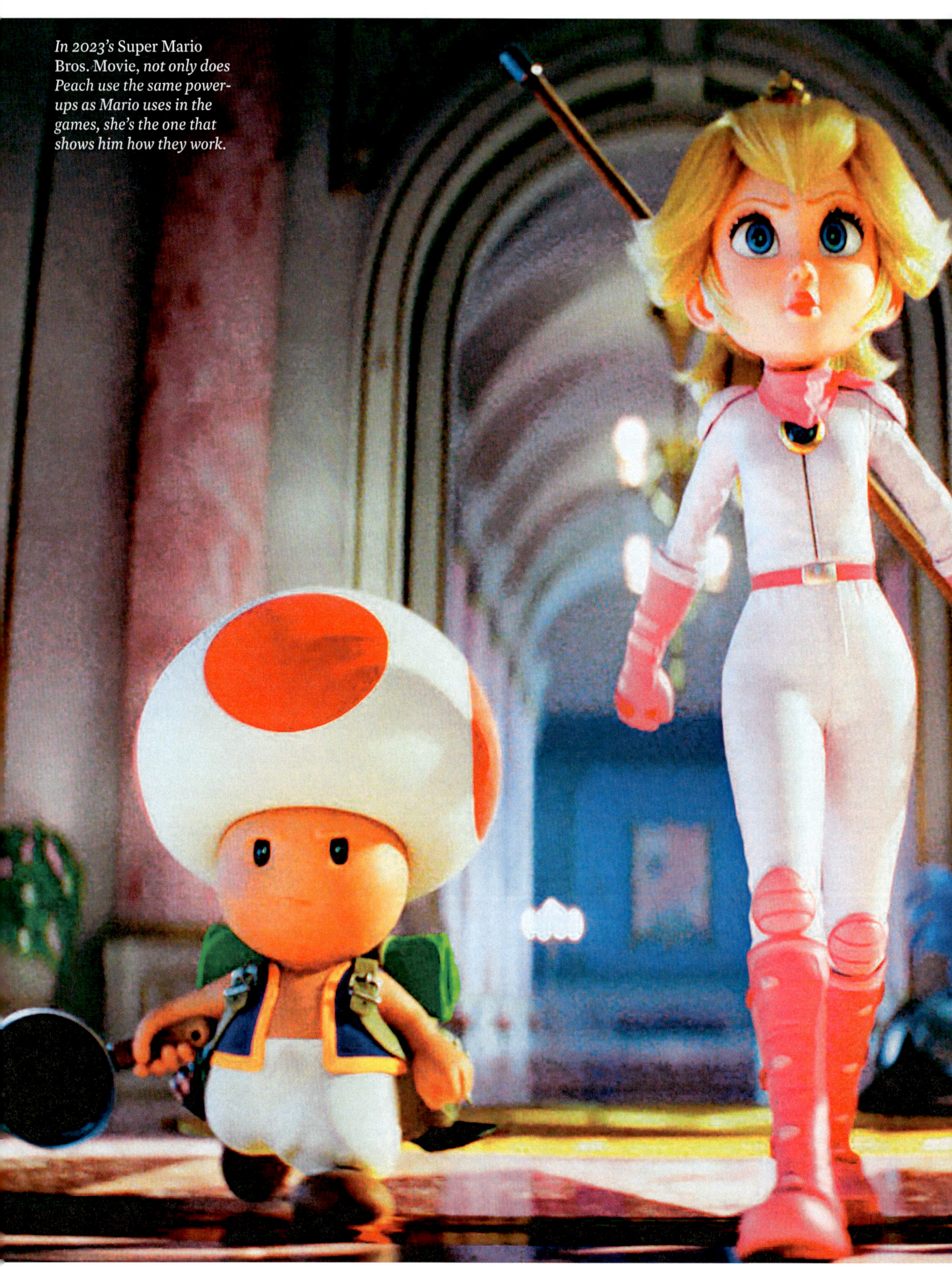

In 2023's Super Mario Bros. Movie, *not only does Peach use the same power-ups as Mario uses in the games, she's the one that shows him how they work.*

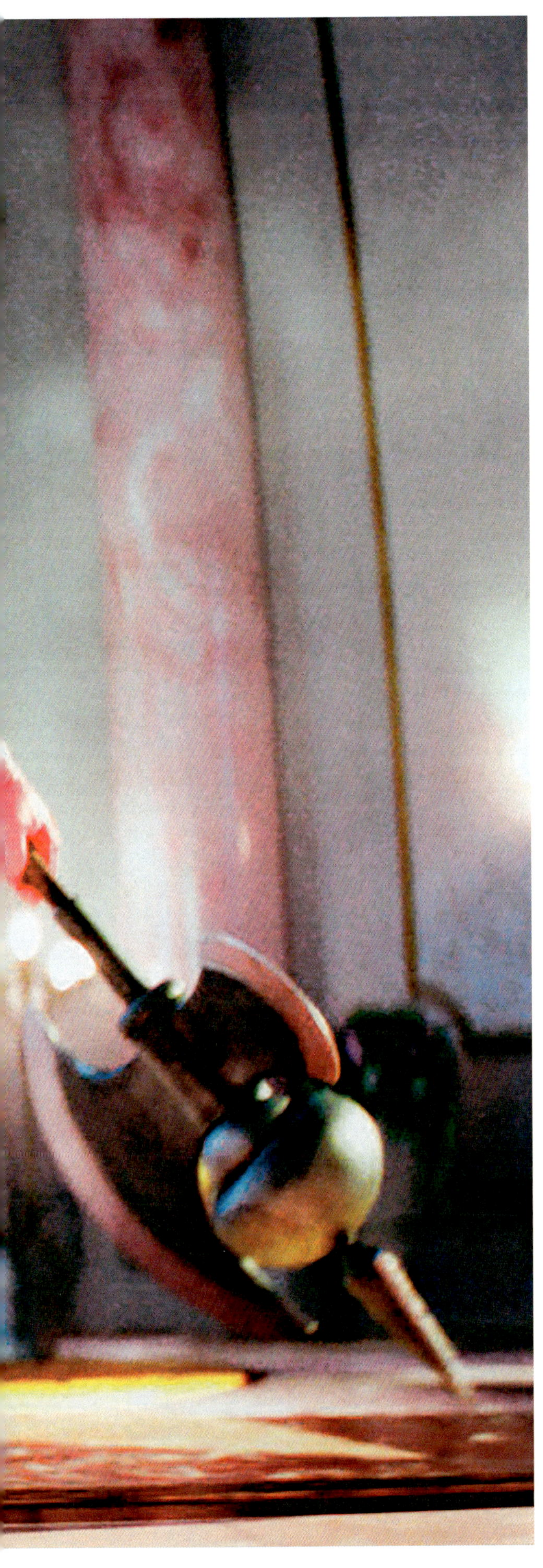

NOT A DAMSEL ANYMORE

Having once held the title of 'most kidnapped,' the franchise mainstay is finally fighting back.

BY COURTNEY MIFSUD INTREGLIA

I AM NOT A COMPETITIVE KARTER. A typical game night with my friends comes with a few guarantees. We'll play some Jackbox games, a round of Catan, or another board game. And we'll certainly be playing *Mario Kart*, specifically *Mario Kart 8 Deluxe* on the Switch. And I'm not very good at it. While my friends race through Thwomp Ruins, I'm spinning out in front of one of the titular Thwomps. As they weave through shortcuts in Cheep Cheep Beach, I'm in the water for the fourth or fifth time. I can't even attempt Rainbow Road without Smart Steering.

According to data scientist Antoine Mayerowitz, I might be playing the wrong character. In April 2024 she released extensive research on which *Mario Kart 8* builds would increase a player's chances for victory. While I often reached for speed demons Bowser and Wario, it turns out that Princess Peach should have been my main girl all along.

Mayerowitz's research examined 703,560 possible builds and employed the Pareto frontier, a set of solutions devised by 19th-century mathematician Vilfredo Pareto to identify the best trade-off between all objective functions. In the case of *Mario Kart 8*, the "functions" include acceleration and speed, while the "objective" is to win. According to Mayerowitz's research, the best build includes Peach behind the wheel.

Nintendo's leading lady retains an array of accolades — she golfs, go-karts, plays tennis, and has even competed in the Olympic Games. She's one of video games' oldest female characters and manages to do it all in her tulip-shaped gown. Yet for the first 38 years of Nintendo's games and media, Peach was woefully underutilized. Despite her athletic proficiencies, Peach's role in the vast majority of Mario games lies solely in her ability to get kidnapped... a lot. But recent entries, such as *Princess Peach Showtime!* and the *Super Mario Bros.* movie, highlight the strength and power of the blond princess.

Since her introduction, Princess Peach has been kidnapped more than a dozen times, namely by Bowser, the dragonlike villain deemed King Koopa. Peach's perpetual plight goes back to her debut in 1985's *Super Mario Bros.* on the NES, in which she was introduced as Princess Toadstool, the ruler of the Mushroom Kingdom. Toadstool appears in *Super Mario Bros.* as less of a person and more of an ambiguous dream. As players complete levels they are told by rescued Toads that "our princess is in another castle!" When you finish the game and rescue her, the princess thanks you and invites you to play again.

But that game's sequel, *Super Mario Bros. 2* brought Peach into the main fold. The 1988 game was the first time that the princess was a playable character. She was given a unique superpower: her pink billowing skirt enables her to hover in the air. And in retrospectives, Peach's role in the franchise's second entry was unique and powerful. "My favorite character, by far, was Princess Peach. I know Toad is the fastest (making for an ideal speedrunning character) and Luigi has the best jump, but Peach could briefly hover in the air, and using that flying technique was my favorite part of the game," wrote Peter Tieryas for Kotaku in 2019, more than 30 years since the game's release. "Princess Peach's flying ability brought a finesse to platforming, making obstacles more forgiving. Miss one of those Trouters jumping from a bottomless waterfall? Have Peach glide until the next Trouter jumps out of the water."

HER FIRST GAME

Nearly 20 years later, Peach finally earned her own game. The 2005 Nintendo DS platformer *Super Princess Peach* was the first, and — until 2024 — only game with Peach as the star. In typical Mario games,

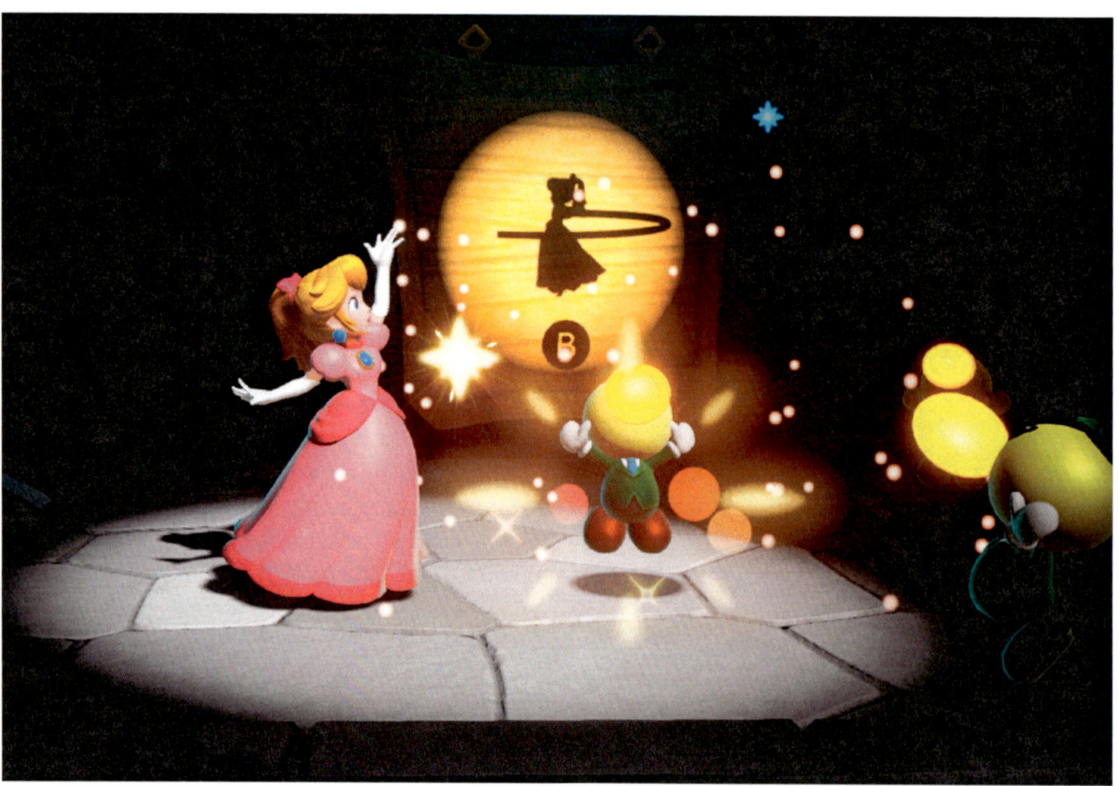

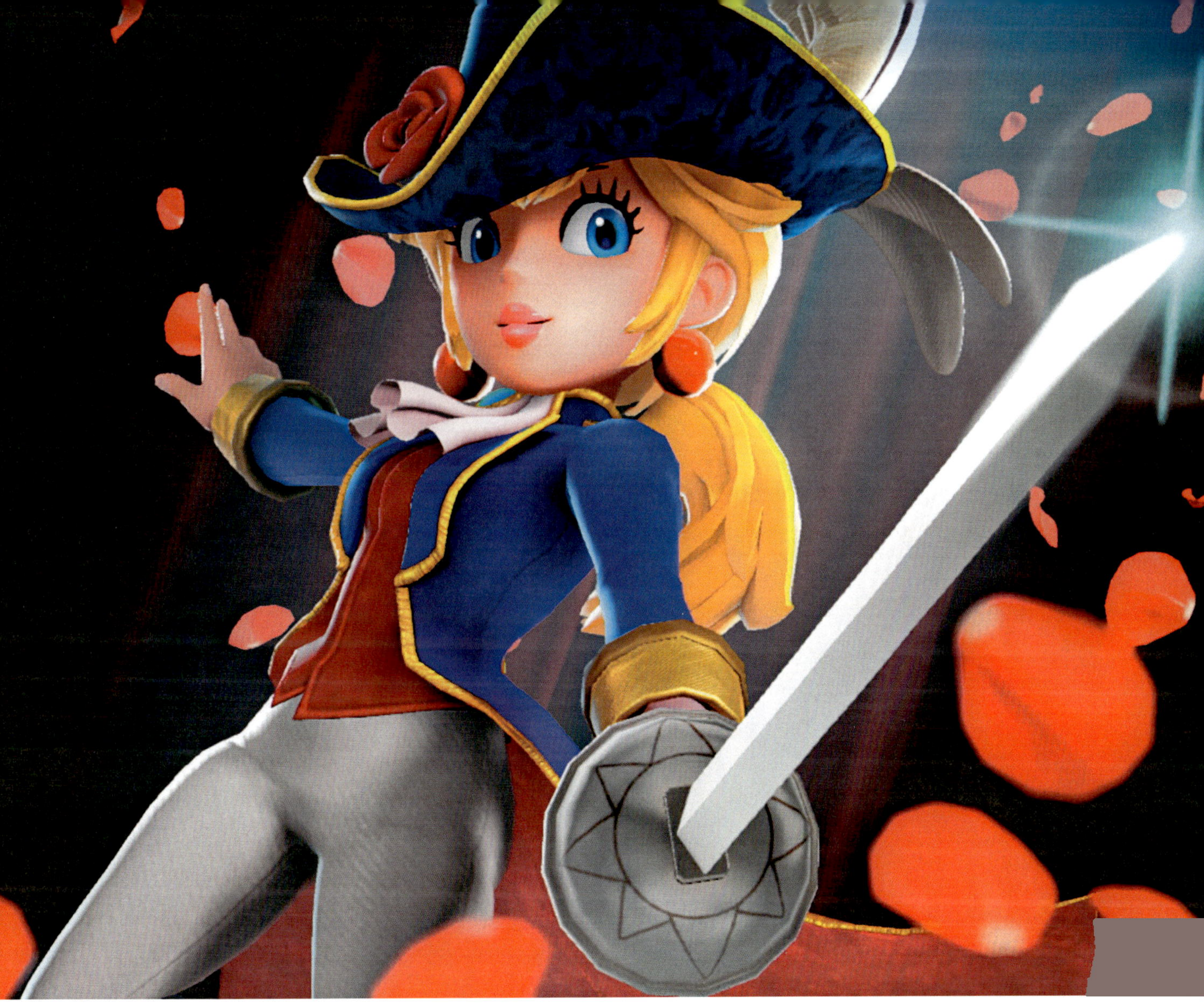

Princess Peach steps into more than 10 roles throughout 2024's Princess Peach Showtime!*, including Swordfighter Peach. Opposite, the helpful Theets work as employees of Sparkle Theater.*

the plumber has his sidekick and brother, Luigi. In *Super Princess Peach* the titular monarch has one too — a boy who transforms into a magical parasol named Perry.

While *Super Princess* plays like most Mario platform games, there's one feature that fuels Peach's powers and utilizes the DS's new touchscreen capabilities. According to Polygon, *Super Princess* was originally planned for the Game Boy Advance, but it was eventually brought forward to the then new Nintendo DS. That transition was evident in the implementation of the DS touchscreen.

As Peach, players can call upon four emotions, or Vibes, as the game describes them: Joy, Gloom, Rage, and Calm. Vibes are accessible by tapping the four corners of the DS touchscreen and letting Peach set objects on fire by tapping into her anger and soaking flames with tears with her dramatic "bawling."

Critic Anita Sarkeesian, in her 2013 video "Damsel in Distress: Part 3," — part of her *Tropes vs. Women in Video Games* series — argued that Super Princess Peach's mood-swing-based powers made the game a "train wreck of gender stereotypes." "Peach's powers are her out-of-control, frantic female emotions," Sarkeesian said. "She can throw a temper tantrum and rage her enemies to death, or bawl her eyes out and wash the bad guys away with tears. Essentially Nintendo has turned a PMS joke into their core gameplay mechanic." Sarkeesian also noted that although *Super Princess Peach* inverted the typical gender roles of the Super Mario games, Peach still manages to take a narrative backseat to her male costar, her sentient parasol. "Peach is not even featured in any of the game's narrative cutscenes, instead they all focus on the back story of her parasol, who it turns out is really a cursed boy named Perry," Sarkeesian said. "The dude in distress role reversal premise here feels like

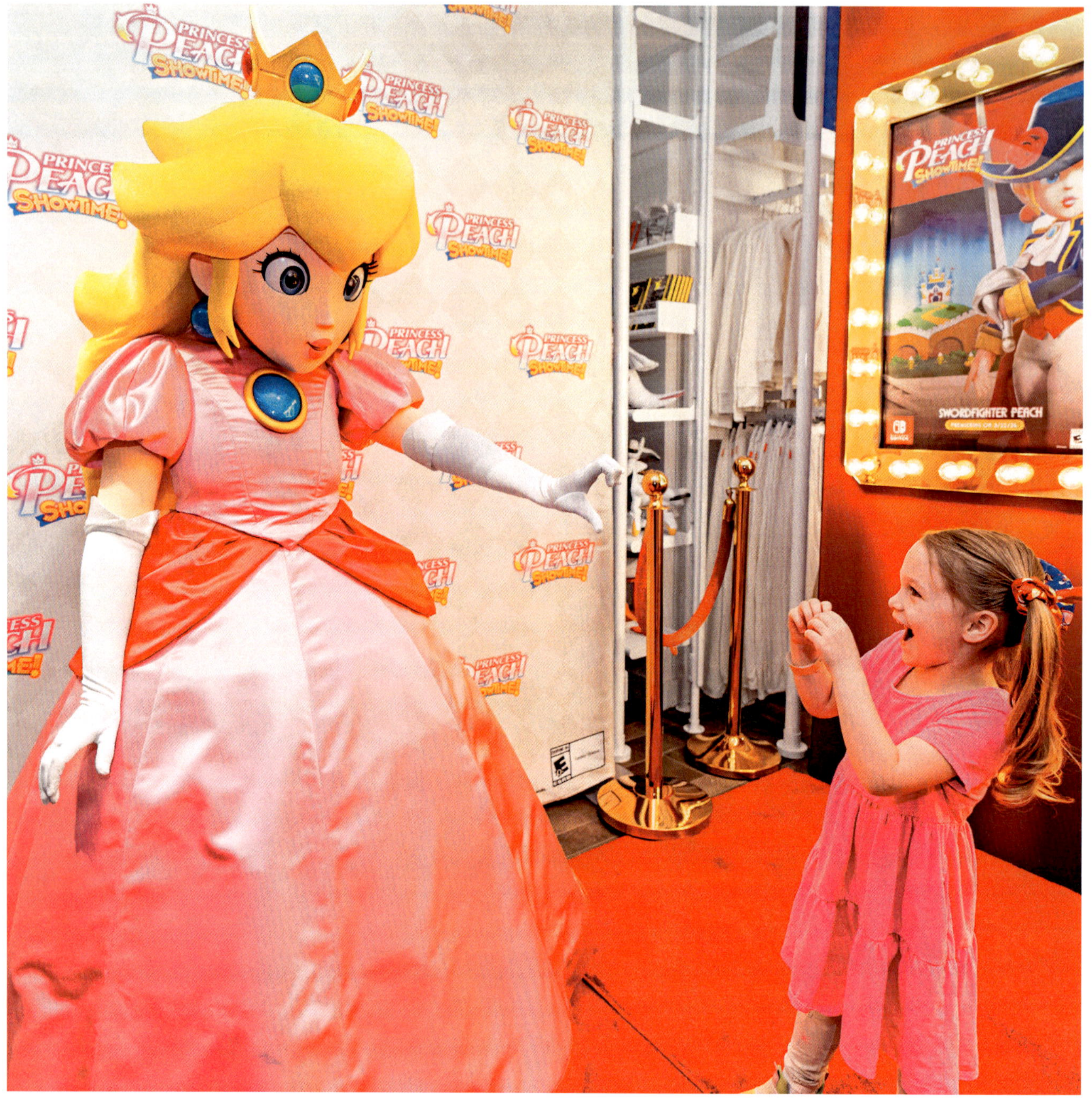

In 2024, in celebration of the release of Princess Peach Showtime!, *Nintendo hosted several meet-and-greets with fans. Attendees were able to play demo versions of the game.*

it's just intended as a lighthearted joke or niche market novelty."

Peach's debut game was an opportunity for the Nintendo audience to explore the character as an individual, but since its early marketing the publisher made clear that this is a "girl game" and added extra touches to promotional copies. "When *Super Princess Peach* arrived in the IGN offices, the box it came in literally permeated the air with an overwhelmingly flowery, peach scent. Call it a clue to where Nintendo's targeting its new platformer," wrote IGN's Craig Harris at the time. "Though the final, released game won't be covered in perfume, it should be clear to you just by the title what you're getting into: a Mario-style game that's more likely than not aimed at a more feminine, and less hardcore, girl audience." *Super Princess Peach* remains one of the lowest-selling Mario titles.

In the years that followed, Princess Peach has achieved playable character status more often, usually in spin-offs like the Mario Kart series of racing games, the Super Smash Bros. series of cross-franchise fighting games and various Mario-branded sports games.

Peach's perpetual victim status draws on a long and storied history regarding the damsel in distress trope. *The Ramayana*, an ancient Indian epic, is a cornerstone of Hinduism that dates back more than 2,000 years. In the tale, Rama must go on a fantastical journey with his brother Lakshmana to rescue his wife, Sita, from a terrifying monster, Ravana. *Super Mario Odyssey*, a 2017 game, has a similar plot, except the Lakshmana character isn't Mario's brother, Luigi, but instead a sentient cap, named Cappy.

A BLOCKBUSTER BEHEMOTH

"I'm taking you to see the princess. She can help you. She can do anything." That was one of the first mentions of Princess Peach in the 2023 blockbuster *The Super Mario Bros. Movie*. Toad greets Mario, who has just warped into the lush Mushroom Kingdom, and hears all about the plumber's plight. When faced with Mario's life or death quest to save his brother, the only answer is to bring him to meet the compassionate, fierce, and benevolent Princess Peach. Video game Peach had "stayed the 'damsel in distress' for a while," Mario creator Shigeru Miyamoto told *Variety* in 2023. "We tried to push [our desires for a more in-control princess in] the movie, and I think it was one of our first conversations, to make her the strong, powerful princess she was always meant to be." In the film, Peach travels to the kingdom of Donkey Kong to champion a wartime coalition against the evil Koopa Kingdom.

AFTER NEARLY 40 YEARS OF BEING SIDELINED AS A DAMSEL, PEACH IS FINALLY COMING INTO HER OWN AS A PRIMARY PROTAGONIST.

Not only is the princess a savvy negotiator, but she knows how to fight, and this time when Bowser and his minions think they've got the upper hand, Peach turns the tables and breaks free on her own. "Peach is more an empowered princess imagined for the current age. She's a respected ruler willing to engage in diplomacy as much as battle in order to protect her subjects and her Mushroom Kingdom," wrote Tracy Brown for the *Los Angeles Times* in 2023. "She's not at all intimidated by Bowser, a fire-breathing bully with a big army. And not only has she already mastered all the skills Mario needs to learn in order to survive his confrontation with their reptilian foe, she can do everything while wearing heels. This Peach is who you want saving you."

During Women's History Month in 2024, Nintendo released the second Peach-fronted game in their expansive library. *Princess Peach Showtime!* begins with Peach and her Toads at the Sparkle Theater — where the Sour Bunch, a troupe of anthropomorphic grapes, attempt to ruin the performance. Peach is separated from her Toad posse and partners up with the theater's guardian, Stella, a magical talking ribbon.

Throughout the game, players explore the game's side-scroller levels as Peach and gather collectibles, unlock boss battles, and progress through the various levels. An invisible audience applauds whenever Peach reaches a checkpoint or does a power pose. Each level is a different play being perfromed in the theater, with Peach as the star. "As a fan of magical girl anime, I enjoyed how, instead of just giving Peach a weapon (like the Poltergust 3000 in *Luigi's Mansion*) or a power-up (like the cat suit in *Bowser's Fury*), Peach activates the unique abilities — or "Sparkla" — of each play's main actor through a Sailor Moon-esque transformation, transfiguring her outfit in a flashy cutscene," noted NPR's Rakiesha Chase-Jackson in her review of the game. "These Sparkla metamorphoses are visually wondrous, but not all are created equal. I hope Nintendo revisits Kung Fu Peach, Ninja Peach, and Dashing Thief Peach in future games. But I dreaded having to play as Figure Skater Peach or Mermaid Peach. As cool as it was to control sea creatures through song or spin through graceful ice choreography, it was way more satisfying to take out guards as a stealthy ninja or navigate puzzling levels as a master spy with a grappling hook."

Despite the pirouettes, *Princess Peach Showtime!* sold a total of 1.22 million units in the first 10 days of its release, according to financial data Nintendo released in May of 2024.

After nearly 40 years of being sidelined as the franchise's main damsel, Princess Peach is finally coming into her own as a primary protagonist. With rumors of a Peach-focused feature film and the potential for new games on the horizon, her story is just getting started. In the meantime, I'll take a cue from data scientist Antoine Mayerowitz and start working on *Mario Kart* builds that involve Peach. Maybe Rainbow Road isn't so daunting after all.

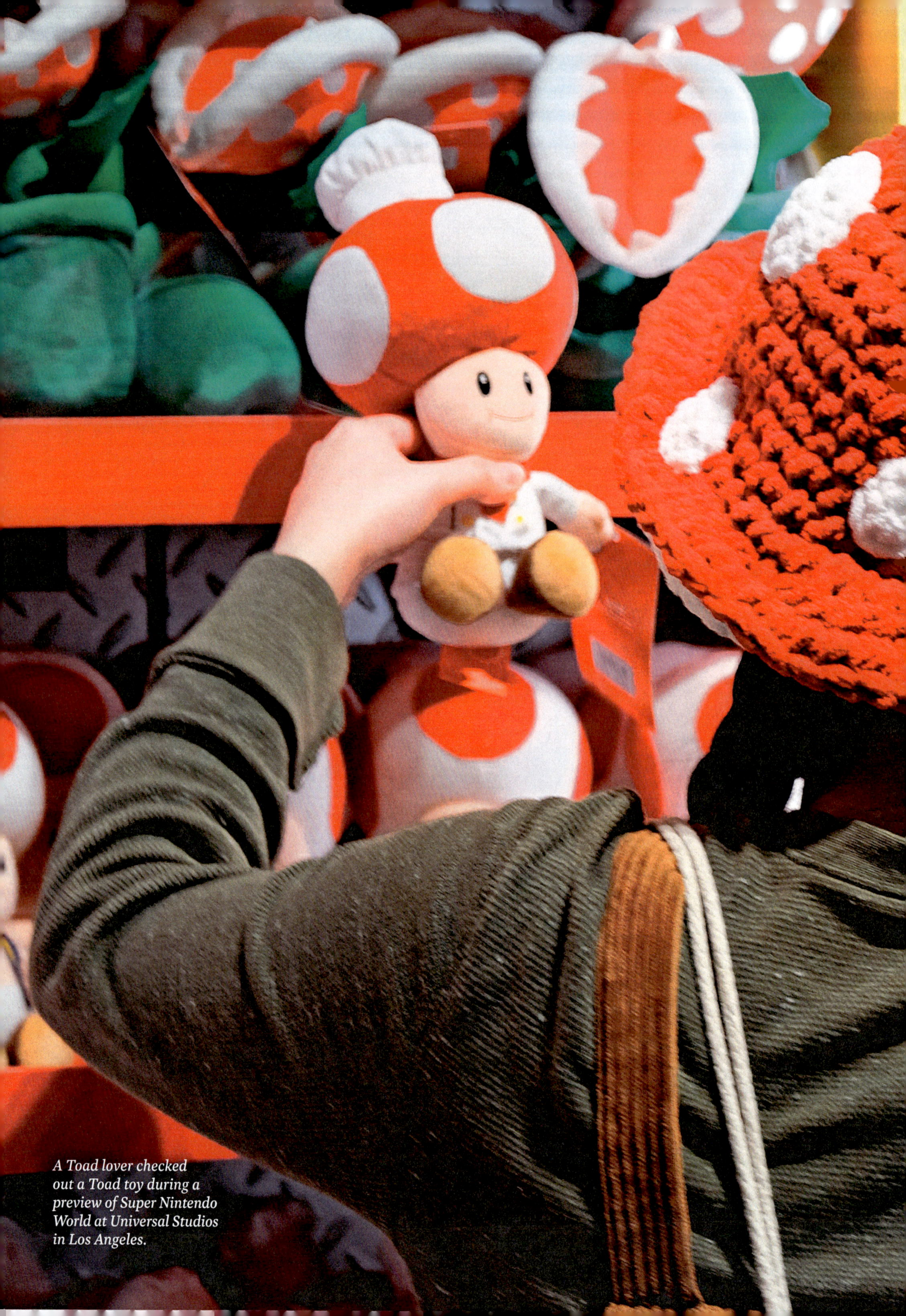

A Toad lover checked out a Toad toy during a preview of Super Nintendo World at Universal Studios in Los Angeles.

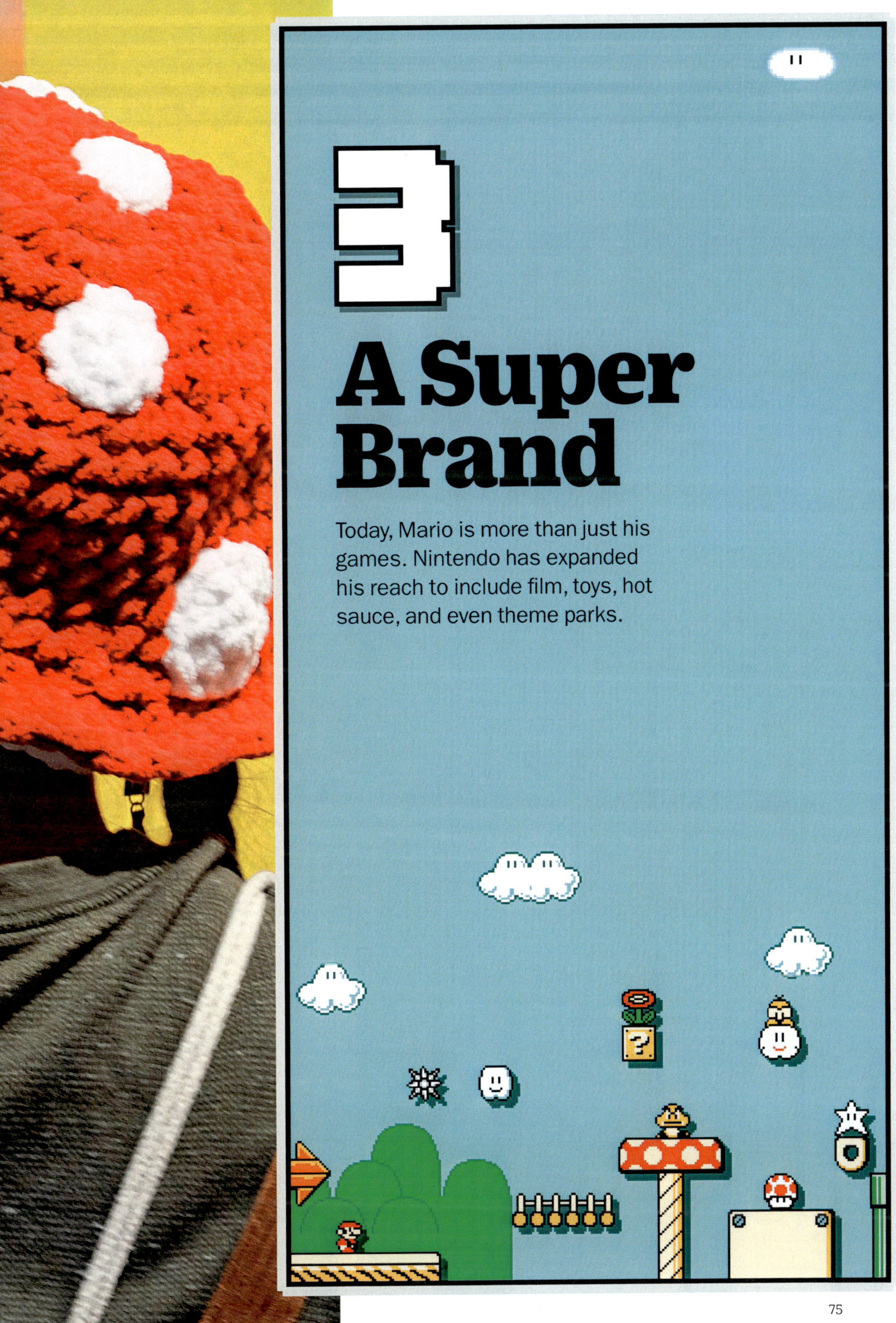

3

A Super Brand

Today, Mario is more than just his games. Nintendo has expanded his reach to include film, toys, hot sauce, and even theme parks.

WHY SUPER MARIO WORKS ON FILM

Video game movies are a tough endeavor to get right. Yet *Super Mario Bros.* figured out a way to perfect the formula.

BY CHRIS NASHAWATY

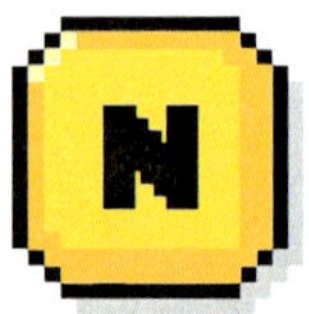

OTHING IS HARDER TO PREDICT than the movie business. Still, what occurred over the first weekend in April 2023 seemed to catch everyone in Hollywood napping. During that extended, five-day holiday frame, theater owners braced themselves for the annual onslaught of ticket buyers who had made a habit out of flocking to the movies over Easter. For the industry, this period each spring had become one of the most lucrative patches of real estate of the calendar year. It was when Universal rolled out its 2015 tentpole *Furious 7*, the latest chapter in its most precious franchise. It's also when Warner Bros. released its 2016 superhero mash-up, *Batman v Superman: Dawn of Justice*, perhaps the most anticipated DC picture of the decade.

By the time that Easter weekend rolled around in early 2023, North America's multiplexes were already doing a brisk business with the latest big-budget offerings from Keanu Reeves (*John Wick: Chapter 4*), Matt Damon and Ben Affleck (*Air*), and a trio of sequels from established franchises (*Scream VI*, *Creed III*, and *Shazam! Fury of the Gods*). Needless to say, these were some of Tinseltown's biggest and most bankable heavyweights. And yet, the film that would end up hijacking the holiday — the entire spring actually — was an animated kids' movie about two Italian American brothers with bushy mustaches and questionable plumbing skills who had first appeared on the pop culture radar in a Nintendo video game back in the 1980s.

During its first week in theaters, Universal's *The Super Mario Bros. Movie* would pull in more than $240 million. And while the reviews weren't over the moon, audiences fell in love again with the outer-borough pipe jockeys, Mario and Luigi. In its blockbuster initial run, the film would rack up $574.9 million domestically and an even more impressive $787.6 million abroad, bringing its total worldwide haul to a staggering $1.36 billion. That's billion with a *b*. When the year finally came to a close, the boys from Brooklyn used their power-ups to claim the No. 2 spot on the list of the biggest box office hits of the year, sandwiched between *Barbie* (No. 1) and *Oppenheimer* (No. 3).

The film's hand-over-fist success was especially astonishing not just because the nation's critics had given it a chilly reception, but also because the last

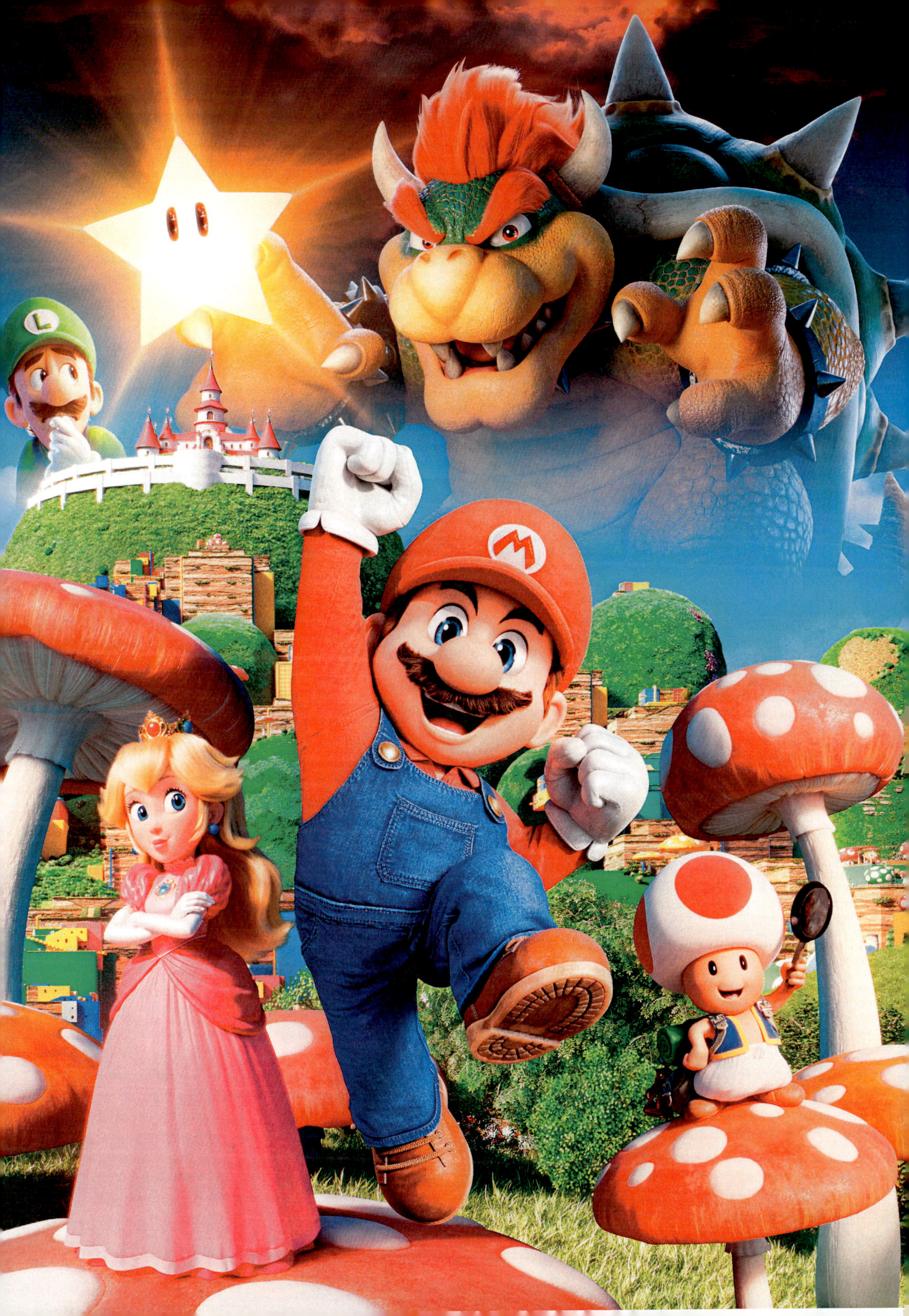

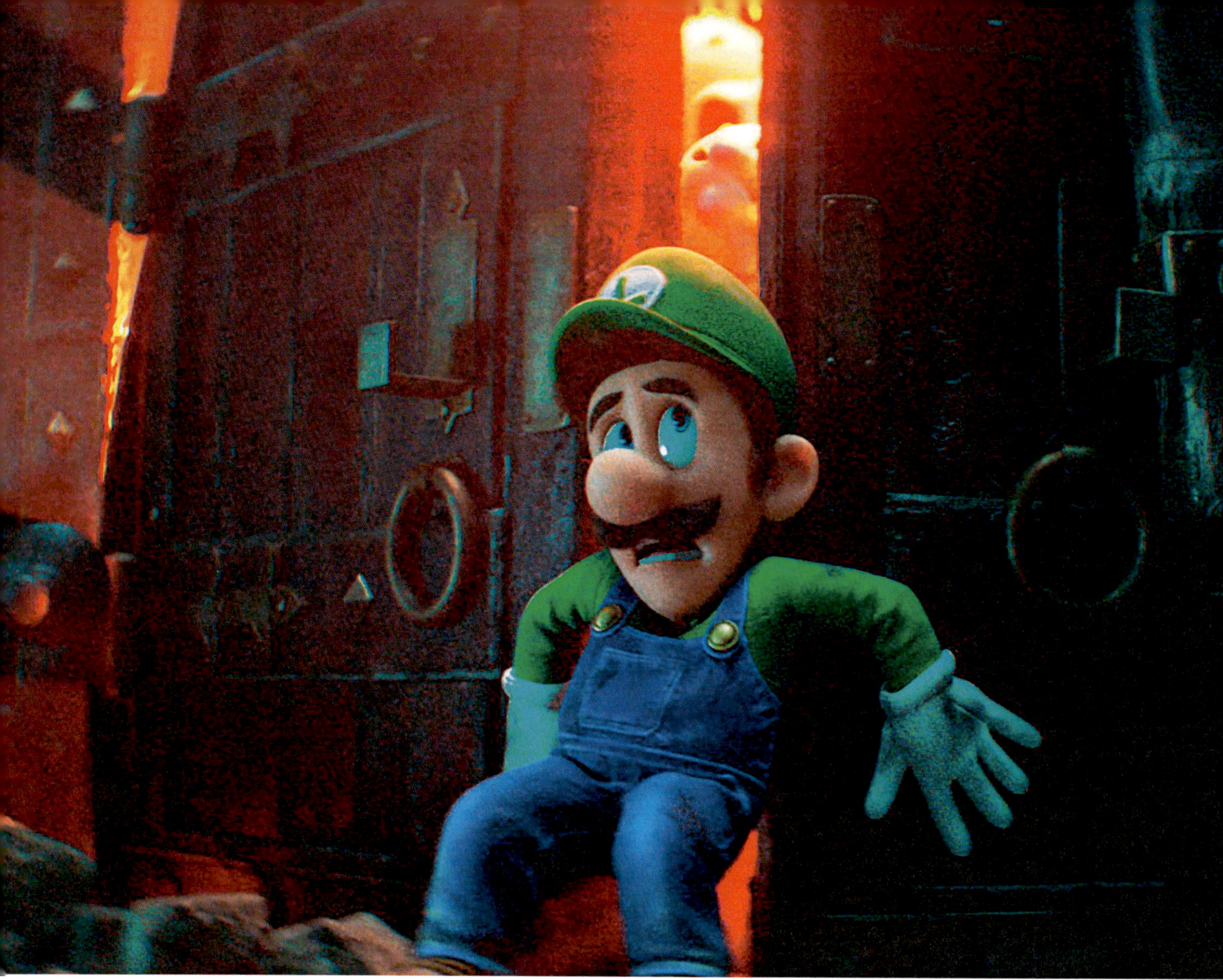

In the film, Luigi is separated from his brother and gets stuck in the Dark Lands. Opposite, Chris Pratt and Charlie Day voiced Mario and Luigi, respectively.

time that the brothers had appeared on the big screen, it did not go nearly as well. As the older gamers out there will recall — some traumatically, no doubt — 1993's live-action *Super Mario Brothers*, starring Bob Hoskins as Mario and John Leguizamo as Luigi, was one of the most reviled box office duds of the '90s. The critics hated it, of course. But so did most of the folks with Nintendo consoles at home who were primed, pumped, and predisposed to love it. Instead, they got what the *Chicago Sun-Times*' Roger Ebert would call "a complete waste of time and money."

Today, the original *Super Mario Bros.* from the '90s is regarded as the first big-screen adaptation of a video game. A trial balloon that came off like a lead weight. And after it quickly slinked its way out of theaters, many predicted that the nascent trend of video game movies was over before it even had a chance to begin. But, in truth, the wave of joystick IP was just getting started. *Street Fighter. Mortal Kombat. Resident Evil.* They just kept coming like an endless string of barrels being hurled by a giant gorilla. *Lara Croft: Tomb Raider. Max Payne. Prince of Persia: The Sands of Time. Assassin's Creed.* The list went on and on. Some of these films would do well at the box office. But few managed to truly spark the imaginations of rabid gamers, especially as their inevitable sequels began to trickle out. Hollywood just couldn't seem to give up on the dream of video game adaptations. Then, in the spring of 2023, the studios' persistence finally paid off.

So why did *The Super Mario Bros. Movie* succeed where so many other video game movies had crashed and burned? Well, the headline of *Variety*'s review of the film hints at one of the main reasons: "Sheer animated fun, and the rare video game movie that gives you a prankish, video game buzz." Yes, *The Super Mario Bros. Movie* was . . . fun. But obviously, there's more to its triumph than that. After all, when a movie makes more than a billion dollars, it tends to be because a number of things went right at the same time — a box office perfect storm. We dug in and came up with eight reasons why Mario and Luigi finally won over old fans and created a generation of new ones along the way.

MAKE IT FOR FANS, NOT CRITICS

If you look up *The Super Mario Bros. Movie* on the popular review aggregator rottentomatoes.com, two numbers will jump out: 59 percent and 95 percent. That first number is the percentage of critics who gave the film a positive review; the second is the percentage of fans who did. That's a pretty big disparity. But the more you think about it, the more it makes sense. Since the earliest days of video games turned into movies, critics have given the impression that they're holding their noses while rendering a verdict. The truth is, some movies just aren't made with critics in mind. This may result in the movie having a green "rotten tomato" splat next to it, but that doesn't take into consideration how fans felt — what is reflected in the film's 95 percent favorability with folks who actually forked over 15 bucks to see it. This is what industry watchers mean when they call a movie "critic proof."

The *Super Mario Bros. Movie* was always targeted at the fans first and foremost. The plot, which serves up some welcome backstory about Mario and Luigi and their Italian American Brooklyn family, tells the story of how the plumber siblings get sucked into a portal underneath New York City and are then separated. Mario winds up in Princess Peach's shiny-happy Mushroom Kingdom, while Luigi ends up in the nightmarish Dark Lands, lorded over by the nasty Bowser. Mario and the Princess enlist the help of Cranky Kong's army (including his son, Donkey Kong) to defeat Bowser and his Koopa-and-Goomba army and get Luigi back safely, all while stopping the smitten Bowser's designs on the Princess and her peaceful homeland. Most of this tracks with the Super Mario canon and won't ruffle the feathers of longtime lovers of the games.

During Marvel's extended reign as Hollywood's box office alpha dog — a reign which kicked off with the release of the first *Iron Man* in 2008 — the studio leaned into "fan service." In other words, it sprinkled in nostalgic references and deep cuts to appeal to its most loyal disciples. These Easter Eggs make fans feel included and appreciated rather than taken for granted. *The Super Mario Bros. Movie* wisely took a page from Marvel's playbook, sprinkling in callbacks like chases that take the characters through labyrinths of pipes, leaping from one floating brick bridge to another, the giddy sights and sounds of power-ups, and a climactic Mario Kart chase along a rainbow track where stray banana peels threaten to send cars off the side of the road. It gives you the

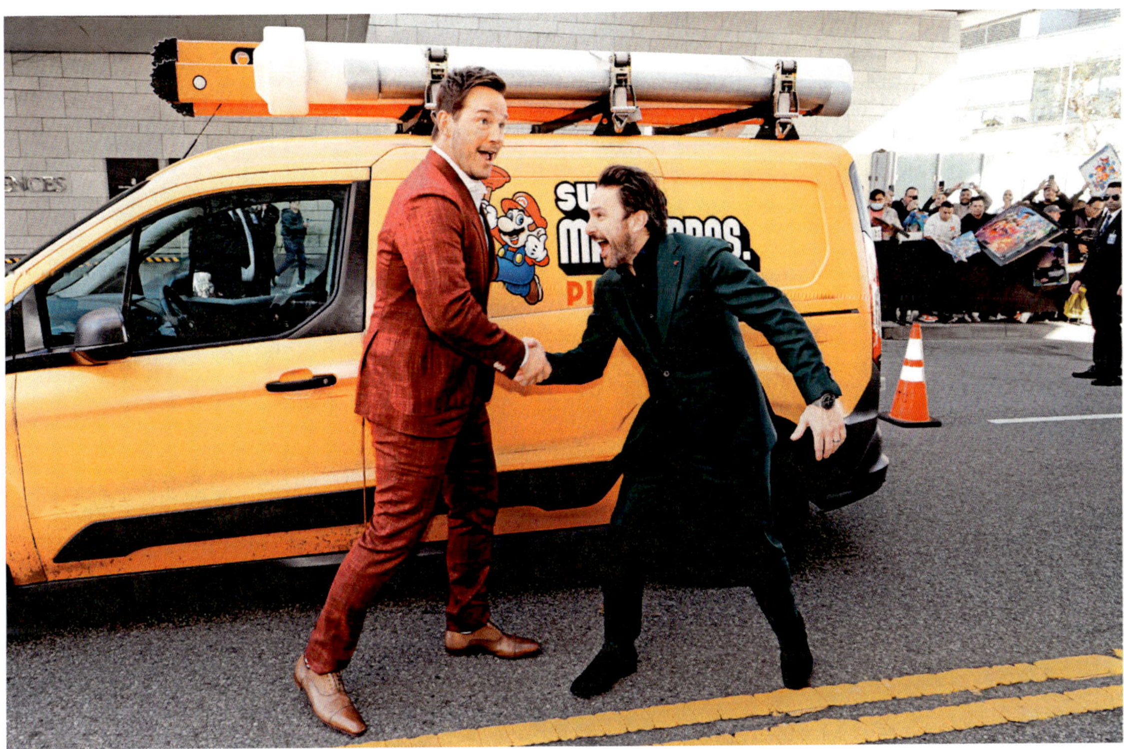

same sensation as playing with your Nintendo Switch — something that the movie's computer animation achieves far better than the 1993 film's live-action. Tossing in well-known characters, like Bowser as the film's villain, helps too.

As a result, young fans in their peak gaming years felt like *The Super Mario Bros. Movie* belonged to them. Which is why many of them watched the movie more than once. Want proof? All you need to do is take one look at how the film fared in its second life after it left theaters. On Netflix, for example, *The Super Mario Bros. Movie* was the streaming giant's fifth-most-watched movie for the first half of 2024. Yes, there were undoubtedly some new viewers factored in to that success, but many of them were returning ones who wanted to watch and parse the movie a second or third time.

MAKE IT FOR KIDS, BUT DON'T FORGET ABOUT THE PARENTS

Opting for animation over live action guaranteed that younger viewers would be the target demo for the film. But quality is important too. Enter the CG wizards at Illumination Entertainment, the house that the Minions built. Illumination isn't just an animation company, it's an imprimatur of quality with the stellar track record to back it up. The studio is responsible for the beloved *Despicable Me* movies as well as the *Sing* films. The *Super Mario Bros. Movie*'s directors, Aaron Horvath and Michael Jelenic, both had previous credits on various *Teen Titans* projects — another franchise that knows how to walk the fine line between frenetic, sugar-rush energy and cheeky, referential humor. Meanwhile, writer Matthew Fogel not only wrote the script for Illumination's *Minions:*

Princess Peach, voiced by Anya Taylor-Joy (opposite), travels to Kong Island to convince its ruler to join her cause.

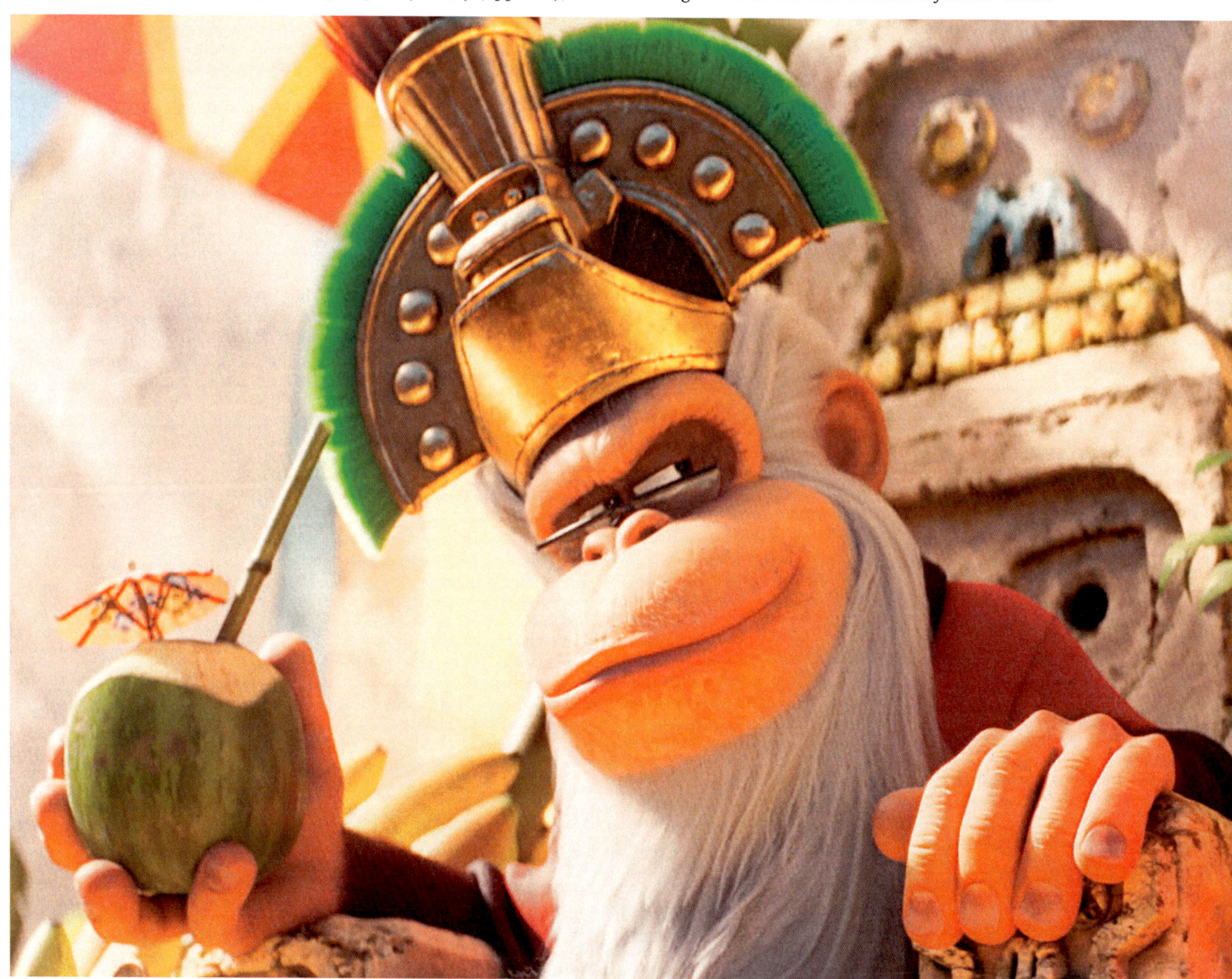

The Rise of Gru, he also penned the screenplay for *The Lego Movie 2,* the sequel to what remains the creative high-water mark of the toys-to-film category.

But if all it took to make a smash hit kids' movie was to barrage the screen with a bunch of caffeinated mayhem and schoolyard jokes for the kiddies, everyone would be able to gross a billion dollars at the box office. It's not that simple. One of the main takeaways from Pixar's domination of the kids' movie landscape for the past three decades is that in addition to serving up laughs to the children in the audience, you also need to give their parents a reason to pay attention and be entertained.

In *The Super Mario Bros. Movie*, that nod to older ticket buyers came in the form of the film's carefully curated retro soundtrack, which included a clever music cue from Quentin Tarantino's *Kill Bill* to introduce an early battle scene, as well as MTV-era tracks by a-ha ("Take On Me"), Bonnie Tyler ("Holding Out for a Hero"), AC/DC ("Thunderstruck"), and the Beastie Boys ("No Sleep Till Brooklyn"). Do throwaway lines like "It's on like Donkey Kong" go over your typical 8-year-old's head? Maybe. But so be it. You've got to keep parents laughing, otherwise they'll file out to the lobby and look at their phones while their kids watch the movie.

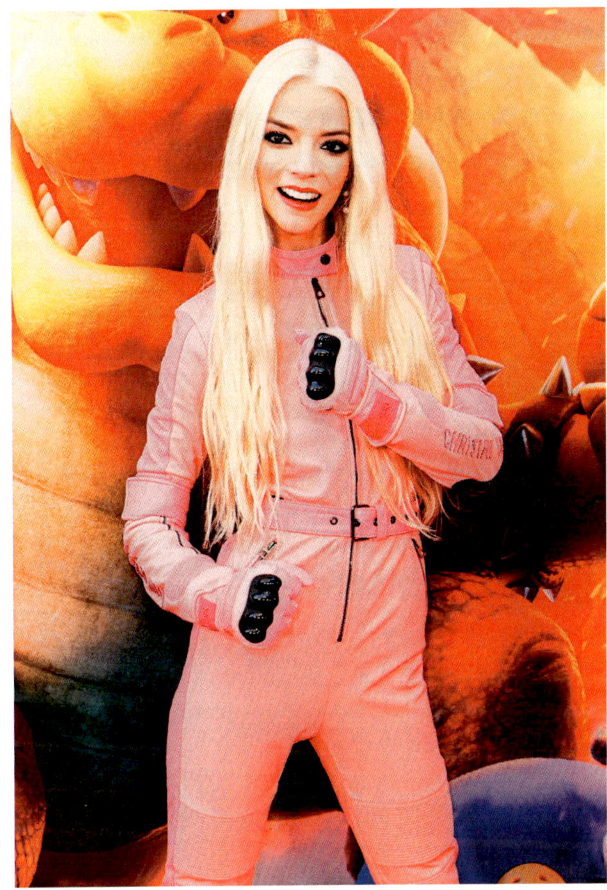

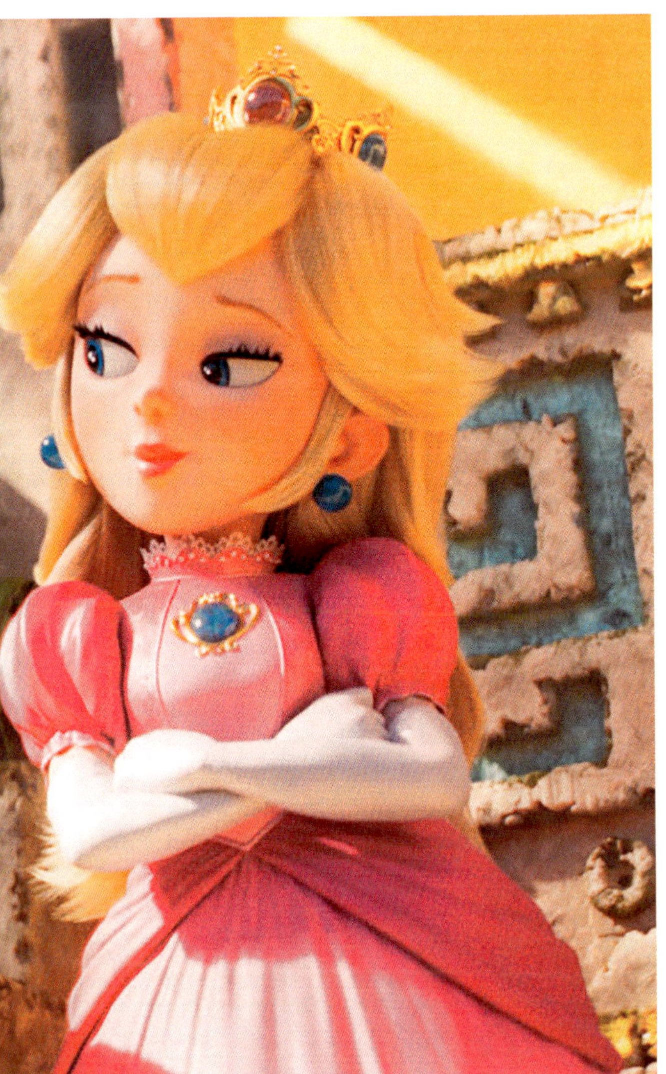

ADD A HEAVY DOSE OF STAR POWER

If you're a Hollywood actor, there's really no better paycheck in the business than the one that comes attached to doing voice work in an animated movie. You can roll into the recording booth unshowered and in baggy, dirty sweatpants. Hiring big-name stars is nothing new when it comes to creating buzz for video game movies, but it isn't a foolproof guarantee of success. All you have to do is look at The Rock's *Rampage* or Kevin Hart's *Borderlands*. Both underwhelming despite the presence of the biggest names in Tinseltown. No, it has to be the right stars, especially in animation, when you don't have the luxury of seeing the voice actor's face.

In *The Super Mario Bros. Movie*, the all-star lineup that lends its tonsils to the picture includes Chris Pratt, who already has a leg up in the genre thanks to his turn as nice-guy hero Emmet in *The Lego*

Movie, not to mention the kid-approved *Guardians of the Galaxy* and *Jurassic World* films. Then there's *School of Rock* and *Jumanji* star Jack Black as Bowser, Charlie Day as Luigi (granted, his claim to fame, *It's Always Sunny in Philadelphia*, is hardly for kids, but he does possess the sort of excitable, helium-pitched delivery that's catnip for tykes) and Seth Rogen, whose kid-targeted vocal credits include *The Lion King*, *Kung Fu Panda*, and *Chip n' Dale: Rescue Rangers*, and who is perfectly cast as the big and lovably dim Donkey Kong in the movie. These stars hit the perfect sweet spot for kids and are instantly recognizable to their parents.

AND A DOSE OF GIRL POWER

As much as video games are stereotyped to be the domain of boy gamers, the truth is girls play them too. And they deserve to be catered to as much as the little guys. While their older sisters can watch the harder-edged exploits of someone like Milla Jovovich in the *Resident Evil* movies, the inclusion of Princess Peach as one of Super Mario's main characters is an incredibly canny move. Even smarter was making the Peach (who's voiced by Anya Taylor-Joy) not just some helpless damsel in distress who requires saving. With her saucer-sized anime eyes, she's a woman with power (she benevolently rules over the Mushroom Kingdom) who is as brave and independent and gung-ho — if not more so — than the bumbling, accident-prone boys from Brooklyn.

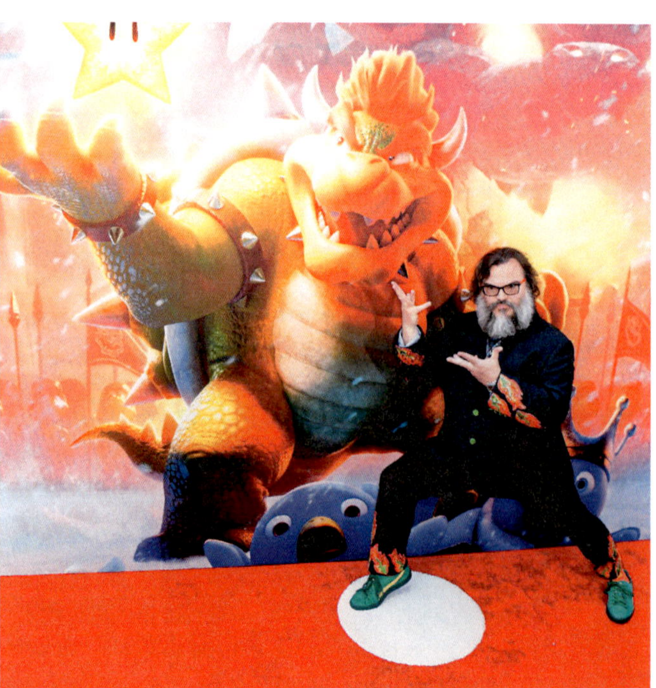

A HANDS-ON NINTENDO

For years, the Japanese gaming behemoth was happy to take a backseat when it came to its participation with big-ticket intellectual property spin-offs like movies. No doubt still scarred from the 1993 Mario disaster, the company merely licensed their products for others to do as they saw fit. Said Mario's creator Shigeru Miyamoto, "We were fearful of all the failure of past IP adaptations, where there's a license and a distance between the original creators and the creators of the films. The fans get outraged and mad because the studios didn't do justice to the original work. We really didn't want a backlash."

But if you're at all concerned with quality control (not to mention fan sentiment), then you have to get your hands a little dirty. Nintendo no doubt paid close attention to rival SEGA's success with 2020's *Sonic the Hedgehog*. The Sonic movie was SEGA's first toe-dip into the world of hands-on movie producing (in partnership with Paramount) and ended up pulling in $319.7 million in theaters worldwide despite being released just a month before Covid darkened multiplexes around the globe. No one knows the universe of Mario better than Nintendo and that comes across on screen thanks to Miyamoto being an active producer on *The Super Mario Bros. Movie*.

THROW IN AN INSPIRING MESSAGE

Another reason why parents were so willing to take their kids to see Mario and Luigi's big-screen hijinks probably has to do with the film's feel-good themes. A ragtag group of outmanned, underdog heroes band together to defeat a powerful and nefarious foe? Check. Hard work, tenacity, perseverance, and positivity pay off? Check and check. But if *The Super Mario Bros. Movie* just treated these wholesome values as mandatory items to be ticked off on a checklist, the film wouldn't work as well as it does — or have the same blast of joy. The lessons in the movie are deeply felt. In fact, you would need to be made of stone not get a lump in your throat when Mario and Luigi are separated in the film and Luigi has a flashback to his big brother sticking up for him against a group of bullies when they were little kids. This was a surprisingly poignant, first-act-of-Pixar's-*Up*-level emotional sucker-punch.

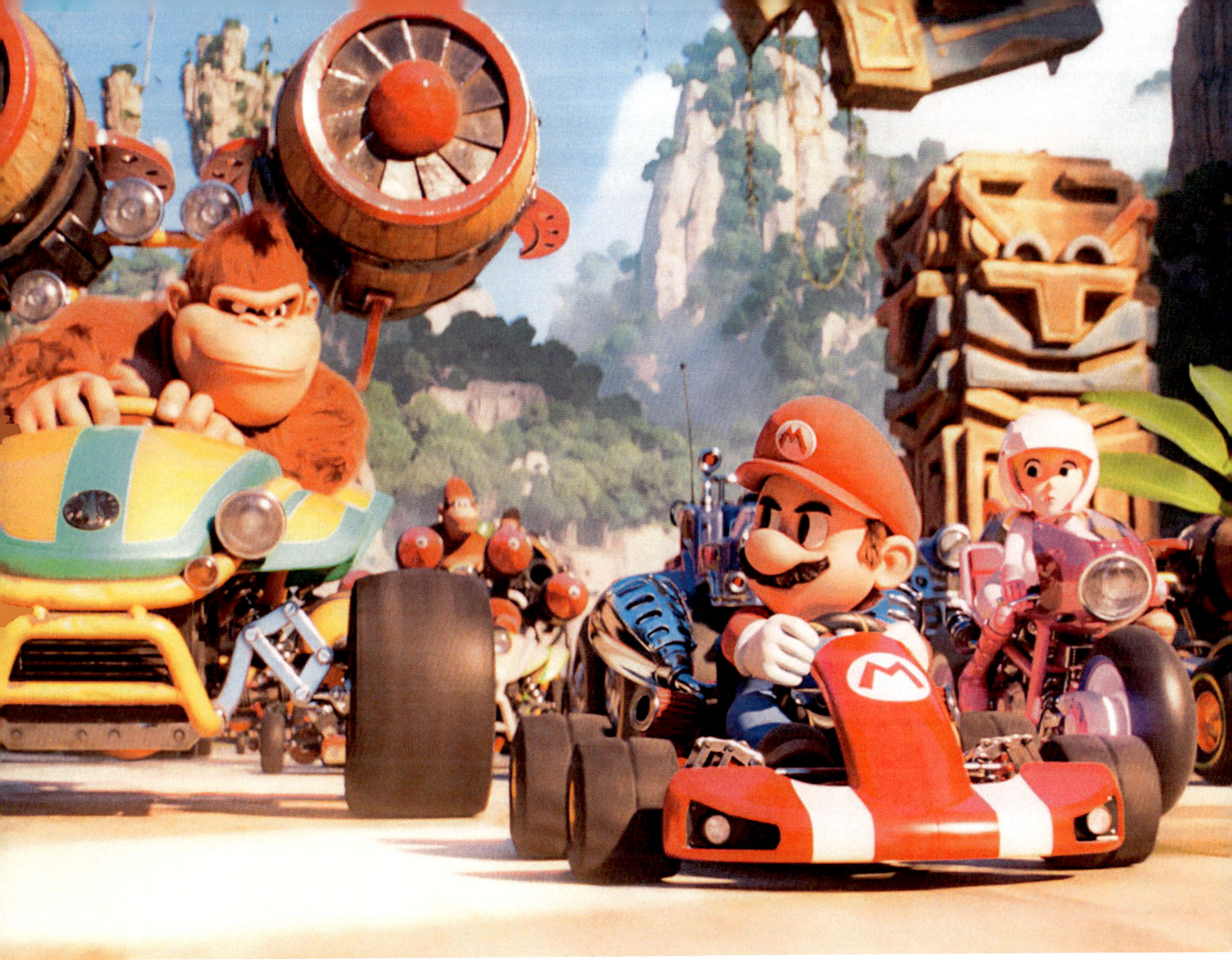

The film nods at the beloved racing game by weaving the Karts into the story's plot. Opposite, Jack Black's portrayal of Bowser was so popular that he released the music video "Peaches."

MEMES ARE YOUR FRIEND

According to TIME.com, memes and social media posts spread like wildfire on the eve of the film's release. "On Twitter and TikTok, hashtags like 'Super Mario Movie' and 'Super Mario Bros' have accumulated nearly 4 billion views." In fact, the movie represented one of TikTok's highest-trending tags in April 2023, the month of the film's initial roll-out. The internet buzz began back when the movie was first announced in 2020. Fans reacted in real time (mostly positively) to the project's casting announcements. And when the trailer dropped in the fall of 2022, thumbs started tapping away, creating the sort of crowd-sourced viral excitement that's impossible to manufacture. Meanwhile, the Mario Reddit thread had 130,000 members, many of whom posted fan art and Super Mario cosplay selfies. That's in addition to the more than 2 million people already active in the Nintendo subreddit. Jack Black's rendition of Bowser's lovesick power ballad, "Peaches," was a viral sensation that led to the creation of its own music video.

LEAVE THE AUDIENCE WANTING MORE

As fans have begun to get primed and pumped for the currently-in-the-works sequel, *The Super Mario Bros. Movie* helped fuel that enthusiasm by taking another page from the Marvel playbook with its post-end-credits bonus scene. Of course, Marvel has been doing this with its Marvel Cinematic Universe chapters for ages. But it's a proven path to future success.

This is obviously harder to pull off with a kids' movie like *The Super Mario Bros. Movie* than *Thor* or *Ant-Man* — I mean, what kid wants to sit through 10 minutes of scrolling, tiny-font names of key grips and second-unit electricians? But those who were able to sit still long enough were rewarded with an unexpected treat that they could take with them out of the theater. In this blink-and-you'll-miss-it bonus scene, a tiny white egg with green spots begins to hatch. Then as the screen goes dark, we hear a squeaky, high-pitched voice yell, "Yoshi!!!"

Flop or Phenomenon?

The top star made a case for the 1993 live-action *Super Mario Bros.* in a 2023 interview with *People* magazine.

BY JEN JUNEAU

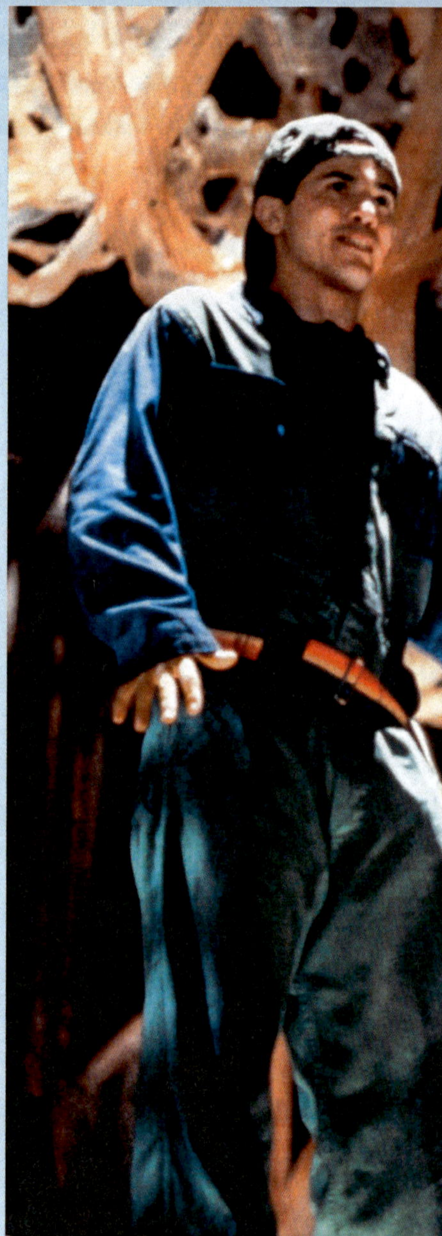

John Leguizamo might be having a bit of a George Bailey moment as he reflects on the lasting impact of his 1993 *Super Mario Bros.* movie.

In a conversation with *People* in conjunction with his 2022 documentary, *John Leguizamo Live at Rikers*, the veteran actor and comedian recalled how his perspective on *Super Mario Bros.*, in which he played Luigi to the late Bob Hoskins' Mario, changed over the years, after attending conventions and meeting fans. "I start[ed] to realize that it was a cultural phenomenon — that it meant a lot to kids who grew up with it," says Leguizamo. And the actor even sees a parallel to another film that didn't gain popularity until later. "You know, *It's A Wonderful Life*, it had the same thing. It was a critical bomb. It bombed at the box office, and yet it became an American staple for Christmas," Leguizamo says. "So you never know. It's fascinating. And I'm glad that I brought joy to kids and was part of their childhood."

Directed by Rocky Morton and Annabel Jankel, *Super Mario Bros.* was the first live-action feature film based on a video game to be released in the United States. While it is now considered a cult classic by many, the movie, which also starred Samantha Mathis and Dennis Hopper, holds just a 29 percent rating and audience score on Rotten Tomatoes.

Rather than a direct adaptation of the story featured in the Mario games released by Nintendo up until that point, the plot follows sibling plumbers Mario Mario (Hoskins, who died in 2014) and his younger brother, Luigi Mario (Leguizamo), as they set out on a quest to a dystopian, dinosaur-laced alternate dimension to rescue Daisy (Mathis) from the evil clutches of King Koopa (the late Hopper) — and meet some fan-familiar friends and foes along the way.

The zany, darker film featured music from Oscar-nominated composer Alan Silvestri, who also famously scored the *Back to the Future* trilogy, *Who Framed Roger*

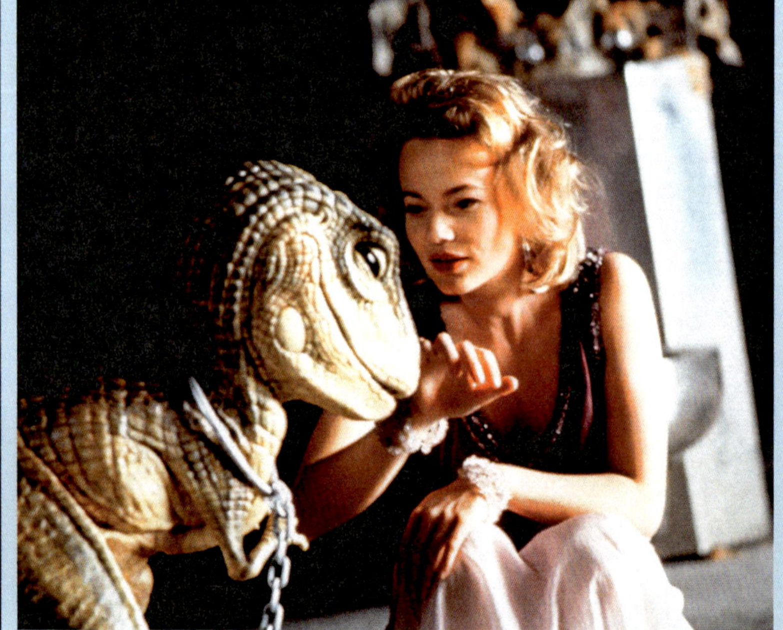

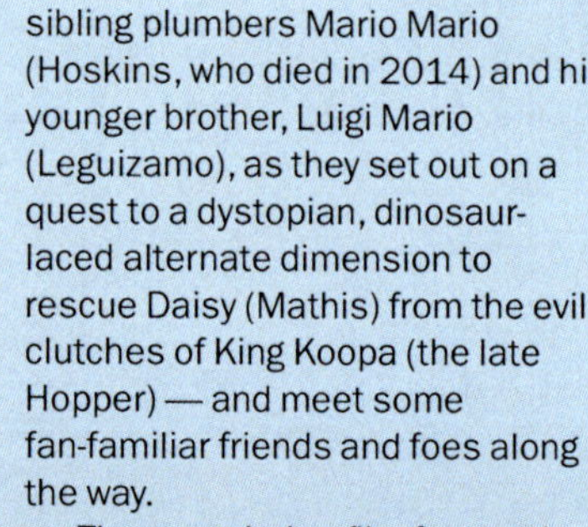

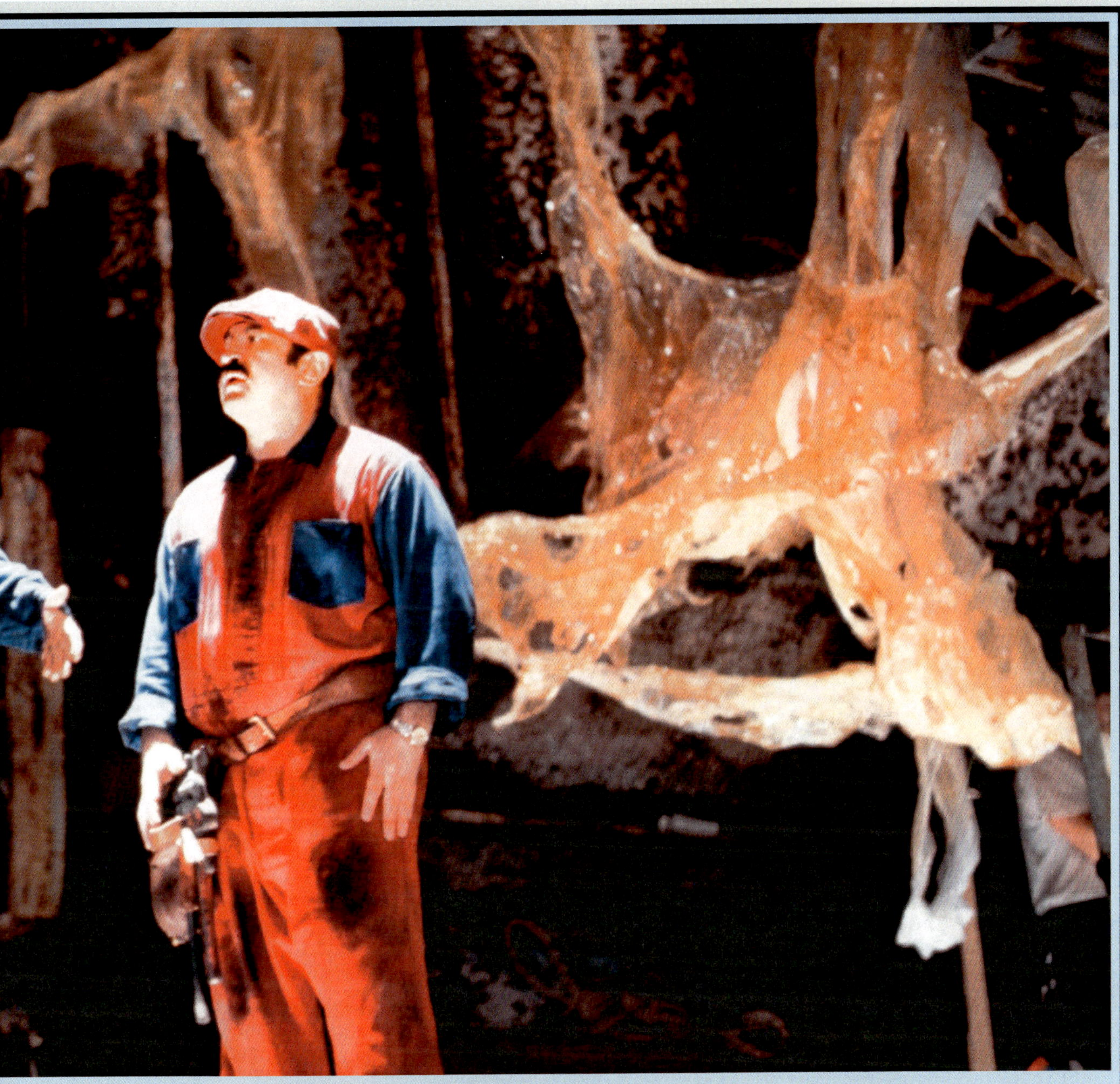

John Leguizamo as Luigi Mario and Bob Hoskins as Mario Mario in Super Mario Bros. *(1993). Opposite: Samantha Mathis portrayed both Daisy and Daisy's mother in the film.*

Rabbit, *Forrest Gump* and more, working often alongside filmmaker Robert Zemeckis. *Super Mario Bros.* was also the first movie to use Autodesk Flame, a CGI software that has since become an industry standard in digital effects, marking a historic jump from practical effects.

But despite its groundbreaking attributes, "I was very down on the movie when it first came out, just because as a young actor, I was like, you just go with the crowd," Leguizamo tells *People*. "And the reviews weren't good. It wasn't a big hit at the box office, so I assumed it didn't have any value."

"And then the years go by and I'm at Comic-Con or some premiere, and there are these kids — well, they're kids to me, but they're in their late 20s and early 30s — and they go, 'Oh my God, you're Luigi. I love that movie. That movie was so everything to me when I was a kid.' "

He also says he believes Jankel and Morton "were really brave and stuck their neck out to get me into the movie. Because it was very hard back then, in the '90s, to be a Latin man and get work, and [to] be a lead was impossible."

The actor also addresses comments made by Seth Rogen (who voices Donkey Kong in the 2023 movie), in which Rogen called the 1993 movie "one of the worst films ever made" during a conversation with *Variety*. "Everybody's entitled to their opinions," Leguizamo says when asked about Rogen's remarks. "That's what he thinks. That's fine. It doesn't hurt my feelings. It doesn't change the quality of the movie . . . I'm cool."

LEVEL UP IN REAL LIFE

The Universal Studios parks that let you step inside the game.

BY AVA ERICKSON

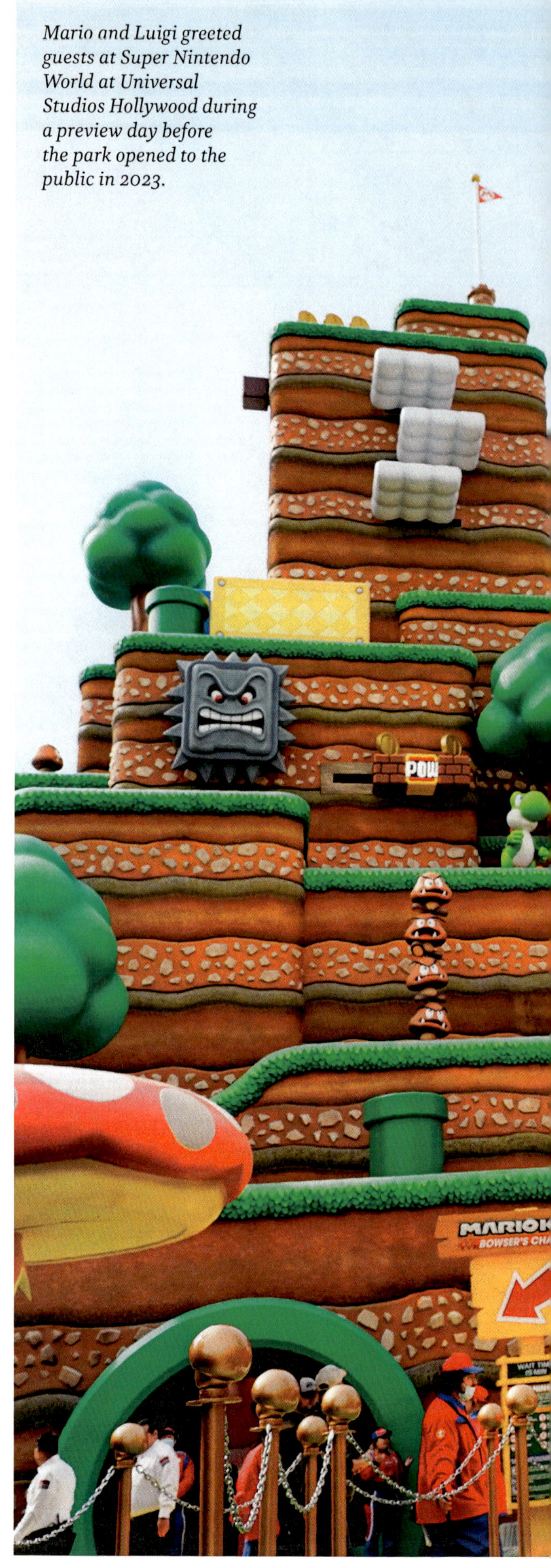

Mario and Luigi greeted guests at Super Nintendo World at Universal Studios Hollywood during a preview day before the park opened to the public in 2023.

DURING THE GROUNDBREAKING ceremony for a new Nintendo theme park at Universal Studios Japan in June 2017, three men took the stage to speak about the plans. But this was hardly a typical groundbreaking ceremony, considering that these businessman heavy hitters were decked out in matching Mario hats and oversized gloves (which made holding their microphones a bit difficult) and were introduced by a giant dancing Mario. During the confetti-filled finale, J.L. Bonnier, CEO of Universal Studios Japan; Shigeru Miyamoto, Nintendo game director; and Mark Woodbury, vice chairman of Universal Parks and Resorts, even struck Mario's signature jumping pose, officially kicking off construction on a new park that would be every bit as fun and extravagant as its groundbreaking ceremony.

After several delays due to the pandemic, Super Nintendo World officially opened its doors in 2021. As the first visitors entered the park, through a green warp pipe of course, they were met with a visually arresting universe filled with all things Mario. "The game world feels alive . . . Goombas walk back and forth, piranha

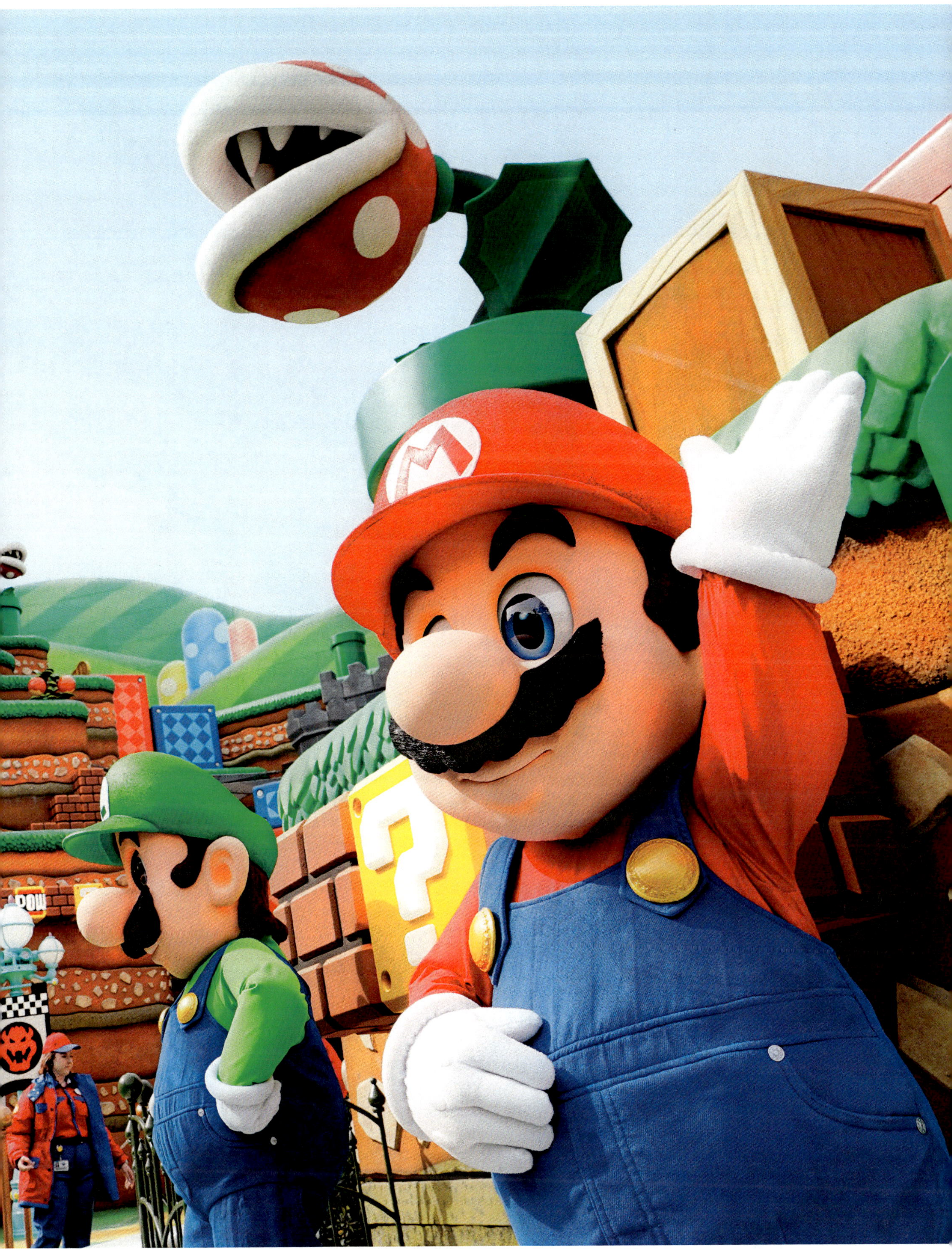

POW

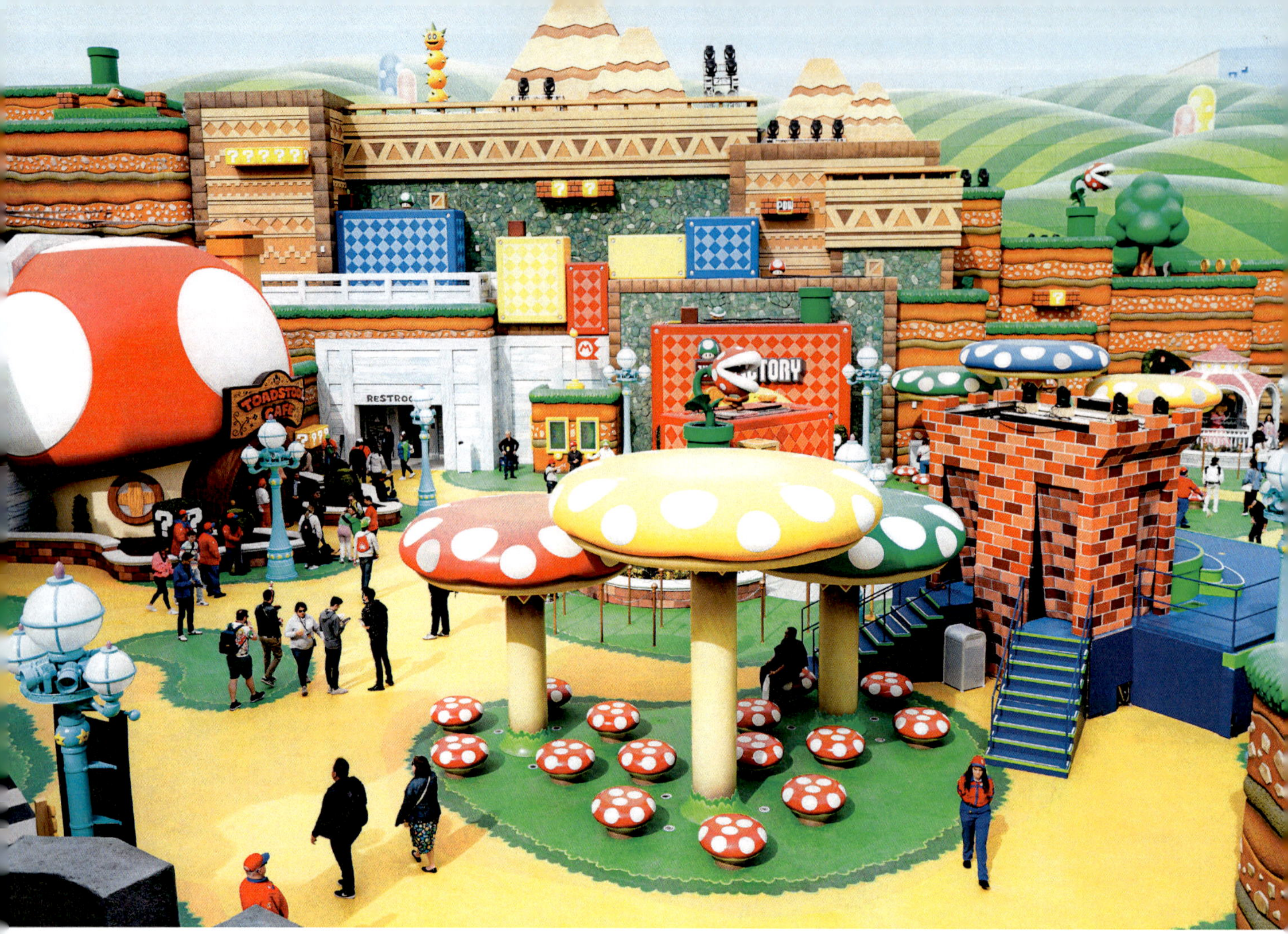

A second park opened in Los Angeles in 2023, here. Opposite, Mark Woodbury, J.L. Bonnier, and Shigeru Miyamoto at the Super Nintendo World groundbreaking ceremony in Japan in 2017.

plants bob and snap at park visitors, coins float in the air and spin, and platforms move from side to side," wrote one reviewer on a blog for Disney and Universal theme parks. "Super Nintendo World feels like being transported from Universal Studios into a 3D Mario land," wrote another blogger.

Every inch of the 76,000 square foot space is packed with elements from across the Mario franchise. From an interactive Mario Kart ride to minigames to blocks that allow visitors to collect virtual coins, Super Nintendo World, which cost upward of $575 million to create, takes theme parks to the next level, blurring the lines between video game and real-life attraction. This is, in part, thanks to the fact that Nintendo game designer Miyamoto was heavily involved in creating the world. "We [Nintendo and Universal] had this shared idea of trying to create something new and impressive, and the idea of wanting to create something that's truly interactive," he told the Verge. "In that sense, our involvement wasn't just a matter of reviewing assets or reviewing designs. But really trying to get down to the nitty-gritty of how people are going to experience this and what their experiences are going to be."

In February 2023, a second park was opened at Universal Studios Hollywood, in California. While the attractions and vibe are similar in the two parks and they were designed in conjunction, after a partnership between Nintendo and Universal was announced in 2015, the U.S. version is significantly smaller.

However, the most beloved attraction appears at both parks. The Mario Kart ride, called Mario Kart: Koopa's Challenge in Japan and Mario Kart: Bowser's Challenge in the U.S., is designed to allow visitors to literally play one of the franchise's most beloved games. It utilizes augmented reality (AR), a type of technology that integrates computer-generated perceptual information into the real world, so riders are literally moving on a track, while seeing virtual components like characters and other elements pulled from the *Mario Kart* game. "You want to be able to go through some of the items in *Mario Kart*, you want to collect things, you want to see the characters fly. Certain things you cannot do with stereo, 3D, or any other kind of projection. It had to be AR," said Thierry Coup, Universal's Creative SVP at the time of the ride's launch.

Visitors wear an AR headset (which looks like a Mario hat) and steer and launch shells at opponents using a real steering wheel attached to the cart. "There's just a lot going on with the Mario Kart ride. It doesn't move very fast, but it feels like it does because the track is often completely simulated. The Rainbow Road section, for example, is incredibly visually intense," wrote a reporter from the Verge who reviewed the Japanese version of the park. "It's overwhelming but a whole lot of fun, and like the rest of the park it seems to be more rewarding if you try it multiple times. I know I'd get a better score the next time around."

According to Universal's VP of Digital Innovation Tom Geraghty, the company has planned for improvement in AR technology, which he says will likely come about before the physical components of the ride wear out. "We know that it's going to advance and come into your home. So we have plans to iterate the tech to support the creative [vision] that we may change."

Aside from rides, the park is packed with interactive elements. To unlock this section of the park, visitors need to purchase a Power Up Band for $40 USD. The bracelet syncs to a smartphone app and allows visitors to collect digital coins, punch question blocks, and play key challenges, which are interactive minigames that allow players to collect virtual keys. If visitors can beat all the games — like Goomba Crazy Crank, where players crank a wheel to push a Goomba away, or Thwomp Panel Panic, where players have to tap panels before a Thwomp mixes them up — they can compete in a final challenge against Bowser Jr. "Think of Super Nintendo World as a life-size, living video game where you become one of the characters. You're not just playing the game; you're living the game, you're living the adventure," Coup told *Forbes* in 2020.

The Nintendo overload doesn't even stop during mealtime—the parks offer a Mario-themed menu at the Toadstool Cafe (Kinopio's Cafe in Japan). Run by "Chef Toad," the restaurant is located inside a red mushroom and screens inside show Toad and friends working away in the kitchen. "Everything on the menu either has mushrooms, looks like a mushroom, has the flavor profile of a mushroom, or is a nod to the Mushroom Kingdom," said Universal Studios Hollywood's executive chef Julia Thrash, the real chef behind the menu at the California park. (Sorry, Chef Toad!) The menus at the different parks are

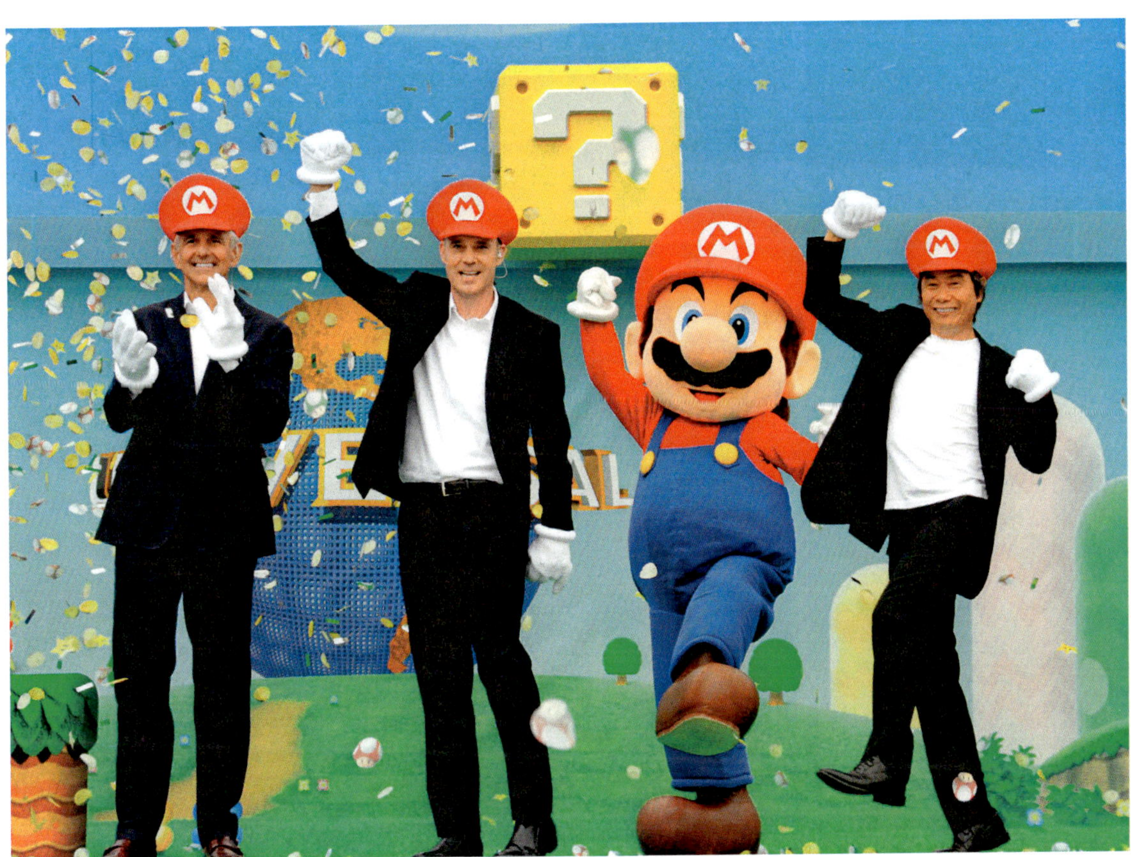

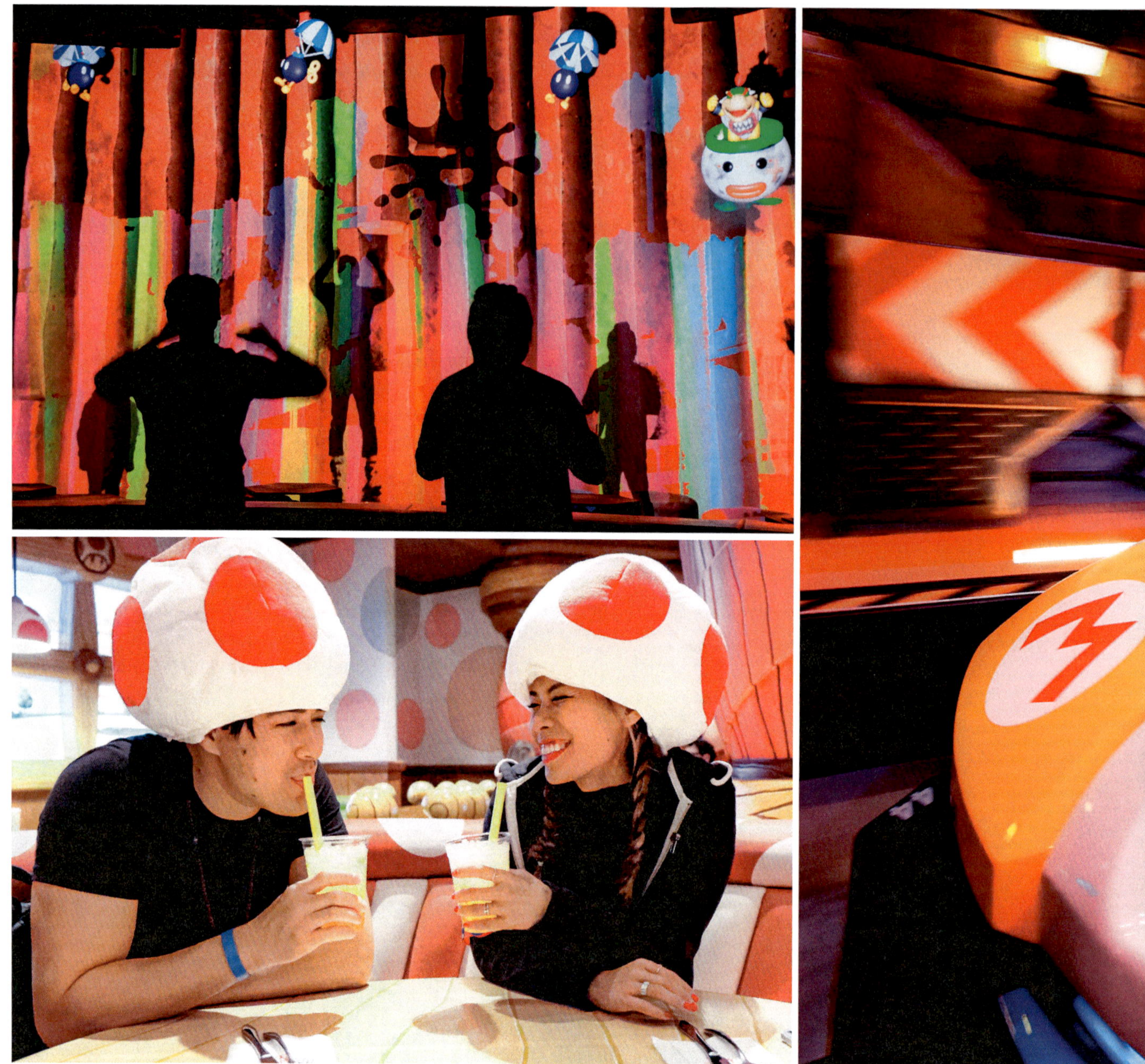

At Universal Studios Hollywood, clockwise from top left: An interactive game; the Mario Kart: Bowser's Challenge ride; guests at the Toadstool Cafe.

slightly different, but they all creatively incorporate the Nintendo IP into plates like the Piranha Plant Caprese Salad, the Question Block Tiramisu, the Super Mushroom Pizza Bowl, or the Teriyaki Chicken & Super Star Rice.

In 2024, an additional dining option, the Power Up Cafe, opened at Universal Hollywood. Located outside of Super Nintendo World in the park's upper lot, the restaurant is completely inspired by power-ups. "We wanted the guests to be able to come in through the park and power up their day," Thrash told Eater Los Angeles. She explained that the menu and decor are inspired by Super Star, Super Mushroom, 1-Up Mushroom, and Fire Flower, with offerings like the Super Mushroom Calzone, the Fire Flower Pretzel, and the Super Star Popcorn Cup (topped with edible glitter).

Because the park at Universal Studios Japan is significantly bigger than the one in California, it boasts some extra features, including Yoshi's Adventure, a slow-paced ride that ambles around a track throughout the park, and the newly opened Donkey Kong Country, a section of the park based on the Nintendo series about the adventures of the tie-wearing gorilla.

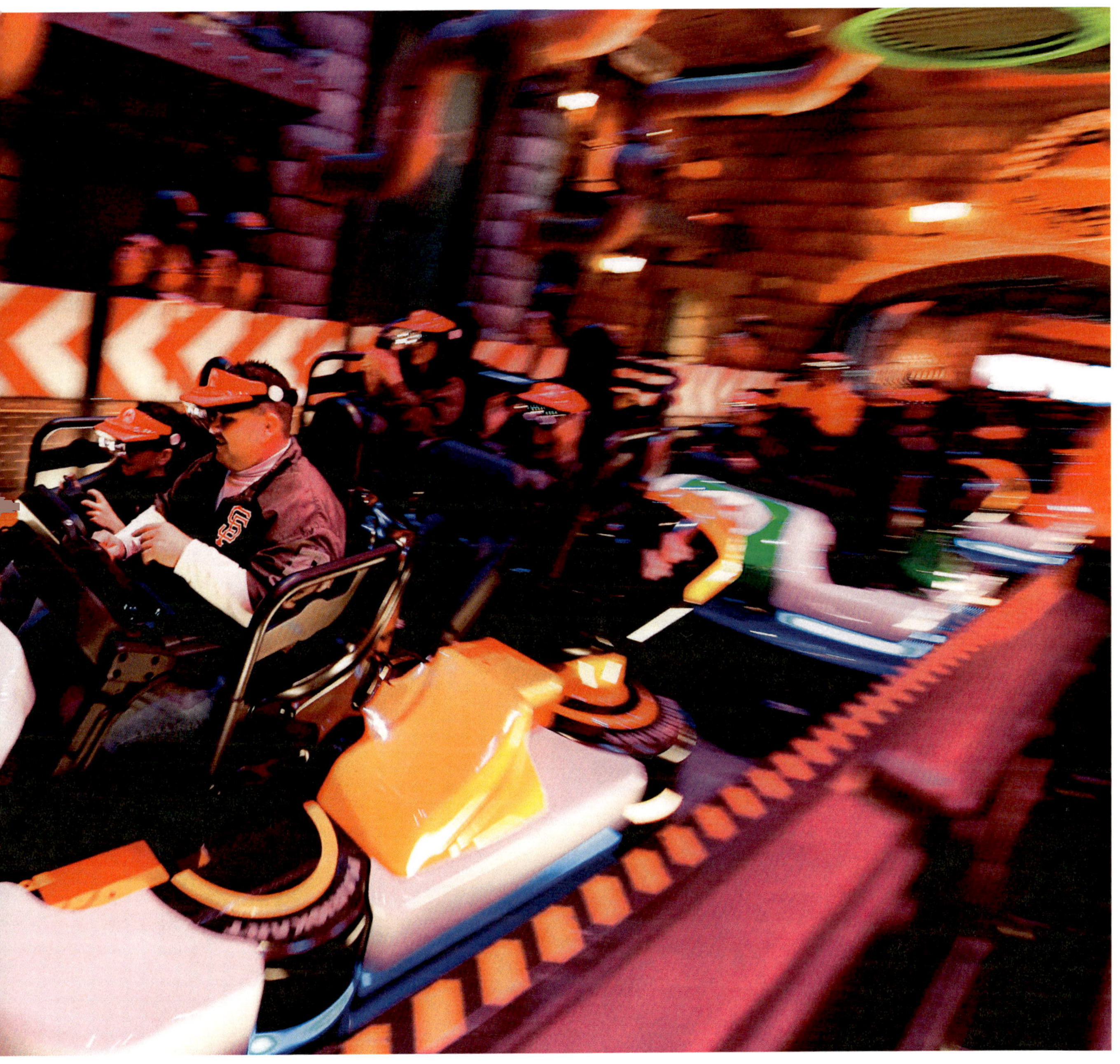

The main attraction in the new area is the Minecart Madness roller coaster, which is designed to look and feel like the cars are "jumping" over broken tracks. Universal patented the design for the ride, which it calls a "boom coaster," back in 2016, and it is also expected to make an appearance in Universal Orlando's Super Nintendo World, opening in 2025.

As soon as the first park in Japan opened in 2021, Super Nintendo World was a smash hit. People traveled from all over the world to experience the theme park that feels like you are in a video game. "The technology was not ready for this," said Coup of the Mario Kart ride. "But one of the incredible things that Universal Parks & Resorts does, we look forward, and we see a technology that could allow us to deliver an experience, and we grab it and we develop it further and make it happen. There is a bit of calculated risk, but we really think that's the only way for us to really stay on the cutting edge of the ultimate experience." With the new iteration opening in Orlando in 2025 and another slated for Universal Studios Singapore in 2026, there's no telling what kinds of attractions are in store for Super Nintendo World.

THE WIDE WORLD OF MERCH

From wacky toys to luxury fashion, there are 40 years' worth of Mario goods out there.

BY AVA ERICKSON

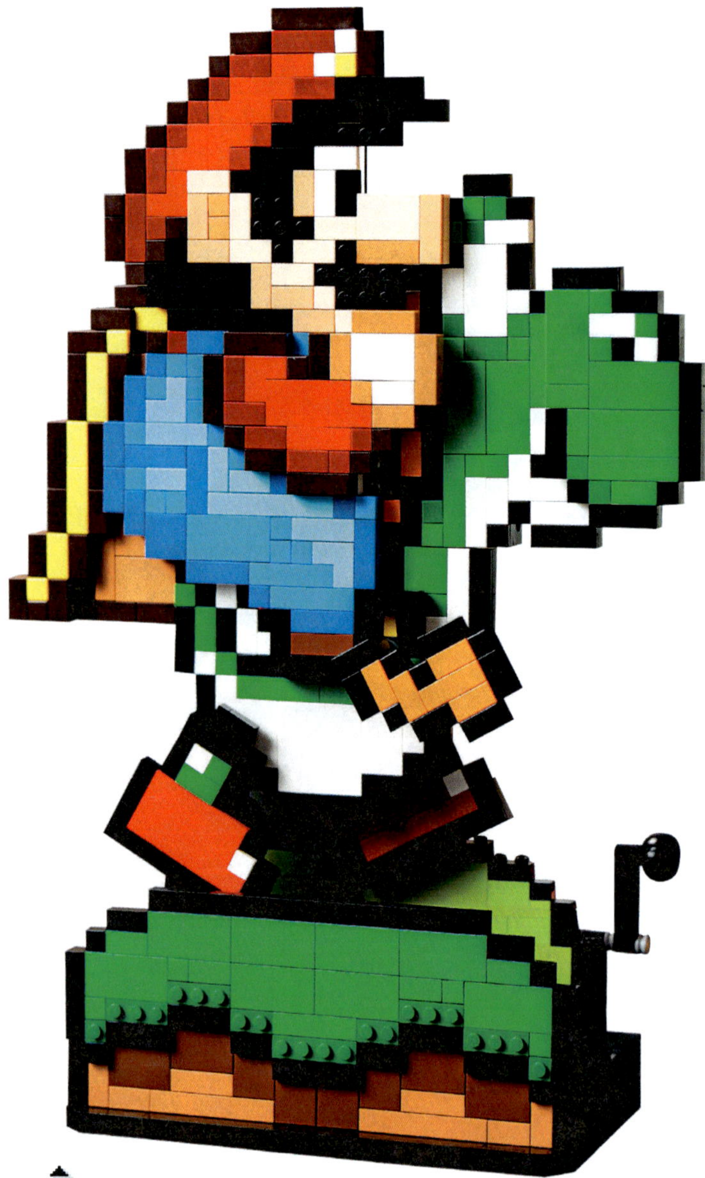

▲

Mario & Yoshi Lego Set

An homage to *Super Mario World*, the 1990 game that saw Mario on a quest to save Princess Peach (and introduced Yoshi), this Lego set has a retro feel with a pixilated image of the two characters and a rich '90s color scheme. Released in 2024, the set is for adults and has over 1,000 pieces. When you're done building, you can even turn a crank to make Yoshi run.

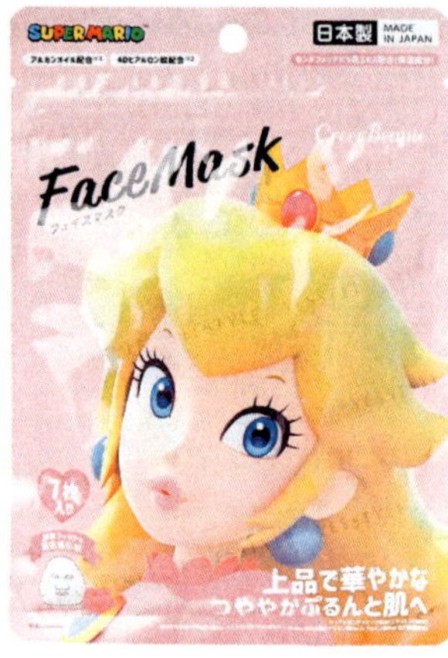

▲

Peach Face Mask

If you're looking to have a Princess Peach–themed spa day, Creer Beaute, a Japanese company that makes character-branded cosmetics, has the product for you. The sheet mask has a rose scent, and one reviewer said, "This is worth it just for the packaging alone!"

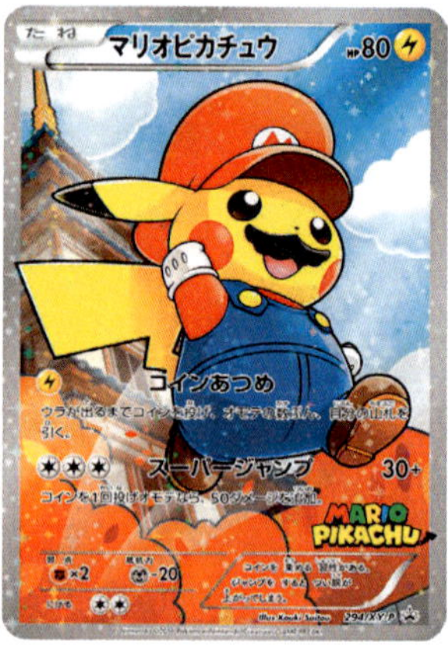

▲

Mario Pikachu

This Pokémon card, released in 2016, saw a crossover between two of Nintendo's most beloved characters: Mario and Pikachu. The card frequently sells for well over $2,000, with the current highest sale at $8,300.There is also a coordinating Luigi Pikachu card with a similar price tag.

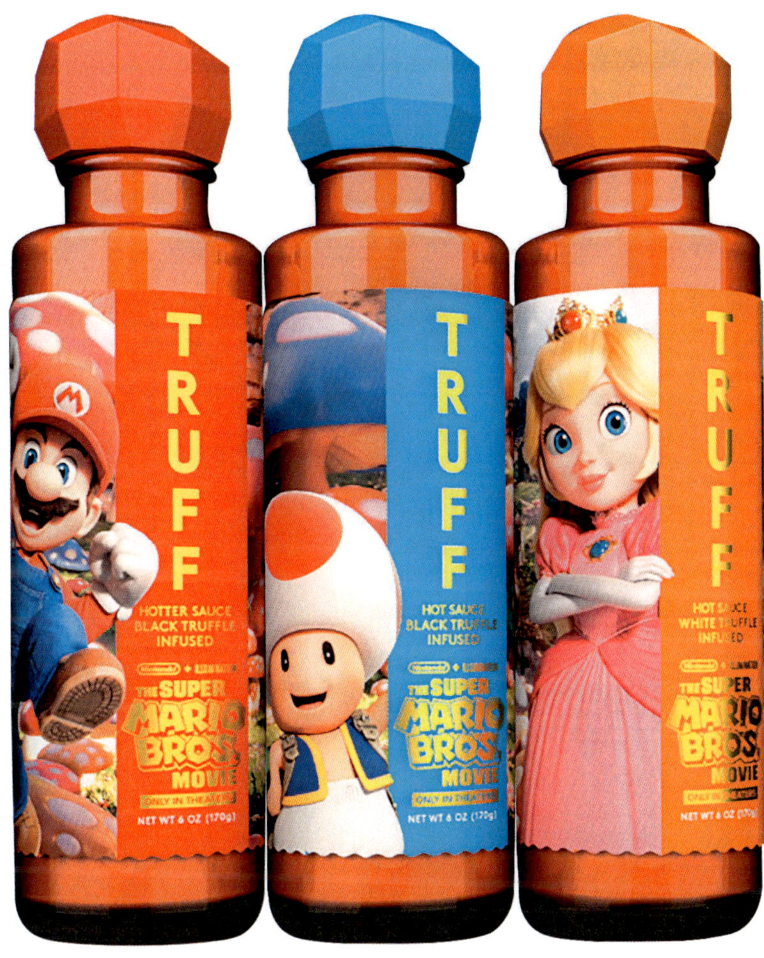

Truff Hot Sauce

By the time the *Super Mario Bros.* movie–themed hot sauce launched in 2023, there were already 20,000 people on the wait list hoping to score a bottle. "Obviously, mushrooms make sense for a truffle sauce brand tie-in," said Michelle Gabe, then director of marketing at Truff, a buzzy hot sauce start-up. Reviewers generally agree that the sauce trio, sold in an Instagram-worthy sleek black box, is pretty tasty.

Pottery Barn Collection

The upscale furniture company teamed up with Nintendo to create a line of Mario home decor with items like a light-up Super Star pillow and this Question Mark Block alarm clock. While you won't get any coins from it, this clock may make waking up a little more fun.

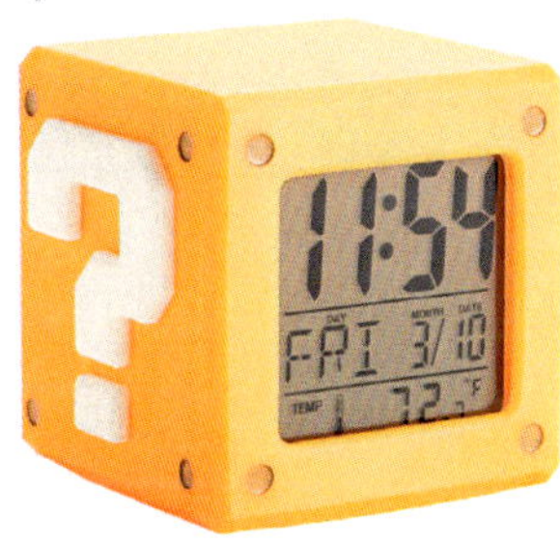

Super Moschino

While Mario is known for his utilitarian overalls, he solidified his place in the world of high fashion in 2015 when Moschino partnered with Nintendo for a Mario line. Complete with graphic shirts and leather bags, the items feature everything from Mario himself to the Goombas.

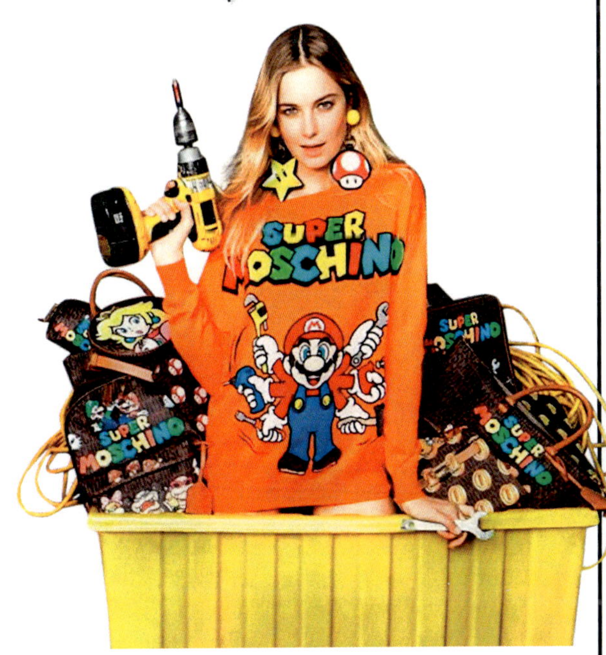

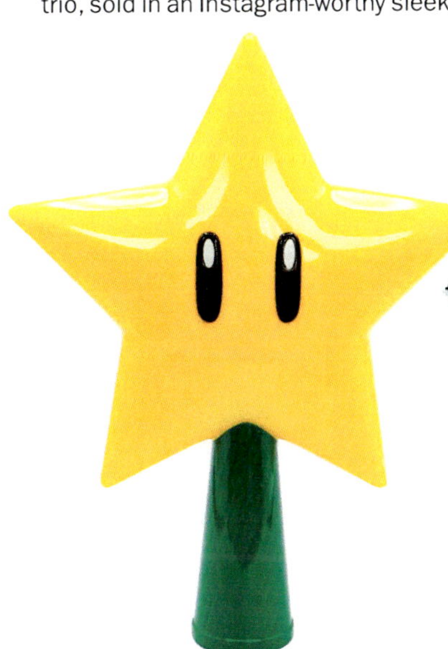

Super Star Tree Topper

Mario fans can now swap their angel tree topper for a Super Star. The 7-inch star, which retails for around $30, lights up. With a plethora of Mario ornaments on the market, from 3D characters to baubles decorated with Mario-inspired art, you can even make your entire tree Super Mario–themed.

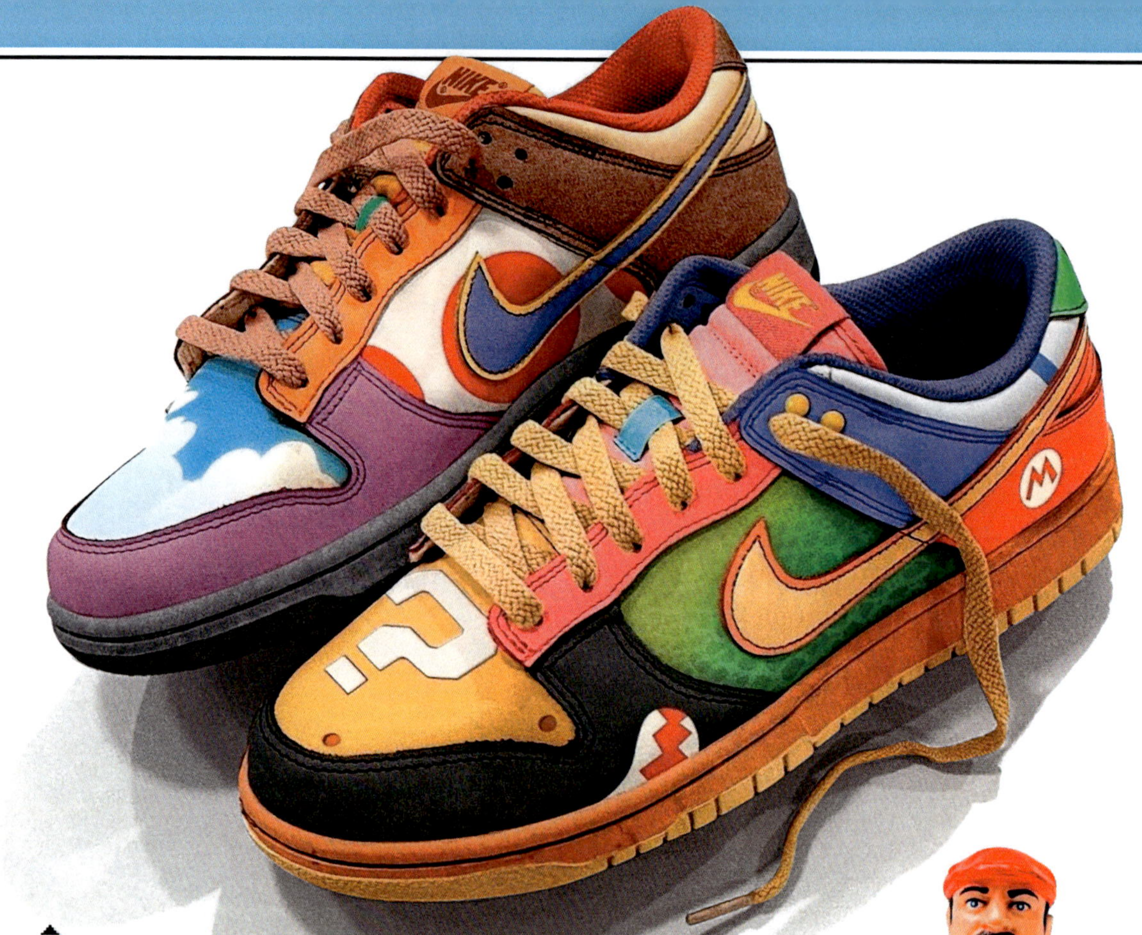

Super Mario Sneaks

In 2023 sneaker designer Andrew Chiou created custom Nike Dunk Lows, which he called "What the Super Mario." Each panel has a subtle nod to a different aspect of the Mario franchise. (Chiou shared inspo pics from the movie and vintage games on his Instagram). The custom kicks had an extremely limited run, and as of December 2024 there was only one pair available on eBay, listed for nearly $4,000.

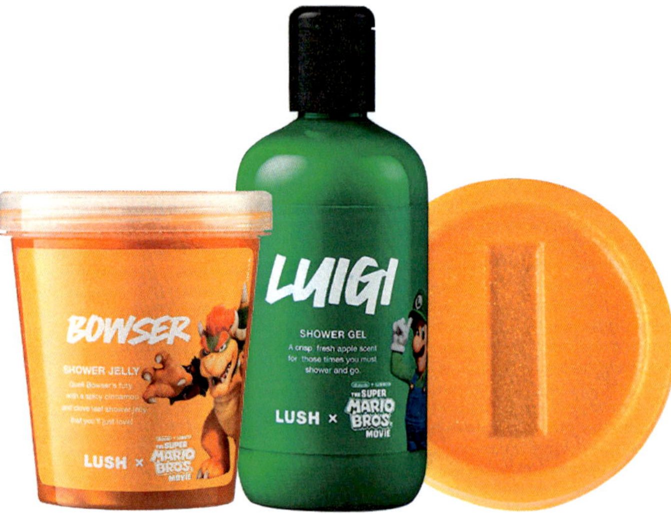

Mario Bath Products

Nintendo teamed up with Lush in 2023 to create a line of bath products. The Mario shower gel has the scent of black pepper and pomegranate, while the Princess Peach body spray has a pineapple and, of course, peach fragrance. The gold coin soap uses the brand's popular honey fragrance.

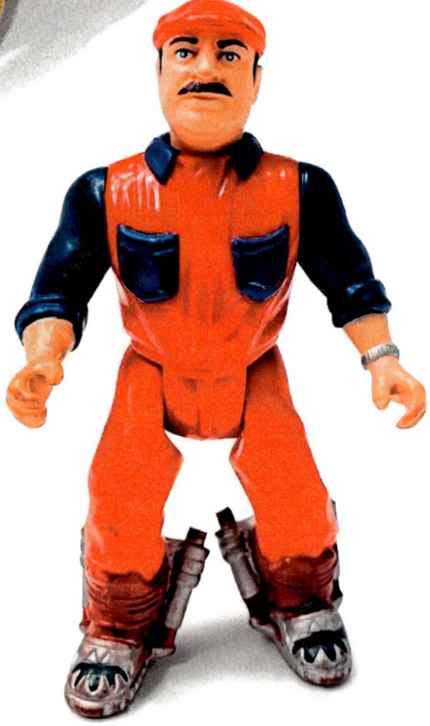

1993 Action Figures

The 1993 *Super Mario Bros.* movie spawned a ton of merch, but perhaps the most infamous were these action figures. Unlike the typical, cartoony renditions of Mario and friends, these action figures were weirdly realistic, and they've now become popular collectors' items.

TIME

Editor in Chief Sam Jacobs
Managing Editor Lily Rothman
Creative Director D.W. Pine

Super Mario

DOTDASH MEREDITH PREMIUM PUBLISHING
Vice President, Editor in Chief Kostya Kennedy
Creative Director Gary Stewart
Associate Photo Director C. Tiffany Lee
Editorial Operations Director Jamie Roth Major
Editor Courtney Mifsud Intreglia
Senior Art Director Lan Yin Bachelis
Senior Photo Editor Louis Pearlman
Writers Ashley Abramson, Lisa Eadicicco, Ava Erickson, Daniel Howley, Courtney Mifsud Intreglia, Jen Juneau, Evan Narcisse, Chris Nashawaty, Matt Peckham
Manager, Editorial Operations Gina Scauzillo
Associate Manager, Editorial Operations Ariel Davis
Copy Chief Tracy Guth Spangler
Copy Editor Joel Van Liew
Researcher Joseph Wilkinson
Production Designer Sandra Jurevics
Premedia Trafficking Supervisor Jacqueline Beard
Premedia Imaging Specialist David Swain
Color Quality Analyst Ryan C. Meier
Production Director Patrick MGowan
Production Managers Ashley Schaubroeck, Trevi Jones, April Gross
Senior Quality Director Joe Kohler
Associate Quality Director Jason Lamb

Vice President & General Manager Jeremy Biloon
Senior Director, Brand Marketing Jean Kennedy
Associate Director, Brand Marketing Katherine Barnet
Senior Manager, Brand Marketing Geoffrey Wohlgamuth
Brand Manager, Brand Marketing Mia Rinaldi
Associate Brand Manager, Brand Marketing Gabby Amello

Special thanks Brad Beatson, Nicoleta Papavasilakis

ADVERTISING AND BUSINESS
SVP & Group Publisher Daren Mazzucca (daren.mazzucca@dotdashmdp.com)
VP & Publisher Donna Lindskog (donna.lindskog@dotdashmdp.com)
Marketing Sandra Salerno Roth, Christine Austin

DOTDASH MEREDITH
President, Lifestyle Alysia Borsa

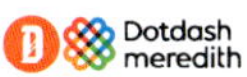
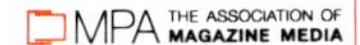

For syndication or international licensing requests, email syndication.generic@dotdashmdp.com. For reprint and reuse permission, email mmc.permissions@dotdashmdp.com.

Printed in the USA.

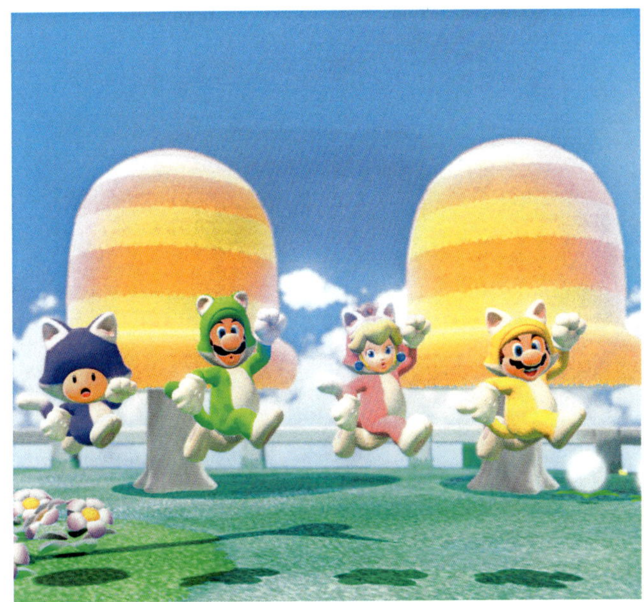

In 2013's Super Mario 3D World, *Mario can obtain the Super Bell, which turns him into Cat Mario. In 2024, the add-on Bowser's Fury Cat Mario can use the Giga Bell to turn into Giga Cat Mario.*

Credits

Front cover
Nintendo of America; E+/Getty Images

Back cover
(from top) Nintendo of America; Everett

Inside covers
Nintendo of America (4)

1 Nintendo of America **2–3** Nintendo of America **4** Chesnot/Getty Images **6–7** (from left) Edward Berthelot/Getty Images; Tom Williams/CQ Roll Call/Getty Images **8–9** (from left) Stanislav Kogiku/SOPA Images/LightRocket/Getty Images; Alison Yin/Invision for Nintendo/Facebook/AP Photo

Mario's Evolution
10–11 (from left) Alamy; Sebastien Berda/AFP/Getty Images **13** Alamy **14–15** Nintendo (3) **16–17** (clockwise from bottom left) beforemario.com; Nintendo; Graham Harrison/Shutterstock; Konektus Photo/Shutterstock **18–19** (from left) LMPC/Getty Images; Alamy; Sankei Archive/Getty Images **20–21** (from left) igdb.com (2); Nintendo of America **22–23** Ralf-Finn Hestoft/Corbis/Getty Images **24–25** (from left) Nintendo; Alamy **26–27** Ralf-Finn Hestoft/Corbis/Getty Images **28–29** Steve Schofield/Contour by Getty Images **30** Matthieu Rondel/Hans Lucas/Redux **32–33** (from left) Nintendo of America; Bob Riha, Jr./Getty Images **34–35** Takaaki Iwabu/Bloomberg/Getty Images **36–37** @ timcook/X **38–39** (from left) E+/Getty Images; Nintendo of America **40–41** Nintendo (8)

Game Time
42–43 (from left) Nintendo of America; Alamy **44–45** Zack Yeo/Unsplash **46–47** (clockwise from bottom left) Nintendo; Alamy; Nintendo/Zuma **48–49** Nintendo of America (2) **50–51** (from left) Nintendo of America; Nintendo **52–53** Kiyoshi Ota/Bloomberg/Getty Images **54–55** (from left) Nintendo of America; Activision **56** Alamy **58–59** Nintendo of America **60–61** Nintendo of America (6) **62–63** Nintendo of America (5) **64–65** Nintendo of America (6) **66–67** Nintendo of America (6) **68–69** Universal Pictures **70–71** Nintendo of America (2) **72** Nintendo of America

A Super Brand
74–75 (from left) Chris Delmas/AFP/Getty Images; Alamy **77** Alamy **78–79** (from left) Everett; Kevin Winter/Getty Images **80–81** (from left) Everett; Leon Bennett/FilmMagic **82–83** (from left) Albert L. Ortega/Getty Images; Universal Pictures **84–85** Alamy (2) **86–87** Chris Pizzello/AP Photo **88–89** (from left) Chris Pizzello/AP Photo; Asahi Shimbun/Getty Images **90–91** (clockwise from right) Chris Delmas/AFP/Getty Images; Rodin Eckenroth/Getty Images; Chris Delmas/AFP/Getty Images **92** (left) Cover Images/Zuma **95** Nintendo of America **96** Nintendo of America

The Greatest of All Time

The chronic kidnapper is the best video game villain ever. It's good to be king.

BY COURTNEY MIFSUD INTREGLIA

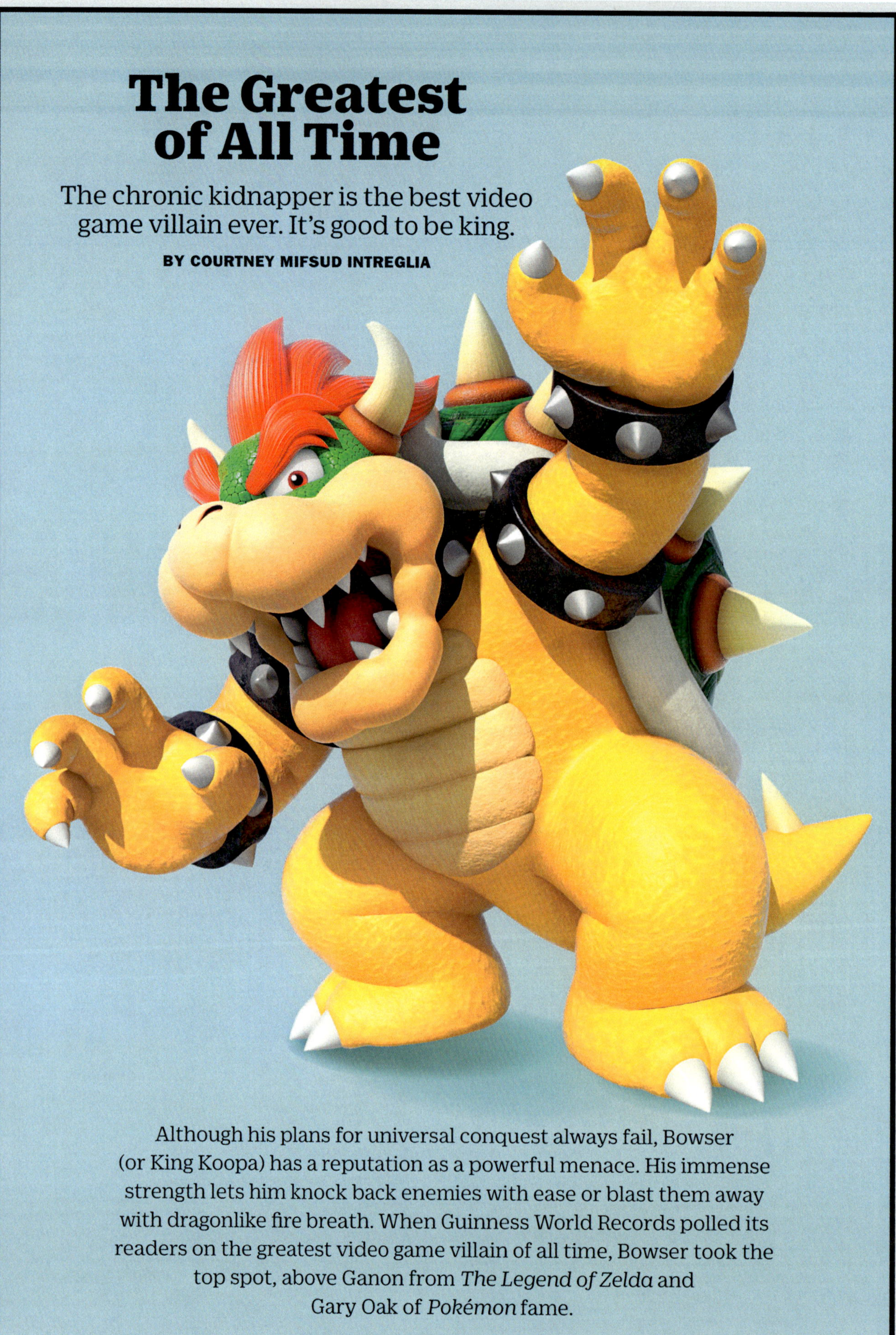

Although his plans for universal conquest always fail, Bowser (or King Koopa) has a reputation as a powerful menace. His immense strength lets him knock back enemies with ease or blast them away with dragonlike fire breath. When Guinness World Records polled its readers on the greatest video game villain of all time, Bowser took the top spot, above Ganon from *The Legend of Zelda* and Gary Oak of *Pokémon* fame.

Made in United States
North Haven, CT
21 March 2025

67071210R00055